Labor in the Public
and Nonprofit Sectors

Labor in the Public and Nonprofit Sectors

EDITED BY DANIEL S. HAMERMESH

Princeton University Press

Princeton, New Jersey

Copyright © 1975 by Princeton University Press
Published by Princeton University Press, Princeton and London
All Rights Reserved
Library of Congress Cataloging in Publication data will
be found on the last printed page of this book
Publication of this book has been aided by the Whitney Darrow
Publication Reserve Fund of Princeton University Press
Printed in the United States of America
by Princeton University Press, Princeton, New Jersey

CONTENTS

Orley C. Ashenfelter is professor of economics at Princeton University and Director of the Industrial Relations Section. He recently served as Director of the Office of Evaluation in the Office of the Assistant Secretary of Labor for Policy, Evaluation, and Research.

John F. Burton, Jr., is associate professor of labor economics in the Graduate School of Business of the University of Chicago. He taught previously at Yale University and served as chairman of the Federal Commission on Workmen's Compensation.

Ronald G. Ehrenberg is associate professor of economics at the University of Massachusetts, Amherst. He has taught at Loyola University in Chicago and worked as a consultant to the U.S. Department of Labor.

Richard B. Freeman is associate professor of economics at Harvard University. He has also taught at Yale University and the University of Chicago.

Donald E. Frey is assistant professor of economics at Wake Forest University. His contribution to this volume is based upon his recently completed doctoral dissertation at Princeton University.

Paul Gerhart is assistant professor of labor economics at the University of Illinois, Urbana. He has worked extensively in the area of public employee labor relations.

Daniel S. Hamermesh is associate professor of economics at Michigan State University. He taught at Yale and Princeton Universities and was affiliated with the Industrial Relations Section of Princeton University.

George E. Johnson is associate professor of economics at the University of Michigan, currently on leave to be Director of the Office of Evaluation in the Office of Assistant Secretary of Labor for Policy, Evaluation, and Research.

CONTRIBUTORS

Hirschel Kasper is professor of economics at Oberlin College. He has taught at the University of Glasgow in Great Britain.

Alvin K. Klevorick is associate professor of economics and law at Yale University. He has been affiliated with the London School of Economics and is a leading expert on problems of regulated industry.

Charles E. Krider is assistant professor of economics at the University of Kansas. He recently completed a doctoral dissertation at the University of Chicago on public-sector collective bargaining.

Melvin W. Reder is professor of labor economics at the Graduate School of Business of the University of Chicago. He has taught at the City University of New York, Stanford University, and the University of Pennsylvania.

Jack Stieber is professor of economics and Director of the School of Labor and Industrial Relations at Michigan State University. He has worked extensively in the area of public employment, specializing in the analysis of the extent of organization of public employees.

Burton A. Weisbrod is professor of economics at the University of Wisconsin, Madison. He has taught at Washington and Princeton Universities, and has done the leading research on the redistributive aspects of the financing of higher education.

viii

The studies in this book were presented at a Conference on Labor in Nonprofit Industry and Government held at Princeton University on May 7–8, 1973. The Industrial Relations Section of Princeton University and the Manpower Administration of the U.S. Department of Labor, under Grant Number 21-34-73-27, sponsored the conference jointly. The points of view or opinions stated in these papers do not necessarily represent the official position or policy of the Department of Labor or the Industrial Relations Section. The Princeton University Conference Office helped in planning the conference.

The rise in government's share of total expenditure and employment has been especially rapid since World War II. Perhaps even more striking and surely more sudden has been the burgeoning of unions in the public sector. Not only has the extent of unionism grown since the early 1960's but union militance, as indicated by the number of man-days lost in strikes, has increased even more. Before 1964 no more than 100,000 man-days of work were lost annually because of strikes by public employees; between 1965 and 1969, the figure averaged nearly 1,000,000 man-days. It is thus clear that problems of labor in this sector are of increased importance.

While there has been substantial study of the institutions of collective bargaining in the public sector and personnel problems there, this sector has received little special attention from analytical economists. This is surprising, since the many issues relating to the demand for labor and the effects of unions should be as amenable to theoretical and empirical work as they have been in the private sector. The purpose of this conference was precisely to begin to fill this gap in the extension of analytical economics to problems of employment in the public sector. By collecting in one place the results of ongoing research on various policy problems in the public sector, we hoped to stimulate other and more detailed studies of these problems by economists.

The book consists of six papers and formal comments by invited discussants. The numerous academic economists and several public employers and union officials who attended provided lively informal discussions following each of the papers. While these were important and useful, it has not proved possible to summarize them in print. Rather, they are reflected in the revised versions of the papers that appear here.

The keynote paper by Melvin Reder is a detailed discussion of how employment and wage determination differ between profit-making industry and the rest of the economy. In a real sense it is the seminal work in this field, as nowhere else has there appeared a serious attempt to isolate those behavioral differences likely to arise when the constraint of the profit criterion is removed. The framework Reder constructs can be useful in analyzing the employment and wage effects of such diverse phenomena as public job creation programs, public employee unionism, etc. He emphasizes political aspects of decision-making in this sector and the need to integrate such considerations into standard economic analysis when discussing behavior. His discussion of cases in which the government will or will not be likely to provide services or shift them to the private sector is particularly interesting. This and others of his ideas should be useful stimuli to empirical work in this field.

Among the important questions about employment in the public sector are those dealing with the effects of wage subsidies and general revenue sharing on public employment. By providing subsidies to state and local governments, the federal government lowers the cost of labor to them and increases their demand for labor. Empirically, however, we have no estimate of the magnitude of these effects. Orley Ashenfelter and Ronald Ehrenberg provide a detailed study of this phenomenon using the theory of consumer demand. The results are the first available measures of the elasticity of demand for different types of labor services in the public sector. In addition to its usefulness for those involved in planning public employment or wage subsidy programs, the paper is a model of how to apply and test a theory developed for one problem (in this case consumers' demand for commodities) to another analogous problem. It should lead to further work to refine their estimates and to test the model on different sets of data covering more detailed occupational breakdowns.

After a detailed comparison of wage and employment determination in for-profit and nonprofit industry, Richard Freeman's paper turns to the specifics of those problems in colleges and universities. He stresses the dual role of tenured faculty—both as employees and employers—and discusses its effects during periods of changing demand for labor in this sector. This study of the academic labor market is the first to base its empirical analysis on a model of behavior of nonprofit firms. The results suggest the existence of demand curves that are by no means completely inelastic. Freeman uses these findings to discuss future developments in this labor market.

If we can discover what determines variations in strike activity, we will have a good leg up on means of improving labor relations in the public sector. John Burton and Charles Krider attempt to do this in their analysis of data on strikes in the public sector from 1968 to 1971 across states. They consider such important factors as the types of law governing public employee labor relations and how these differences affect strike activity. While their results are somewhat discouraging insofar as definite answers are concerned, they do point out the need for further work in this area and the way that work should proceed. Most interesting is the evidence from their paper that the extent of private unionization in a labor market has a bearing on the willingness of public employees to strike. The negative result that laws prohibiting strikes do not appear to lower the number of man-days lost is itself of great interest.

Donald Frey's detailed study of the market for teachers in New Jersey is useful both as a theoretical model of how quality interacts with quantity in the demand for labor and as an empirical study of wage determination in a narrowly defined occupation. His finding that the presence of a collective bargaining agreement appears to have little effect on wages is consistent with other, less detailed and thorough work on the wage effects of public-employee unions. The very small effects of differences in family income and tax base on wages paid to teachers suggest that the important factors causing variations in the quality of educational services arise from differences in the nonpecuniary attractiveness of higher-income school districts to prospective teachers. This in turn implies that equalization of property tax rates across areas will by itself have little direct effect in equalizing the quality of schooling. While a number of previous studies have measured the wage effect of public employee unions, none has attempted to separate differences in the types of services operated publicly from differences caused by public versus private ownership of the same service. In his study of local transit, construction, and a sample of workers from all occupations, Daniel Hamermesh provides this separation. The results suggest that there is a small extra wage effect produced by public-employee unions over what is gained by a union in the same service in the private sector. Perhaps more important, the study isolates this problem and provides ways of analyzing it that can be extended to other services using detailed data from carefully selected cities.

The papers presented here are complete and self contained, each being concerned with some aspect of labor in the public sector. On the other hand, they are only a beginning insofar as they are the first attempts to provide such thorough analysis of this sector of the national labor market. As such, in addition to their inherent usefulness for policy makers, the demonstrated fruitfulness of the approach should encourage work by other economists who recognize the increasing importance of this sector.

Labor in the Public
and Nonprofit Sectors

MELVIN W. REDER

The Theory of Employment and Wages in the Public Sector

Since no later point will be convenient, at the outset I should like to contrast the quality of the recent work in the area of this conference with the early pioneering efforts at analyzing interindustry wage differentials in the immediate post-World War II period. In theoretical conception, econometric technique, and wealth of data analyzed, the work to which I shall refer is incomparably superior to the efforts of only a quarter century ago. However, my role is not to dwell on how far we have come, but on how far we have still to go.

I. Introduction

I propose to organize my discussion around the following question: Why should there be a wage differential between the public and nonpublic sectors for "comparable" workers? The quick and largely correct answer is that among workers who are truly comparable there will be no such differential in the long run. The critical point, obviously, is what is meant by "comparable."

Roughly, in order to be truly comparable, workers should be alike in respect of embodied human capital, tastes, and location. Alike in respect of "embodied capital" means, in practice, alike in respect of age, years of (relevant) experience, years of schooling, and all natural endowments not fully reflected in the measures of the other characteristics. For workers to be alike in respect of tastes means that a per-hour, equalizing, pecuniary wage differential between any two jobs would be the same for any pair of workers. Location is a significant attribute of a job, and

Note: I thank Professor Victor Fuchs for the tabulations underlying the data in the Appendix. Some of my discussion takes account of Professor Klevorick's helpful comments.

"equalizing differentials" between otherwise identical jobs may arise simply because the jobs have different locations; workers will be comparable only after such locational differentials have been taken into account.

Thus defined, hourly wage differentials between *comparable* workers would seem incompatible with competitive equilibrium.[1] Yet such differentials may, and I suspect do, exist between public and other types of employment. The explanation lies in the peculiar characteristics of public employment that make jobs that are superficially similar to those in the private sector have appreciably different marginal products and supply prices.

Originally I had hoped to relate the theoretical considerations developed to observations on the differences in wage rates actually paid comparable workers in the public and private sectors. However, this intention has been frustrated. The differences in job characteristics, effort expended, and the like between superficially comparable workers in the public and private sectors are too important from the standpoint of the theory advanced to permit any useful confrontation of theory with data now available. Accordingly, I have described the data now available on public and private sector hourly earnings in the Appendix. The reader should consider it solely as background information.

This paper focuses on the public sector. The hypothesis upon which the discussion is based is that all decision makers are utility maximizers. The inferences drawn from this hypothesis are very simple and, save for one or two duly noted exceptions, follow directly from the assumption that the public-sector decision makers are successful utility maximizers operating under static conditions and with no "political rent." The assumption of static conditions means that public-sector decision makers act as though there were no difference between present and expected future values of variables subject to control. The notion of political rent is a bit more complicated and can best be discussed later.

The public-sector employer may be a federal, state, or local

[1]Throughout the paper I shall abstract from wage differentials associated with length of work week. For simplicity, and at the price of some inaccuracy, I shall assume that the price of an hour of labor of given quality is the same whatever the number of weekly hours hired.

government or any type of special-purpose governmental unit. For convenience, let the definitive characteristic of a governmental unit be possession of some power to levy taxes on persons within its zone of authority. The demand function of a governmental unit, for labor of any given kind, will vary with the political characteristics of the unit. Thus the demand function of the federal government will (or may) differ from that of a state government, which in turn will differ from that of a local government. Most of the extant empirical research on public employee wages refers to local governments; however, an explanation of public-private wage differentials should be as broadly applicable as possible. Our explanation of public-private wage and employment differentials proceeds under these headings: differentials arising in the production of a single product in the absence of unionism; differentials arising from differences in product-mix; and differentials attributable to unionism.

II. Public-Private Wage and Employment Differentials in the Production of a Single Product

A. Utility Maximization by a Public-Sector Employer

It is tempting to regard the demand for labor of a given quality by a governmental agency as simply an application of the theory of household demand for inputs. For example, this is the spirit in which Ehrenberg (1972) proceeds. In effect, he treats a governmental decision-making unit as a household whose resource constraint reflects a process of utility maximization in which it or some higher body funding it decides the fraction of the constituency's resources to be devoted to supporting the governmental activities under discussion. The allocation of resources between the governmental unit and other uses is assumed to be "strongly separable" from the allocation of the governmental unit's resources among alternative inputs.[2] This assumption permits

[2] That is, the optimal input-output combinations chosen under any set of input and output prices are independent of whatever resource allocations are made within or between any other sector or sectors of the economy.

3

focusing attention entirely on the optimal mix of publicly produced goods and services from a given governmental budget, with the resulting derived demand for a given kind of labor being determined by the maximization of some utility or objective function subject to a budget constraint with given input prices. As Ehrenberg shows, this leads to a set of interrelated derived demand functions for various kinds of labor that is formally analogous to household demand functions for goods.

This procedure precludes consideration of the *political* factors that bear upon government behavior. It is the premise of this paper that normally political factors are important in determining government wage-employment decisions. In some cases it may be expedient to abstract from them, but this should be done explicitly and only with specific justification. In analyzing behavior in the public sector, political considerations can never be treated as incidental.

What follows is a sketch of a model that purports to explain the politically determined behavior of a governmental decision maker. Consider first its objective or utility function that relates the utility of a government, U, to its *expected* number of votes, V:

$$(1) \qquad U = f(V, a_1, \ldots, a_q).$$

For simplicity, abstract from lags and consider only static relationships. (It will often be useful to measure V as a percentage of eligible voters.) In general, $U'_V > 0$ for all V, though, as we shall see there may be discontinuities and inflection points.[3]

[3] As written, (1) implies that a government has no tradeoff between votes and pecuniary payoffs for its members. At least in some circumstances this is descriptively inaccurate. Its justification for the present purpose is the assumption that there is a fairly steady rate of exchange between dollars and votes. That is, it is assumed that a political party can convert sure dollars into probabilistic votes by various combinations of advertising and personal canvassing (both purchasable) and also can trade votes of its "dedicated supporters" for dollars of contributions from outsiders by joining coalitions, endorsing outside candidates, etc.

As a rule actions that increase a government's expected V will also increase its contributions, and vice versa. An exception should be made for crude sellouts that enrich government members but disgust voters. This last case aside, what improves the government's vote prospects is likely to

The empirical characteristics of the transformation function between dollars and votes obviously is a matter of great practical interest and, in my judgment, is eminently researchable. For the present purpose I assume that the government chooses an optimal mix of disposable dollars and votes, and that its actions are selected so as to reach this optimum, given the constraint of its political resource endowment. That is, I assume the government selects a course of action such as to make its marginal rate of substitution between dollars and votes equal to the rate at which they can be exchanged for one another. It is assumed that the rate of exchange between dollars and votes is independent of wage and employment decisions. Everything said of (1) refers to a political party out of office as much as to a government; however, our primary interest is in the behavior of governments, i.e., parties in office.[4]

The parameters $a_1, \ldots, a_q$ are "ideological parameters," which are determined exogenously. They reflect the fact that a government gets utility not only by adding to its votes but also by avoiding (engaging) in certain types of actions that it considers ideologically offensive (attractive). Normally there is some trade-off between attracting votes and pursuing ideological objectives, but this is irrelevant to the present theme.

Depending upon the specific characteristics of the electoral system, at particular values of V, U'_V may have a saltus. For example, in a two-party situation, the marginal utility of an additional vote that puts a party over 50 percent will be very much greater than that of a vote that puts it over 40 or 60 percent.

---

increase its receipts which, in various ways, can be converted into increased consumption for its members. Hence vote maximization is taken to be a reasonable first approximation to a government's behavior function. The issue of government objectives is explored in greater depth by Barro (1972).

[4] The classic discussion of optimization by political parties is Downs (1957), but during the past few years a number of papers have been devoted to formal development of this theory. Two of the better ones are Wittman (1973) and Hinich and Ordeshook (1970). I cite these not only because of their inherent value but also because their footnotes give many references to the literature.

Such salta sometimes cause great sacrifices of ideology to get a few extra votes.

In principle, a party will have some discretion in choosing combinations of ideological position and number of votes; it is assumed that there is some finite tradeoff between the two. In practice, this apparent discretion will be greatly limited by the exigencies of political competition, which normally compel a party to approximate vote-maximizing behavior fairly closely if it is to win elections.[5] Parties with strong ideological commitments may *survive*, but their chance of winning and becoming a government is very low and therefore, for our purposes, may be ignored.[6]

Political parties with a substantial probability of success may have some long-run options as to the combination of victory-probability and ideological position that they choose. This is analogous to the type of option that entrepreneurs may have between maximizing pecuniary income and pursuing other utility-yielding objectives in cases where they are earning rent. However, as in the case of a competitive industry, it is assumed that the range of tradeoff options compatible with continuing political contention is so narrow as to be negligible, with the result that all relevant parties are assumed to maximize expected votes.[7]

Analogous to the situation where competitive entrepreneurs may earn large temporary quasi-rents, transitory disturbances may give a political party a comfortable vote margin for achieving victory at the next election (or put it in a position where victory is unattainable). In either of these cases an entrepreneur may temporarily deemphasize his quest for pecuniary income in favor of other sources of utility, and, analogously, political parties may relent in their efforts to attract marginal votes in favor of a more

[5] A good discussion of political competition and related matters is Barro (1972). Barro's analysis is in many ways deeper than mine, but it is not directly relevant to wage and employment behavior.

[6] Clearly, the survival prospects of governments and parties with greater and less ideological rigidity is an interesting and important matter, but one that cannot be discussed here.

[7] By "continuing political contention" I mean that the party has a sufficient chance of victory for its leaders to make winning elections the major determinant of behavior whether in or out of office.

intensive pursuit of ideological purity. Although recognizing these possibilities, I abstract from them and argue as though governments normally behaved like maximizers of expected votes subject to the constraint of maintaining a certain (constant) degree of ideological purity.[8] (The analogy to the assumption that firms behave as if they were maximizers of money profits is obvious.) The assumption of vote maximization has no greater claim to descriptive accuracy in regard to political behavior than has profit maximization as a description of ordinary business activity; indeed, it may well have less. However, it is an extension of economic theory that should at least be tried.

B. Vote Maximization and Public-Sector Labor Demand

Now let us turn to the vote function:

$$(2) \qquad V = \phi \, (Q(p), p, X_1, X_2, X_3, T, C, S, w_1, w_2, r),$$

where the X are inputs, r is the cost of capital, and C are resource contributions. Let us consider the arguments of (2) *seriatim;* for simplicity, assume the government produces one good in quantity Q which it sells at a price, p. Assume that p and Q are selected so that their values always lie on the demand curve $Q = Q(p)$.

It is assumed that V_p' is negative. The rationale is that, *ceteris paribus,* a voter is more favorably disposed toward a government the lower the price at which it furnishes him a good.[9] Hence, lowering p will tip some marginal voters toward the government.[10]

---

[8] Formally, this would mean rewriting (1) so that $U = F(V)$ subject to a set of constraints $a_i \geqslant A_i$, $i = 1, 2, \ldots, q$, where A_i increases with the "purity" of the party's stand on the ith issue. This formal development is not needed for this paper.

[9] I assume that voters have short memories, otherwise they would remember the failures of the "outs" during their last period of incumbency. Also voters would heavily discount actions taken immediately prior to an election. Our argument, like any that explains political behavior as inspired by a desire to attract votes, must posit: 1) some positive association between current performance and voter expectation of future behavior; and 2) rather short voter memories. However, the detailed structure of such models cannot be considered here.

[10] It is assumed that the probability of any voter casting his ballot in favor of the government in the next election is a function of a number of variables including the price, p. The probability of an individual voting

7

Given the assumption that the government's policy is to adjust output so as to stay on the demand curve, Q is determined once p is set. Since lowering p will increase the consumer surplus of buyers, it will increase the probability that they will vote for the government.

This line of reasoning might be thought to suggest that a rational government should set all prices at zero or even charge negative prices, but this would ignore taxes, T. The higher an individual's tax burden, the less likely he is to vote to retain a government; i.e., $V_T' < 0$. For convenience, assume that T is a vector of tax payments for all n taxpayers, and that the tax burden of individual i, $T^{(i)}$, is a unique and increasing function of the general tax level, T.[11] Let S be a vector of payments to citizens for reasons other than provision of factor services. In general, the effect of S upon V is the mirror image of that of T, hence $V_S' > 0$.

Assume that deficits are not permitted; all government payments must be financed by sales or taxes. (This restrictive assumption prevents consideration of the political economy of inflation.) In effect, this makes government expenditure subject to a receipts constraint:

(3) $$E \equiv pQ + T \equiv X_1 w_1 + X_2 w_2 + X_3 r + S,$$

where E is government spending.

Suppose the government goods were produced at a rate that made marginal cost equal to the price charged. To reduce its price and continue to supply the quantity demanded it would be necessary to increase outlays on factor inputs $(X_1 w_1 + X_2 w_2 + X_3 r)$ by more than the increment in receipts from selling the required outputs. Other things equal, this would necessitate an increase in T which would reduce V. Thus the effect of a reduction in p on V includes a favorable effect on voting through buyers of

---

for the government is a non-increasing function of pQ, given the values of the other arguments of his voting function. In principle, from individual voting functions one could calculate the expected gain in votes from a small decrease in p.

[11] This simplifying assumption enables us to avoid some complex questions on the distribution of the tax burden.

the product and an unfavorable effect through taxpayers.[12] (Later we shall consider the impact of p on V that arises from the effect through employment and wages, but for the moment we shall assume that this is negligible.)

The impact of government decisions concerning price and output upon votes is both direct and indirect, via contributions of resources. Resource contributions, either in cash or services (which have a cash equivalent) are an argument of (2), ($V_C' > 0$) and must satisfy:

$$(4) \qquad\qquad C = c_1 + \ldots + c_n.$$

The contribution of individual i is given by:

$$(4') \qquad\qquad c_i = c_i(T_i, S_i, p),$$

where $c_{i_{T_i}}'$ and c_{i_p}' are negative, and $c_{i_{S_i}}'$ is positive. If the government's price-output behavior injures its purchasers sufficiently, they may respond by reducing their contributions or even making them negative.[13] The indirect effect of a price change on the government's expected vote, via contributions, may be greater

[12]Obviously, voters may be both buyers and taxpayers. We assume that each voter responds more to the stimulus of one variable than the other, depending upon his marginal tax rate and the importance of the government good in his budget. Symbolically, the effect on V of reducing p is given by:

$$\frac{dV}{dp} = \frac{\partial V}{\partial p} + \frac{\partial V}{\partial Q}\frac{\partial Q}{\partial p} + \frac{\partial V}{\partial T}\frac{dT}{dp}.$$

From (3):

$$\frac{dT}{dp} = -\left[p\frac{dQ}{dp} + Q\right],$$

and from the demand function:

$$\frac{dQ}{dp} = \frac{\partial Q}{\partial p},$$

so that:

$$\frac{dV}{dp} = \frac{\partial V}{\partial p} + \left[\frac{\partial V}{\partial Q} - p\frac{\partial V}{\partial T}\right]\cdot\frac{\partial Q}{\partial p} - Q\frac{\partial V}{\partial T}.$$

[13]A negative contribution is one made to a political opponent.

9

than the direct effect; the relative size of direct and indirect effects depends both on the impact of the price change on contributions and on the impact of contributions on votes.[14]

Our primary concern is not with the effect of vote seeking on the pricing of public-sector output, but on the wage rates the public sector pays and the amounts of labor it uses. In a conventional, nonpolitical model of public-sector wage and employment behavior, X_1, X_2, and X_3 would be related to Q and to one another via a production function such as:

$$(5) \qquad Q = G(X_1, X_2, X_3).$$

with G'_{X_1}, G'_{X_2}, $G'_{X_3} > 0$ and G''_{X_1}, G''_{X_2} and $G''_{X_3} < 0$.

The input prices w_1, and w_2 and r would either be treated as parametric constants or, where the public sector was large enough, as increasing functions of the quantities used, as in:

$$(6) \qquad \begin{aligned} w_1 &= W_1(X_1; \theta_1); \\ w_2 &= W_2(X_2; \theta_2); \\ r &= W_3(X_3; \theta_3); \end{aligned}$$

with W'_1, W'_2, and $W'_3 \geqslant 0$.

In such a model Q would (or might) be treated as exogenous and the X's deduced from (5) and (6) on the assumption that (3) is minimized for given Q, S, θ_1, θ_2 and θ_3. The thetas are parameters of the various factor supply functions reflecting, inter alia, rates of pecuniary reward outside the public sector, the effect of unionism on rates of remuneration in the public sector, and relative nonpecuniary advantages of employment in the public and private sectors.

If such a model were to be used to explain the existence of wage differentials for comparable labor employed in the public sector relative to that employed elsewhere, it would be necessary to posit either a relative taste (nonpecuniary advantage) for being employed in the public sector or a differential impact of unionism in the public sector. While it is possible that a relative taste for public-sector employment per se does exist, such an hypothe-

---

[14] Equation (4') is derived from constrained maximization of contributor i's utility function.

sis has never been proposed and I see no reason to consider it seriously. Differential impact of unionism is the explanation of public-private wage differentials most in keeping with the spirit of the recent empirical work on public-sector wage behavior, and it is commented upon in Section IV.

An approach I consider more promising is to treat vote-getting explicitly as the primary activity of government with the output of the public sector as a produced input in the vote production function:

$$(2') \qquad V = \overline{\phi}(X_1, X_2, X_3, p, T, C, S, w_1, w_2, r),$$

derived from (2) by substituting (5) into (2). The technology underlying (5) is assumed to be the same as that available elsewhere in the economy, so that the marginal product of any quantity of labor in terms of Q is the same in the public sector as elsewhere. (For convenience it is assumed that Q is also produced and sold under competitive conditions in the private sector.) The marginal product in terms of V, expected votes, has no obvious counterpart outside of the public sector.

The theory of public-sector factor demand is not altered by making the impact of any X on U occur in two steps, through Q to V and from V to U, instead of directly from Q to U. What does alter it is the assumption that the X affects V directly as well as through Q. This assumption implies that even if Q were produced in the private as well as in the public sector with the same technology and factor prices, the derived demand for any X at given Q would be different in the public sector because of the direct effect of X on V.

The direct effect of, for example, X_1 on V arises from encouraging or even requiring as a condition of employment that public-sector employees furnish political campaign labor. The importance of this effect will vary, with their effectiveness as political workers, from one class of employee to another, from one governmental unit to another, and with laws, customs, and regulations restricting the political activity of government employees.

For given w_1 a rational public-sector employer should be able to obtain an amount of employee effort per hour from a given worker equal to what would be supplied to a private-sector employer. Therefore, if the terms of public-sector employment required that some effort be expended in political activity, the marginal product of X_1 in terms of Q would be lower than in the private sector. That is, the equilibrium condition that there be equal advantages of employment in alternative activities implies that if: 1) the ratio of pecuniary compensation in the public and private sectors are equal; and 2) the value of the marginal product of time devoted to political activity in votes is positive, $\overline{\phi}'_{X_1} > 0$ for similar workers, the value of the marginal product of X_1 in terms of public sector Q will be lower than the private-sector marginal product of Q.[15] If public-sector workers vary in their allocation of time between political activity and production of Q, then, among workers embodying equal amounts of human capital *and* paid equal pecuniary compensation per hour, there will be an inverse association of time spent on the job and time devoted to political activity.

This is not to argue that all public-sector employees engage in political activity. For some workers, possibly very many, the relative importance of public-sector services to consumer-voters may be so great that the marginal vote product of time spent in direct politicking would be negligible compared with the votes they may produce through increasing nonpolitical output, Q. Such workers would engage in no political activity.

C. Taxes and Related Limitations upon Vote Production

Statutes punishing political activity by public employees, such as the Hatch Act of 1940, function as a tax upon use of public employees' time as an input in vote production, thereby discouraging such use of their time. That is, these statutes encourage specialization of public employees in producing Q. Similarly, statutes protecting the jobs of civil servants from the arbitrary or politically motivated decisions of elected officials or

---

[15] This argument is analogous to that of Alchian and Kessel (1962), who contend that regulated firms and those otherwise prevented from maximizing pecuniary profit tend to pay wage premia to workers for characteristics that render utility to their managers but are irrelevant to stockholders' concerns.

their agents reduce the expected increment in votes a government can obtain by offering a marginal hour of employment in the public sector.[16] This discourages use of tax dollars, which have a vote cost, for putting people on the public payroll to get them to produce votes.

Thus taxes, including at the limit outright prohibitions, on political activity by persons holding public jobs may reduce or possibly eliminate such activity.[17] Inter alia, this would alter the equilibrium relation between w_1 and G'_{X_1}, which varies with the tax rate levied upon political activity by public employees. Even if such activity by public employees could be completely prevented, it would not follow that "vote production" could be separated from public-sector wages and employment.

For example, a government might trade a job that paid its incumbent more than his marginal product in the private sector in exchange for a cash contribution to its political war chest. At the extreme, such jobs might be outright sinecures. Moreover, the contribution need not be in cash nor made by the person who gets the job. That is, jobs may be sold to intermediaries (friends or relatives, possibly at second or third remove, of contributors) as a way of inducing contributions. Taxes or regulations on contributions in cash or in kind will act as impediments to this method of vote production and tend to encourage use of public funds to "overpay" public employees as an indirect method of getting them to produce votes.

So long as political success has utility, and an increase in the expected number of votes increases the probability of political success, the marginal vote product must be positive for all methods

[16] They do this by increasing the cost of enforcing promises to engage in vote-producing activities in the future by persons seeking public-sector jobs. That is, statutes that make it difficult to dismiss or worsen the terms of employment of a public employee once he is hired also make it difficult (costly) to punish him for reneging on a promise to render political service.

[17] We adopt the convention that curbs on or deterrents to political activity may be interpreted as specific taxes that function as the price of a license to engage in it. Attempts to circumvent curbs on political activity are analogous to black-market activities to circumvent price controls. For discussions of black markets see Bronfenbrenner (1947), Gönensay (1966), and Gould and Henry (1967).

13

of vote production in use. Moreover, the marginal vote product of a one dollar cash contribution must be equal to the marginal vote product that could be obtained by a contributor's devoting a dollar's worth of his time to vote-producing activity and to the marginal vote product that a potential contributor could purchase by hiring a dollar's worth of labor to engage in vote producing.[18]

Attempts to restrict political activity of public employees, their cash contributions to political funds, or the cash contributions by others are on all fours with other sumptuary legislation. The welfare aspects of such attempts to restrict the use of private wealth are beyond the purview of this paper, though obviously not trivial. However, such attempts have the effect of encouraging vote production by use of private resources (e.g. having votes produced by individuals on payrolls of private firms in which employers contribute employer services) in lieu of cash contributions and/or higher taxes to finance public employment of vote producers.

Penalizing the use of private resources to induce others to engage in vote production discourages specialization and division of labor in the production of votes. By discouraging use of the market in the production of votes, society imposes a discriminatory tax on vote production by use of nonhuman capital relative to use of human capital. For example, the services of a great entertainer to raise funds or attract votes for a "cause" tend to be treated as a commendable use of his personal liberty, while a cash contribution of equal value by an unentertaining "fat cat" is condemned and legally proscribed.

Formally, this argument may be expressed by modifying (2′) in the following way: divide X_1, X_2, and X_3 into hours used to produce votes and hours used for all other purposes. Let the hours used to produce votes be designated with a superscript, $X_1^{(V)}$, $X_2^{(V)}$, etc. Also let those hours in the public sector that are used to produce votes be designated by a second superscript, $X_1^{(GV)}$, etc. Where a tax is imposed on vote production by public em-

---

[18] This statement abstracts from transactions costs, which may be very important in this context.

ployees of type 1, their employment cost will be $w_1[1 + t_1^{(GV)}]$; if the tax is imposed on vote production in the private sector, the employment cost will be $w_1[1 + t_1^{(V)}]$. (Appropriate notation can be introduced if vote production is taxed in part but not all of the private sector, etc.) The indicated modification of (2′) is given by:

$$(2'') \quad V = \bar{\phi}([X_i, X_i^{(V)}, X_i^{(GV)}; w_i[1 + t_j^{(V)}], r[1 + t^{(V)}];$$
$$w_j[1 + t_j^{(GV)}], r[1 + t^{(GV)}]; w_j, r; \text{etc.}), i = 1, 2, 3; j = 1, 2.$$

Those variables unaffected by the modification are indicated by "etc."[19]

The effect of a "t" is (potentially) to shift the optimal combination of inputs from what it would have been had t been zero; a change in a t acts like an exogenous change in a factor price. The "ordinary" discussions of wages and employment in the public sector, which assume votes to be independent of resource use, may be interpreted as applying where either: 1) $\bar{\phi}_{X_i}^{\prime(V)} \equiv \bar{\phi}_{X_i}^{\prime(GV)} \equiv 0$; or 2) Both $t_j^{(V)}$ and $t_j^{(GV)}$ are set so high as to make the demand for X_i for use in vote production equal to zero in both the public and private sectors. Satisfaction of the first condition would imply that no one ever engaged in vote production on behalf of anyone outside of his household for any reason other than enjoyment of the activity itself.

Obviously, neither of these conditions is likely to be satisfied. The important question is how important are the violations of these conditions, and where they occur. In general, given total expenditure on vote production and relative input prices, an increase in the ratio $t_j^{(GV)}/t_j^{(V)}$ will have the conventional substitution and wealth effects on relative input quantities. There will be a shift toward relatively greater use of private-sector inputs of i in the production of votes.[20] This means that an increase in the tax upon use of public employees to produce votes relative to the tax

---

[19] In principle, (2″) should be derived from the conditions of expected vote maximization of the government. However, the formal derivation is trivial and its implications obvious. Therefore, I assume these implications are built into (2″) without going through their derivation.

[20] It is assumed that use of household time to produce votes increases with household wealth.

levied upon use of private employees for this same purpose will lead to a relative increase in the use of the latter. To use private-sector labor in vote production means either having workers on the payrolls of business firms engage in political activity or paying households for the political activity of their members, the means of payment coming as contributions from businesses or other households.

The t's are in essence transaction taxes levied upon the hiring of resources or upon the contribution of means to pay for hired resources to engage in vote production without transactions; i.e., production by households for direct satisfaction. Studying the effect of such taxes on the level and kinds of political activity that take place would constitute an interesting and important investigation but one that cannot be undertaken here.[21]

To summarize briefly, consider the effects of such taxes in cases where they are not so great as to prevent completely the joint production of votes and ordinary public-sector output, i.e., where public employees engage in political activity. If the marginal vote product is positive, and the marginal nonvote products in the public and private sectors are equal, the hourly wage rate in the public sector must exceed that in the private sector for labor embodying equal quanta of human capital.[22] The implied difference between public- and private-sector wage rates will reflect compensation for the extra effort required for vote produc-

---

[21] There is a substantial and growing bibliography on the explanation of political behavior as the result of some sort of vote-seeking. While this literature is theoretically elaborate, I have not yet found a way to make use of its results in the present context. Moreover, so far as I am aware, this literature has not appreciably influenced students of wage and employment behavior in the public sector. Therefore, for the purpose of getting the discussion off the ground, I have ignored complications and restricted myself to what may prove to be an overly simple model.

[22] Throughout this paper it is assumed that the marginal vote product of employment in the private sector is negligible. There are circumstances, e.g., when corporate managers divert time normally used for company business to political activity, where this assumption is contrary to fact. However, it will not be disputed that time devoted to political activity and paid for by the employer is much more common among public-sector workers.

tion. Still further, at any given set of input prices and with constant returns to scale, the input of X_1 per unit of Q will increase with the marginal vote product of X_1. If vote output is ignored, it will appear that inputs of X_1 per unit of Q, observed as variations in productivity, will increase with X_1's marginal vote product.

In short, the unmeasured effect of public-sector inputs on votes may generate either or both wage differentials and differences in equilibrium inputs per unit output for comparable labor in the public and private sectors. If effort per hour is the same in both sectors, it will be necessary for the public sector to make jobs more attractive than those offered to comparable labor in the private sector in order to be able to require workers to contribute some combination of extra effort to be used in vote production and money to be used for buying vote-producing inputs.[23]

Allocating the public-sector "excess" net advantage per hour between pecuniary wage difference and difference in required political effort is a difficult and complicated matter with which I shall not attempt to cope. Wherever part of this excess is used to reduce hourly effort required on public-sector jobs relative to private, there will be an increased input of hours of the relevant kind of labor at given levels of public sector outputs. Except where the effect of increasing returns is very strong, this will lead to an increase in hours of employment of a given kind of labor per unit of public-sector output.

To give the above remarks empirical content would require far more data than can be obtained from census-type surveys that gather information on earnings, weekly hours, age, education, sex, race, etc. To correct hourly wages for differences in intensity of effort and/or uses of time as between vote production and production of public-sector output, it would be necessary to study work patterns in considerable detail, as is done in time-and-motion studies. While such studies are feasible, few have yet

---

[23] It would be incorrect to infer from this that the *measured* wage rate for given quality labor will normally be higher in the public sector. It is possible that public-sector wage rates would be lower than private, but that the effort required to produce public-sector output would also be less than what is required elsewhere.

17

been made, so that use of this theory to explain empirical phenomena must be left to the future.

D. Political Transactions and Vote Production

What is suggested here is that we make the theory of public-sector wages and employment, insofar as it differs from that applicable to the private sector, part of a theory of behavior in which votes and goods are produced jointly. Some readers may be moved to object on the ground that most public job holders do not feel that their jobs confer any special benefits and do not feel themselves under any pressure to engage in political activity. To such an objection I would suggest that many public-sector jobs are not "sold" directly to their incumbents, but are made available through various political functionaries who arrange for their friends to have differentially advantageous access. This might mean nothing more than advance or very early knowledge of vacancies, so that political favor would involve only a differential reduction in search cost. This consequence of political favoritism might be reflected only indirectly, if at all, in public-private wage or productivity differentials.

Another way in which political favoritism confers advantage upon certain public job holders is by giving them jobs above what their ability, industry, and training would obtain in private industry. This would be reflected in a tendency for the public sector disproportionately to attract and retain individuals having bad employment histories or possessing only *pro forma* competence.

To estimate the importance of this selection bias, it would be necessary to compare some or all of the following: 1) earnings histories of public employees prior to their entry into public employment with histories of otherwise comparable workers remaining in the private sector; 2) public- and private-sector employees having equal earnings and equal experience in respect of "ability," as measured by school grades, test performance, or some index other than earnings; 3) public- and private-sector employees in respect of effort expended, as indicated by, for example, time-and-motion studies; 4) the hiring and selection processes for public-sector jobs to ascertain the strength of the association between political connections useful in obtaining a job with subsequent job performance. Unless these and other channels of differential performance are taken into account, public-private wage and employment differences will not be properly analyzed.

There are other important channels through which government vote-seeking influences the terms of public employment. For example, on many Civil Service examinations provision is made for favoritism to members of particular groups, e.g., veterans, local residents, U.S. citizens, handicapped persons, members of groups favored by "Affirmative Action Programs." The particular individuals who benefit by such favoritism incur no individual political debts, but the groups to which they belong, voluntarily or otherwise, do. The organizations that lobby for such favors are politically active and use their alleged influence over their members' votes as material for political trading. Obviously, many beneficiaries of this type of political trading act as "free riders," but not all of them do.

As we note in part E below, public employers tend to operate with a shorter time horizon than private. Moreover, public-sector funds often must be spent by a given date or be returned to the treasury. As a result, public jobs are frequently filled in a hurried fashion with little opportunity for considering either the marginal vote product or the marginal public-sector output of those hired. At other times, transitory excesses of public-sector job applicants or deficiencies of public-sector vacancies make each vacancy a treasure to be "auctioned" for what it will fetch. These fluctuations in the state of the public-sector job market introduce a large and erratic transitory component into the relation between public-sector wage rates and the marginal vote product of public-sector employees; the relative importance of this component increases with the intertemporal variability of expenditure by the relevant public employer and with intertemporal variations in labor market tightness.[24]

---

[24] Labor market tightness is relevant because in a loose labor market, where jobs are hard to find and search costs correspondingly great, job opportunities are prized and tend to be sold or traded rather than more or less given away.

The relative proportions of public employees' time that are devoted to vote production or to public-sector output vary from one worker to another and from job to job, with complete specialization a distinct possibility. As already indicated, concentration on vote production will be associated with a relatively low contribution to public-sector output. Because the public sector tends to specialize in tasks where output quality is difficult to measure, concentration on vote production will often be reflected in low quality rather than scant quantity of output.

This does not mean that quality standards are nonexistent in the public sector, but their enforcement is erratic. To a large extent such standards must be enforced by "voice" rather than by seeking alternative suppliers.[25] Complaint about public-sector quality of service will be effective to the extent that it is persistent, articulate, and emanates from sources able to affect votes. Effective complaint is likely to increase the resources devoted to the service complained about as well as, or instead of, increasing hourly productivity, but in any event it will set some sort of floor under worker performance.

The use of complaints to improve the quality of public service involves an investment of time and trouble by the complainant. Such investment is likely to occur only where contact with the offending government agency is expected to continue. Therefore, one would expect performance to be better, both because of greater resources per unit of output and more effort per man hour, where an agency's clientele is dominated by repeaters rather than by "one-shot" contacts.

One would also expect that frequent transactors would develop special relationships reinforced by gratuities with appropriate employees to improve the quality of the service rendered to them.[26] Such relationships will increase real earnings and also

[25] "Voice" here refers to complaint by dissatisfied recipients of the government service. The concept of "voice" was introduced by Hirschman (1970).

[26] Thus payment by results enters the public sector through an illegal backdoor. The comparative roles of bribery and complaint in maintaining service quality in different branches of the public sector are obviously a matter of interest. In principle, a user would optimize by an appropriate combination of complaint and bribery, varying with costs and circumstances.

20

increase effort expended; however, to some extent the increased effort on behalf of "gratuity" payers will be offset by reduced effort on behalf of others. Obviously, some jobs will yield more gratuities than others, which will make them more coveted and a source of influence to those with power to assign them.

In short, to understand wage and employment behavior in the public sector it is essential to explore in some detail the set of activities associated with each job and the net advantages to the job assigner of assigning a particular job to a given individual. Otherwise, differences in productivity and output quality among different branches of government and on different jobs will never be properly understood.[27] (Indeed, to a lesser extent, surreptitious use of incentive payments and related phenomena also exist in the private sector.) While such differences are measurable, they cannot be inferred from a manning table or a payroll sheet.

Where public-private differences in compensation and employment per unit of output of otherwise comparable labor exist, they are due to the production in the public sector of an unmeasured output—votes. In some unknown fraction of public-sector jobs, the production of votes does not require an expenditure of effort sufficient to offset the other advantages of public-sector employment. Where such excess of net advantages occurs, it is imputable to an input into the production of votes made by third parties whose benefits are transferred or traded, directly or through intermediaries, to the public-sector workers.

E. A Digression on Optimization by Politicians and Profit Seekers

Opposition to increases in w_i and X_i (Q fixed) comes from voter opposition to tax increases and client resistance to deteriora-

---

[27]What is needed is the analogue of time-and-motion studies of the work behavior of appropriately selected individuals; in particular, it is necessary to study the time and effort spent in dealing with the various clients of the governmental entity employing the job holder. Also, the difficulty of filling particular jobs should be analyzed; jobs where nonpecuniary or hidden pecuniary benefits are important should be easier to fill than others. This should be reflected in lower average intervals during which such jobs are vacant, in lower quit rates and in above average qualifications of incumbents on these jobs relative to others having the same organizational rank.

tion of public output. The strength of this opposition is exaggerated by the requirements of (3), which constrain the government to a continuously balanced budget. This precludes consideration of an important facet of behavior that distinguishes the public and private sectors. In the private sector an entrepreneur normally expects to pay his own debts and generally to bear the consequences of his behavior. Even if he anticipates selling his business, the effects of actions currently undertaken will be reflected in the sale price of his equity.[28] This serves to hold him reasonably close to the mark of cost minimization.

In the public sector it is often quite different. When defeated in an election, a politician and his party have virtually no liability for whatever fiscal mess is left behind. (We shall assume that voters have short memories so that current fiscal misbehavior has no long-term effect on a party's appeal to the electorate.) Consequently, the difference in utility between victory and defeat at the next election is usually large enough to swamp fear of facing any but the largest fiscal disasters in the event of victory.[29]

Because political rationality often leads politicians to behave as though the world will end next election day, there is a tendency for them to "buy" votes by raising w_i and X_i and running deficits in lieu of tax increases to the fullest extent possible.[30] The realization of this tropism is partly responsible for the imposition of statutory limits on government debt and deficits. It is these limits and the fear of credit deterioration, rather than prudence, that operate as the immediate restraints on government deficits.

This contrasts with the behavior of private firms, which, having longer time horizons, can more readily anticipate approaching difficulties and engage in anticipatory adjustments than can public decision makers.[31] This suggests that, other things equal,

[28] The only exception to this is where he anticipates going bankrupt.

[29] One reason for the emphasis on victory in the next election is the danger that a defeated leader or clique will be ousted from party control.

[30] How then can one account for the behavior of politicians and parties who parade their fiscal conservatism? A full answer is not possible here, but the argument would lead to the prediction that such parties would be "relatively unsuccessful."

[31] Highly speculative private enterprises striving to expand faster than the growth of their equity capital comfortably permits will behave much

22

public-sector expenditure and employment will vary more abruptly through time than private.

A further important difference between the public and private sectors is the frequent separation in the former of responsibility for raising funds from authority to spend them. This separation of spending and funding authority is masked by the excessive aggregation of the variables we have been discussing. Not one government, but a number of governmental bodies have joint and imprecisely allocated responsibilities both for spending and for funding. Hence, political rationality often suggests to one body that it undertake expenditure for political gain, leaving to others responsibility for providing the funding. Similarly, the complexity of government accounting often encourages the hiding of obligations incurred, secret trenching on reserves, and generally the minimization of currently levied taxes.

Yet a further consequence of the diffusion of authority within the government is the propensity for "making gestures" and "passing the buck." (Modeling this would go well beyond anything attempted here, so I shall merely comment ad hoc.) To gain votes, the executive branch will sometimes recommend and legislatures vote for measures they really oppose, in the hope that the other branch of government will prevent final enactment. Sometimes this buck-passing "works" in the sense that the other branch accepts the onus of having blocked the measure, but sometimes both entities acquiesce in what neither desires. It is rather obvious that this game is likely to generate an upward bias relative to what is desired in expenditure and a downward bias in taxation.

At bottom, the difference between the behavior of the private and the public sectors in the raising of capital lies in the fact that contingent obligations of a business firm are rapidly capitalized by the equity market, while those of a public body may be

---

as the governmental units we are describing. The argument of the text assumes that such enterprises do not normally characterize the private sector, though they may become quite prominent during speculative booms. However expansionary private firms may become, they are not likely to be tempted to "overpay" labor to the same degree as the public sector.

hidden for substantial periods of time. Together with the very uncertain character of a politician's or political party's "property rights" in the government, this encourages a tropism for buying votes with borrowed resources and camouflaging both the resulting debt and the responsibility for incurring it.

This tropism is countered at government levels below the federal by a combination of legal limits on indebtedness and voter resistance to the increase in interest rates that must be paid by local authorities if their indebtedness rises faster than their tax base. At the federal level, budget deficits trigger increases in the money supply, which generates inflation. While, given time to adjust, voters may accept a wide range of rates of inflation, rapid increases in the rate have a strong, adverse effect on the vote for incumbents.

III. The Output Mix of the Public Sector

A. Comparative Advantage and Public-Sector Production

As in the private sector demand for labor in the public sector is derived from demand for final output, depending upon relative input prices and technology. As used here, "technology" includes not only technical know-how but also the political feasibility of using various methods of employing and paying labor. Only to a limited degree would knowledge of the menu of final goods and services provided to households by the public sector suffice to determine the kinds and quantities of activities performed by individuals on the public payroll. The productive activities carried on in the public sector depend largely upon which intermediate stages of production are performed by workers on the public payroll aided by publicly owned instruments and which are contracted out to firms in the private sector. A country in whose final output public goods bulk large will not necessarily employ much of its resources in the public sector.[32]

To illustrate this point, consider the public good *par excellence*—the lighthouse. For obvious reasons it is impossible to exclude nonpayers from benefiting from lighthouse service; this

---

[32] Pashigian (1972, pp. 1–3) has a good discussion of this point.

makes it necessary for the government to raise the funds required through levying taxes, charging port fees, or using other fiscal means. But the *operation* of a lighthouse may be contracted out to a profit-seeking firm on any mutually acceptable basis of compensation.

It is not necessary to contend that all activities normally carried on within the public sector could be contracted out to private firms, but many of them can be. The question of which activities will be retained within the public sector and which contracted out is not decided entirely by considerations of cost minimization as costs are normally measured. However, cost minimization and comparative advantage do play an important role in determining the relative importance of public and private employment of productive resources. For example, the public sector can hire certain types of labor more cheaply than the private. This would seem to be the case for a small number of high-level jobs. Usually these jobs are highly visible in the sense that the activities of their incumbents receive a substantial amount of news coverage or at least attract a great deal of attention from members of their own professions. This attention serves as a nonpecuniary benefit of the job, enabling a public employer to hire a given quality candidate at a lower wage than he could obtain in the private sector.[33] As most of these glamorous jobs tend to be "political" and therefore of short duration, the pecuniary sacrifice involved is usually of brief duration. Thus the public sector *can* set wages on certain of its jobs that are below what the private sector would normally pay for comparable talent, but why should it do so?[34]

In part, the explanation lies in the recognition by all con-

---

[33] Among workers at or beyond their peak earning years, recruits for these jobs frequently will accept actual pecuniary wage reductions not usually compensated by subsequent higher earnings. These workers must obtain consumption utility as part of their compensation. Among young workers, jobs of this kind are often a way of accumulating human capital in the form of reputation that later pays off in higher earnings.

[34] This statement refers to annual earnings. On an hourly basis the statement holds a fortiori as the holders of these jobs normally work as long or longer hours than they would in the private sector.

25

cerned that these jobs afford such great nonpecuniary attractions as not to require pecuniary rewards equal to what a suitable candidate could earn elsewhere. Over and above considerations of parsimony, compensation in the public sector is subject to a "ceiling effect" of the salaries of legislators, governors, mayors, cabinet members, and the like. Understandably these functionaries, who are critically involved in public-sector wage setting, are resistant to the suggestion that their organizational inferiors should receive as much or more than they. While violations of an unwritten ceiling may be permitted, they will be scrutinized unsympathetically, and the larger the fraction of a given budget used to pay such salaries, the more difficult it will be to get it adopted. This creates a bias against paying such high salaries. Where such salaries are needed to attract appropriate manpower, the tendency will be to "contract out" the activity to the private sector where they can be paid. The effect will be to shift "high-salary" intensive activities to the private sector.

I shall not attempt to explain why legislators and executives resist the paying of higher salaries to others than they themselves receive. Such resistance exists in the private sector as well as in the public, and is probably rooted in feelings of envy. What is more to the point is to ask why those with legal power to set salaries do not raise their own rather than hold down those of their organizational inferiors. The answer probably lies in a feared adverse political reaction, a negative effect on votes, to such salary increases. If this surmise is correct, then fear of an adverse voter reaction to paying high salaries to elected officials, combined with an unexplained resistance to paying appointees more than their elected appointers, leads to a bias against retaining activities in the public sector that require numerous high-salaried personnel.[35]

B. Government Subsidy versus Public Production

A type of situation in which the public sector has a comparative advantage is where cost-price relations are such that equity

[35] This implies that politicians are not so averse to high salaries for employees of government contractors as they are to high salaries for government employees. This kind of payroll illusion acts as a negative transaction cost, encouraging contracting out.

capital cannot earn a competitive rate of return. In such cases, if the activity is to be conducted at all, it must either be subsidized or carried on in the public sector. This means that the capital must come either from the public or from the private not-for-profit sector. For simplicity, we will assume that the government will finance only what other sectors will not or cannot handle.

For our purpose, the critical choice for the state is between subsidizing an activity and engaging in it directly. There are few activities where superior technology or ability to buy productive services gives the state a comparative advantage in productive activity. Almost any of the essential activities of the government, raising revenue, maintaining order, providing for the national defense, may and have been subcontracted to the private sector. The right to collect taxes has been sold to tax farmers; private police have flourished at various times and places; authority to settle disputes has been delegated to private tribunals; the right to raise and equip armed men and use them for private gain has been delegated to privateers, and so on.

Indeed, the notion that some activities necessarily must be performed by the state is more a matter of how "state" is defined than a refutable proposition. For example, if we contend that the ultimate power to enforce laws and exclude would-be intruders to the enforcement process must rest with the state, how are we to interpret the exercise of such power by feudal nobility? To argue that the local nobility were the local government is to make the matter definitional; to argue that they were exercising delegated authority is to concede that the enforcement power is capable of alienation.

Rather than chop logic, for the present purpose let it suffice to posit that there would be grave difficulties for the head of state in enforcing contracts with private employers of military forces. To avoid these difficulties, governments attempt to make the commanders of these forces identify with the state, by means of great honors, special oaths of loyalty, etc. One of the devices to insure loyalty is to place commanders of the armed forces on government payrolls. How far down the chain of command this attitude of loyalty must go is a question we need not answer here. Clearly, soldiers and junior officers have been hired from abroad on a basis

27

of contract, but always subject to some local control from within the government.

Apart from this exception, no activity per se need be performed by government. Those activities that become part of the agenda of government are those at which the public sector has some sort of comparative advantage. As already noted, one source of such advantage is the ability to hire or purchase productive agents at lower prices than other sectors. For example, factor services may be commandeered through eminent domain for use in the public or private not-for-profit sectors more easily than for the profit-seeking sector. Normally, political resistance to compulsory sale or rent of a productive instrument would be much greater if it were to be used by a profit-maker than if it were alleged to be used in the public interest, or in an otherwise "worthy" cause.

Thus in the present context, labor may be conscripted for the armed services at less than a market wage, or hired on a voluntary basis at less than the supply price to profit-seeking firms for public-service activities such as the Peace Corps, environmental improvement, and the like. One comparative advantage of both the public and private not-for-profit sectors lies in their ability to offer their employees the nonpecuniary satisfaction of "doing good." The effect of this is to make public-sector wage rates for the relevant kind of labor lower than the private; the nonpecuniary satisfactions offset the lower pay.

To a limited extent the not-for-profit sector provides capital for activities in which cost-price relations are such that a competitive rate of return cannot be earned. Government tax abatement policies may subsidize these activities, but tax relief and, even more, cash subsidies are limited to situations where there is voter approval or at least tolerance of the beneficiaries. Subsidies are properly perceived as transfers from taxpayers that yield a gain in votes only when their recipients are accepted by voters as "meritorious." Without such acceptance, the activity cannot be financed by subsidies and must either be abandoned or performed by the government directly. It is assumed that direct government production is not normally perceived as a subsidy.

28

C. Some Examples of Public Production

The political economy of government choice between the options of subsidizing private production and engaging in public production are well illustrated by the example of public, pre-college education. Manifestly, schools can be run privately; however, the volume of expenditure per student that advocates of education have persuaded governments to finance entails costs per student well above what most parents would pay in a free market. Consequently, subsidies, public instruction, or both, have been required. However, if subsidies, other than those from one governmental unit to another, are to be paid, who is to receive them?

In the nineteenth century, the strongest potential sources of alternative educational supply to public schools were religious organizations; subsidies to these were and are politically unacceptable. Private-for-profit schools were too varied in character, and state policing machinery too rudimentary, to hold profit seekers effectively to acceptable minimum educational standards.[36] Its rivals blocked, public instruction flourished. Once established as the dominant mode of instruction, public schools had the further advantage of momentum. Economies of scale and an established organization made public schools seem vastly superior to actual or potential small-scale private competitors. So great has the apparent superiority of public schools become that, with negligible exceptions, profit seekers have not challenged their hegemony. Apparently, actual and potential profit-seeking educational entrepreneurs have considered the probability of obtaining a public subsidy so small as not to be worth the effort of a serious campaign.[37] In short, neither profit-seeking nor

[36]"Too rudimentary" means that the marginal policing cost was unacceptably high. The assertions of this paragraph are offered as speculative reconstruction of "virtual history," what would have happened if history had been different, and not as an historical account. For a good historical discussion see West (1967).

[37]Such competitive challenge to public education as has arisen has come mainly from not-for-profit organizations, co-operative and church-affiliated schools.

private-nonprofit schools have been considered politically eligible for a subsidy. The massive tax support for public schools has resulted in public instruction becoming the dominant mode of pre-college education.

Occasionally the state shifts from subsidizer of private production to producer of last resort when the vote cost of the taxes requisite to financing a subsidy sufficient to induce supply from the private sector becomes greater than the vote cost entailed by public production. For example, in public transportation declining volume has tended to raise unit costs, causing losses and prompting demands for subsidized loans to improve rolling stock, avert bankruptcy, meet wage demands, etc. In cases such as this, if there is a private profit-seeking supplier of a "publicly needed" service for which the demand has been permanently reduced, the situation is one of virtual bankruptcy with market considerations suggesting termination of production, but political considerations preventing the government from accepting such an outcome. The government attempts to induce the private supplier to continue operation somehow, with the size of the subsidy serving as the principal item of negotiation. Sometimes no terms acceptable to both the supplier and the government can be found, and the government takes over as "producer of last resort." The effect of such takeovers is probably to make wage rates higher and man-hour productivity lower than would otherwise be the case. This is because vote-seeking politicans are far more responsive to the pressure of unions and general public opinion to treat employees of *failing enterprises* "fairly" than are profit-seeking stockholders.[38]

The need to preserve jobs is yet another reason why government sometimes takes over and keeps in operation production processes that the private sector would abandon. To put the same thing in a different way, government will continue operations under financially less favorable circumstances than would private producers. Political considerations will lead governments to

---

[38] The statements of this paragraph are intended as conjectures. They are not incompatible with the findings of Pashigian (1972), but they imply a much more specific hypothesis than his data could test.

avoid reductions in force and/or wage reductions that profit seekers would require as a condition of continuing operations; this tends to make losses of public enterprises bigger than those that would be incurred by private firms under comparable cost and demand conditions.[39] Looked at in a slightly different way, what I am conjecturing is that public bodies are less prone to destroy the specific capital of their employees than are private employers. If true, this makes for relatively smaller variances and probably higher average earnings in the public than in the private sector.[40]

D. Employer of Last Resort

Yet a further situation in which the public sector has a comparative advantage vis-à-vis profit makers is as employer of last resort. In recent years the government has had no real competition in this field. We assume that "employer of last resort" is taken literally to mean that a job on a public payroll at a specified wage rate and given working conditions will be made available to anyone upon application. Then no worker need fear being dismissed from such a job, because by definition another would be available with negligible search cost. Discipline and productivity on such jobs could not be higher than what suits the workers' convenience, since fear of dismissal would be removed.

If the wage rate on last resort jobs were set at what is paid per hour in the private sector for the services of comparably trained workers, the disutility and productivity of workers in private jobs would decline to the level obtaining on the public jobs; otherwise workers would shift to the public jobs in pursuit of greater net advantages of employment. This would lead to some

[39] In effect, the government obtains working capital from the taxpayers on more favorable terms than private entrepreneurs can get from private or public sources. This is a testable conjecture; what is suggested is that legislative bodies will accept operating losses from publicly operated enterprises bigger than the subsidies they will provide to privately operated firms.

[40] This statement might not hold in the long run if workers are risk-averse and treat the lower risk in the public sector as a net advantage, thereby increasing relative supply to the public sector.

reduction in the number of hours of work demanded privately, and to an increased rate of hourly compensation for those hours still demanded so as to make private employment sufficiently attractive relative to last-resort employment for private workers to fear dismissal in the event of poor performance. Varying with the response of the nominal money supply, this would lead either to: 1) a general rise in all wage rates and product prices to restore initial equilibrium relationships, making the wage rate on last-resort jobs too low to attract many workers; or 2) a compression of the hourly wage structure with a consequent reduction in supply of applicants for those types of training that would be submarginal at the reduced wage differentials.[41]

It may be protested that an argument such as this implies an unfair interpretation of the "employer of last resort" concept. The laws did not intend that jobs should be available for the asking, regardless of past or current work performance, but only that a certain number of jobs should be available on specified conditions. Whether the first interpretation or something like that suggested in the previous sentence is more nearly correct may remain moot; but if the latter interpretation is correct, then the conditions under which last-resort jobs can be obtained and held become critical determinants of the economic effects of any program of last-resort employment. Indeed, until these conditions are specified, the meaning of "employer of last resort" is not determined. If access to a certain class of public-sector jobs is a matter of right, then they have no sale value to the government. Therefore if the government were to offer unlimited access to one class of jobs, political rationality would lead it to develop a superior class conditionally available to the same type of worker in exchange for political support. By the same reasoning a politically rational government faced with a positive cost of taxing will resist any unconditional guarantee of jobs as politically wasteful. Whatever it pretends, ultimately a government will

---

[41] The above remarks on the effect of an "employer of last resort" work guarantee on wage rates are very inadequate. Such a guarantee affects the risk of quitting and the cost of obtaining job discipline and productivity in a quite complicated manner that has not been adequately explored in the literature.

want admission to the payroll to be restricted and priced by its functionaries.

E. Methods of Payment and Sectoral Specialization

Let me venture the following speculative argument: If paid on a cost plus fixed fee basis, and with little or no risk of audit, few producers would be likely to strain themselves to hold down costs. The converse would hold where there was payment by a fixed fee for a rigidly specified task, with producers reaping all gains of cost reduction. In general, producer concern with cost minimization is likely to vary directly with the strength of the relation between reward and effectiveness in limiting cost.[42]

In the public sector it is only rarely, if ever, that anyone is given a task that is so defined that he has an incentive to minimize costs. Tasks are almost never defined so that performance can be judged in terms of cost-effectiveness. Indeed, spending less than the total of one's annual budget is likely to serve as a signal for a subsequent budget cut. Saving resources to go beyond one's assigned target in order to achieve unassigned objectives may result in punishment for exceeding one's authority.

There is per se nothing about the activities in which the public sector engages that compels it to avoid payment by results. It is rather that tasks where payment by results is feasible tend to be contracted out to the private sector. One reason for this is that it is on these tasks that large profits can be made, and where contractors seek opportunities to participate. Another reason is the fear of civil servants that high earnings by any government employee will attract hostile inquiries from the legislature or the press. Moreover, the possibility of getting assignments that yield unusually high earnings would create opportunities for favoritism and/or corruption that would be very destructive of civil service morale.

---

[42]Such a relation need not involve direct incentive payments. For example, if it is known that promotion within an organization is closely related to effectiveness in limiting costs, efforts in this direction may be quite as strong as though "cost savings" were shared with the employed manager or worker responsible.

The implications for the specialization pattern of the public sector are: since public employers tend to avoid activities that involve payment by results, workers who prefer to be employed in situations where they can increase their earnings per time period by expending extra effort or by using unusual skill will tend to avoid such employment. That is, among workers embodying equal amounts of human capital and of the same cohort, those who will accept relatively low earnings in exchange for a relatively undemanding job will tend disproportionately to find employment in the public sector. This creates a bias toward lower earnings and lower productivity per hour in the public than in the private sector among otherwise comparable workers.

F. The Size Bias of the Public Sector

One distinguishing characteristic of the public sector is that its employing units are likely to include very few entities analogous to the myriad of small firms that populate the private sector, especially the service trades. One reason for this is the greater economies of scale in the public sector caused by the detailed record keeping required for the disbursement of public funds. Another is that exemption, either de jure or de facto because of non-enforcement, from laws governing compensation and working conditions applies only to small firms in the private sector and not to small governmental units. A third reason is the political pressure on public bodies as on large private firms to act as exemplary, i.e. high-wage, employers.

In other words the private sector is a haven for employers who seek to pay relatively low wages to workers of little skill and/or education. The public sector tends to pay workers of this kind, when it does hire them, more than the private. I suspect that the resulting differences in productivity are slight, if any; hence the public sector is tilted away from the activities in which small, low-wage firms survive.

IV. Unionism

Much of the empirical work on public-private wage differentials has focused on estimating the effect of unionism on public-sector wage rates. I devote relatively little attention to this topic because of my dissatisfaction with the theoretical explanation of how unionism affects wage rates in the public sector. Many of my remarks apply to unionism in the private sector as well, but they apply with special force to unions of government employees.

It is generally conceded that unionism has the effect of raising the hourly wage rate of workers in the relevant bargaining unit, but the mechanism by which this is accomplished is not clear. The usual account would rationalize this effect as the result of replacing a competitive labor market with a monopoly union. Without necessarily denying the relevance of this explanation of the wage advantage associated with unionism, let me suggest a more specific hypothesis: unions tend to raise the relative wages of workers who would otherwise receive less than the average for individuals of their socio-economic characteristics, especially the average of those in comparable jobs.

The pressure of unions on wages envisaged in this hypothesis might operate either through the "supply of unionism," through the labor demand function, or both. On the supply side, low-paid workers feel relatively deprived and are therefore easier to unionize.[43] On the demand side, the tolerance of public opinion for strike action is greater where the strikers are "relatively underpaid"; this would tend to reinforce the supply of unionism effect. If this argument has validity, we would, for example, expect unionism to raise the lower quartile of hourly earnings of employees relative to the mean, in addition to any effect it might have on mean earnings.

Treating unionism as exogenous to the wage-employment determination model may, though, be a source of specification error. One of the important channels through which unionism operates on wage rates in the public sector is by creating a political climate favorable to higher wage rates. However, the ability of unions to do this depends upon the political predisposition of the voters toward higher wage rates; this predisposition is

---

[43] However, employers who use relatively deprived workers may be unusually resistant to unionization. Obviously this possibility must be considered along with that mentioned in the text.

likely to be correlated with their attitude toward unionism itself. If so, the measured effect of unionism on wage rates is likely to include not only the "true effect" but also the correlation between tolerance of unionism, and therefore low costs of recruiting union members, and willingness to pay high wages to public employees.[44]   That is, it is possible that this latter correlation could produce the illusion of a union effect on wage rates, even though such an effect would not appear if political attitudes were held constant.

The practical significance of this argument is that the effect of unionism on public-sector wage rates cannot be appraised properly except in the context of an explicit model of government decision making that determines, inter alia, wage rates and labor quantities hired.   This is not to offer a counsel of perfection; obviously, estimates of the effect of unionism on wage rates will improve along with estimates of the coefficients of other relevant variables. What is urged is greater care in constructing models of public decision making, and particularly in specifying the interaction of other variables with both unionism and wage rates.

Specifically, let me note the interesting finding of Ehrenberg (1973b) that, other things equal, firefighters' annual salaries are higher, hourly wage rates lower, and annual hours greater in cities run by city managers than in those governed by mayor-council arrangements.   Ehrenberg also found that cities run by elected commissioners paid lower hourly wages to their firefighters and worked them more hours per year than "mayor-council cities." My quarrel is not with the substance of this finding, but with the absence of an acceptable rationale for choosing this characteristic of political structure as relevant to explaining intercity differences in firefighters' wages. Indeed, as Ehrenberg notes, the direction of the effect of the city-manager form of government

---

[44] A further, and important, source of specification error is the probable association of tolerance for unionism and desire to hire above-average quality workers. What appears to be a positive association of unionism and wage rates may be due entirely or in part to an association of desire for above-average quality workers and relatively low cost of organizing.

was in a number of cases opposite that hypothesized, and it was often statistically insignificant.[45]

In conclusion, it is important to specify carefully labor supply equations to the public sector. Some public-sector workers, notably teachers, firemen, and policemen, are more prone to hold second jobs than are workers generally; hence intercity differences in public-sector wage rates may be related to earning opportunities in secondary employment through their effect on labor supply. The better the employment opportunities for second jobs in a city, the lower the supply price of labor to its public sector.[46]

[45] Ehrenberg (1973b) argues that if, as is often supposed, city managers are more efficient than elected officials, this should be reflected in superior bargaining tactics that result in lower wage rates. This is plausible only if worker quality is held constant. If, as is quite likely, managers have a comparative advantage in utilizing highly trained workers, they may opt for higher wage rates to get lower unit costs through greater productivity. Furthermore, it is not clear how the greater capacity of city-managers relative to elected officials interacts with the incidence of unionism. It might be that they can make better deals with a union, but these might take the form of buying greater productivity gains for given increases in hourly labor costs than elected officials can obtain. The result would be a rational decision by managers to accept unions and pay higher wages than elected officials.

[46] See Perrella (1970, p. 61): "Persons who were protective service workers (policemen, security guards and firemen, for example) and farmers on their primary jobs had the highest multiple job holding rates."

The main body of the paper contains a number of speculations about differences in wage rates between workers in the public and private sectors that are not related to any body of statistical data. In this Appendix we present estimates of hourly earnings (in 1959 and 1969) of employees in various parts of the public and private sectors. These estimates are presented in total and for white males, nonwhite males, white females, and nonwhite females separately. Raw estimates and those corrected for differences in age, education, and region are listed; these data do not pretend to reflect differences in effort expended nor in nonpecuniary benefits received per hour of employment. Moreover, they are not specific as to industry or occupation of the workers represented; consequently they bear an uncertain relation to the data needed to test the various conjectures offered in the text. For this reason I make no attempt to interpret the data in this Appendix by means of the theory presented in the text; the discussion here is intended as no more than a description of the data in the tables.

The data are taken from 1 in 1000 samples of the 1960 and 1970 U.S. Censuses of Population. "Public-sector workers" includes all employees of any governmental unit—federal, state, or local. "Private-sector workers" include all persons receiving wages or salaries but not employed in the public sector. The calculation of average hourly earnings is described by Fuchs (1967, pp. 4–5).

As Table 1 shows, both in 1959 and 1969 average hourly earnings were higher in the public sector than in the private; in 1959 the average hourly earnings of all public sector workers exceeded those of all private sector workers. When workers are classified by their age in 1960, in all but two categories average hourly earnings are greater for public- than for private-sector workers.

The relative earnings advantage of public employees increased

TABLE 1. Average Hourly Earnings in the Public and Private Sectors,
by Age: 1959 and 1969

	1959			1969		
Age	Private Sector	Public Sector	% Differential	Private Sector	Public Sector	% Differential
14–19	$1.26	$1.35	5	$1.97	$2.19	11
20–24	1.65	1.79	8	2.61	2.82	8
25–34	2.31	2.30	0	3.62	3.77	4
35–44	2.58	2.56	−1	4.05	4.27	6
45–54	2.55	2.61	2	3.95	4.25	8
55–64	2.52	2.56	2	3.80	4.13	9
65–	2.32	2.35	1	3.24	3.70	14
All	2.36	2.45	4	3.62	3.94	9

% Differential = (Public − Private)/Private.
Source: U.S. Census; 1 in 1000 Sample, 1960 and 1970. Computations,
courtesy of V. R. Fuchs.

during the 1960's so that by 1969 the percentage hourly earnings differential in favor of public-sector workers was greater than a decade earlier in every age class. The 1960's also eliminated and reversed the private-sector advantage of the two exceptional age groups in 1959. There is no obvious age pattern to the size of the public-private sector earnings differential either in 1959 and 1969.

Breaking down the aggregated data of Table 1 by race and sex we find in Table 2 that in both 1959 and 1969 black males and females of both races had higher average hourly earnings when employed in the public sector. This statement holds for every age-race-sex cell in 1969 and for almost all of these cells a decade earlier. Among blacks of both sexes, the percentage differential in favor of the public sector declined during the decade. For white females in all age classes save one in 1959, average hourly earnings were higher in the public sector in both 1959 and 1969. In general, the percentage differential for white females increased during the 1960's. For white males in 1959, average hourly earnings were greater in the private than in the public sector. This statement holds not only for all white males taken together but, except for the two youngest, for each age group separately.

TABLE 2. Average Hourly Earnings in the Public and Private Sectors, by Age, Sex and Race: 1959 and 1969

	White Males					
	1959			1969		
Age	Private Sector	Public Sector	% Differential	Private Sector	Public Sector	% Differential
14–19	$1.36	$1.62	19	$2.02	$2.28	14
20–24	1.83	1.90	4	2.88	2.89	0
25–34	2.59	2.41	− 7	4.07	4.07	0
35–44	3.04	2.83	− 6	4.78	4.81	1
45–54	3.07	2.80	− 9	4.83	4.90	1
55–64	3.00	2.69	−10	4.62	4.54	−2
65–	2.87	2.52	− 9	3.97	4.03	1
All	2.77	2.63	− 5	4.27	4.44	3

	White Females					
	1959			1969		
Age	Private Sector	Public Sector	% Differential	Private Sector	Public Sector	% Differential
14–19	$1.19	$1.16	− 3	$1.93	$2.02	5
20–24	1.47	1.78	21	2.29	2.84	24
25–34	1.67	2.17	24	2.64	3.57	35
35–44	1.68	2.23	33	2.66	3.50	32
45–54	1.64	2.45	33	2.61	3.48	33
55–64	1.62	2.48	53	2.53	3.85	52
65–	1.37	2.17	58	2.44	3.17	30
All	1.60	2.27	30	2.52	3.43	36

	Black Males					
	1959			1969		
Age	Private Sector	Public Sector	% Differential	Private Sector	Public Sector	% Differential
14–19	$ .97	$1.70	75	$1.97	$3.20	62
20–24	1.24	1.44	14	2.60	2.67	3
25–34	1.71	2.03	19	2.95	3.16	7
35–44	1.87	2.15	15	3.19	4.07	28
45–54	1.71	2.12	24	3.05	3.33	9
55–64	1.72	1.94	13	2.78	2.91	5
65–	1.54	1.50	− 3	2.03	3.01	48
All	1.67	2.02	17	2.91	3.39	16

TABLE 2. Continued

| | Black Females | | | | | |
| | 1959 | | | 1969 | | |
Age	Private Sector	Public Sector	% Differential	Private Sector	Public Sector	% Differential
14–19	$ .88	$1.47	67	$1.61	$2.36	47
20–24	.97	1.43	47	1.88	2.52	34
25–34	1.02	1.97	93	2.09	2.98	43
35–44	1.07	1.87	81	2.10	3.20	34
45–54	.92	1.87	103	1.83	2.90	58
55–64	.91	1.81	99	1.90	2.71	43
65–	.79	2.03	157	1.52	3.56	134
All	.99	1.85	87	1.96	2.94	50

By 1969, the private sector's advantage had been more than cancelled, with average hourly earnings being slightly higher in the public sector for all age groups combined and, save for one, for all age groups taken separately. In both decennial years, the public-private sector differential in average hourly earnings was largest for black females, next largest for white females and smallest for white males.

Disaggregating by years of schooling reveals a different aspect of the differential in sectoral earnings than disaggregating by age. As shown in Table 3, in both 1959 and 1969 average hourly earnings in the private sector were greater for virtually every schooling class. In percentage terms, between 1959 and 1969 the earnings advantage of the private sector shrank in all but two education classes. This earnings advantage by education class of the private sector contrasts sharply with the earnings advantage of the public sector among all workers combined indicated by Table 4.

Now let us consider the behavior of the public-private earnings differential within race-sex categories. Both in 1959 and in 1969 earnings of white males in the private sector exceeded those in the public sector for all education classes; however, in almost all classes the 1969 percentage difference was smaller. These statements do not hold for other race-sex categories; in 1959 female hourly earnings for both blacks and whites were greater in

TABLE 3. Average Hourly Earnings in the Public and Private Sectors, by Years of Schooling: 1959 and 1969

| | All Employees | | | | | |
| | 1959 | | | 1969 | | |
Years of Schooling	Private Sector	Public Sector	% Differential	Private Sector	Public Sector	% Differential
< 9	$1.96	$1.87	− 5	$2.89	$2.82	− 2
9–11	2.17	2.16	0	3.20	3.16	− 1
12	2.29	2.21	− 3	n.a.	3.38	…
13–15	2.81	2.52	−10	3.96	3.78	− 5
16	3.80	2.94	−23	5.70	4.64	−19
17	4.05	3.23	−20	5.88	5.08	−14
⩾18	4.07	3.55	−13	6.47	6.16	− 5
All	2.36	2.45	4	3.62	3.94	9

Source: Same as Tables 1 and 2.

TABLE 4. Average Hourly Earnings in the Public and Private Sectors, by Years of Schooling, Sex and Race: 1959 and 1969

| | White Males | | | | | |
| | 1959 | | | 1969 | | |
Years of Schooling	Private Sector	Public Sector	% Differential	Private Sector	Public Sector	% Differential
< 9	$2.31	$2.03	− 8	$3.42	$3.15	− 9
9–11	2.52	2.36	− 6	3.75	3.65	− 3
12	2.69	2.44	− 6	4.01	3.92	− 2
13–15	3.23	2.89	−11	4.58	4.36	− 5
16	4.16	3.23	−22	6.28	5.24	−17
17	4.38	3.34	−24	6.23	5.21	−16
⩾18	4.37	3.67	−16	6.89	6.41	− 7
All	2.77	2.63	5	4.27	4.44	4

| | White Females | | | | | |
| | 1959 | | | 1969 | | |
Years of Schooling	Private Sector	Public Sector	% Differential	Private Sector	Public Sector	% Differential
< 9	$1.35	$1.54	14	$2.04	$2.19	7
9–11	1.47	1.67	13	2.28	2.37	4
12	1.67	1.86	11	2.52	2.80	10
13–15	1.78	2.19	23	2.79	3.09	11
16	2.18	2.78	22	3.46	4.18	21
17	2.16	3.15	46	3.96	4.94	25
⩾18	2.40	3.42	43	4.23	5.44	29
All	1.60	2.27	42	2.52	3.43	36

TABLE 4. Continued

| | Black Males | | | | | |
| | 1959 | | | 1969 | | |
Years of Schooling	Private Sector	Public Sector	% Differential	Private Sector	Public Sector	% Differential
< 9	$1.58	$1.62	2	$2.55	$2.43	− 6
9–11	1.69	2.03	20	2.96	2.88	− 3
12	1.72	2.04	16	3.03	3.29	9
13–15	2.06	2.17	5	3.23	3.72	15
16	2.05	2.63	28	4.15	4.77	15
17	2.51	2.70	8	5.89	5.27	−11
≥18	4.00	3.08	−23	4.01	6.09	52
All	1.67	2.02	21	2.91	3.39	16

| | Black Females | | | | | |
| | 1959 | | | 1969 | | |
Years of Schooling	Private Sector	Public Sector	% Differential	Private Sector	Public Sector	% Differential
< 9	$ .82	$ .98	19	$1.44	$1.90	32
9–11	1.03	1.49	31	1.91	2.09	9
12	1.11	1.65	49	2.15	2.52	17
13–15	1.38	1.86	35	2.49	3.10	24
16	1.61	2.57	60	3.99	4.08	2
17	.80	2.71	239	4.10	4.69	14
≥18	2.49	2.65	6	6.53	5.07	−22
All	.99	1.85	87	1.96	2.94	50

the public sector in every education class. In 1969 the same statement applies except to the most highly educated black females, for whom average earnings in the public sector exceeded those in the private. In all female education classes, except blacks with less than 9 years of schooling, private-sector earnings rose by a greater percentage between 1959 and 1969 than public-sector earnings. In 1959 black men did better in the public sector than in the private in all education classes except the highest. In 1969 private-sector earnings of black men exceeded those in the public sector in three of seven educational classes.

As shown in Table 5, the black-white differential in average hourly earnings is greater in the private sector than in the public,

TABLE 5. Black-White Differentials in Average Hourly Earnings Between Individuals of the Same Sex and Given Years of Schooling in the Public and Private Sectors: 1959 and 1969

	Percent Differentials							
	1959				1969			
Years of Schooling	Males		Females		Males		Females	
	Private	Public	Private	Public	Private	Public	Private	Public
< 9	32	20	39	57	25	23	29	15
9–11	33	14	30	11	21	21	16	13
12	36	16	34	11	24	16	17	10
13–15	36	25	22	15	29	15	11	0
16	51	19	35	8	34	9	−15	2
17	43	19	63	14	4	−1	− 4	5
⩾18	9	16	4	23	42	5	−54	7
All	40	23	38	42	32	24	22	14

both in the aggregate and within most education classes. For males this statement applies both in 1959 and 1969, but for females it holds only in 1969. In the private sector the black-white differential for all education classes combined was lower in 1969 than a decade earlier. During the 1960's this differential declined for males in all but the highest educational class. Among females the differential declined in all education classes, and in the three highest became negative, i.e., average hourly earnings of blacks exceeded that of whites.

Table 6 compares average hourly earnings of employees of state and local (S–L) governments with those of all governmental units; it should be compared with Tables 3 and 4. In 1959 S–L employees obtained average hourly wages 4 percent below those in the private sector who in turn received 4 percent less per hour than all public-sector workers. By 1969 S and L workers received the same average hourly earnings as those in the private sector, but the earnings of federal workers had advanced even faster, so that all public workers combined received 9 percent more than those in the private sector.

S–L hourly earnings among white males were less than in the private sector in every class in both census years, and the differential shrank during the decade. With but a few exceptions a

TABLE 6. Average Hourly Earnings Among Employees of State and Local
Governments by Sex, Race and Years of Schooling: 1959
and 1969

| Years of Schooling | All Employees 1959 | | 1969 | |
	State & Local	% Differential with Private	State & Local	% Differential with Private
< 9	1.88	− 4	2.82	− 2
9–11	2.15	− 1	3.30	3
12	2.15	− 6	3.32	. . .
13–15	2.44	−13	3.70	− 7
16	2.88	−24	4.85	−15
17	2.91	−28	4.71	−20
⩾18	3.61	−11	6.05	− 6
All	2.26	− 4	3.61	0

Source: Same % Differential = (State and Local − Private)/Private.

| Years of Schooling | White Males 1959 | | 1969 | |
	State & Local	% Differential with Private	State & Local	% Differential with Private
< 9	1.97	−15	2.98	−13
9–11	2.26	−10	3.65	− 3
12	2.31	−14	3.63	− 9
13–15	2.63	−19	4.05	−12
16	3.12	−25	5.26	−16
17	3.11	−29	5.14	−17
⩾18	3.74	−14	6.35	− 8
All	2.39	−14	3.96	− 7

| Years of Schooling | White Females 1959 | | 1969 | |
	State & Local	% Differential with Private	State & Local	% Differential with Private
< 9	1.70	21	2.39	17
9–11	1.70	16	2.33	2
12	1.80	7	2.38	− 6
13–15	1.98	11	2.89	4
16	2.35	8	3.95	14
17	2.38	10	3.17	−20
⩾18	3.17	32	4.40	4
All	1.89	18	2.86	3

TABLE 6. Continued

| | Black Males | | | |
| | 1959 | | 1969 | |
Years of Schooling	State & Local	% Differential with Private	State & Local	% Differential with Private
< 9	1.34	−15	1.89	31
9–11	1.99	18	2.35	23
12	1.97	15	3.48	62
13–15	2.92	42	3.71	49
16	2.79	36	4.21	6
17	2.71	8	5.07	24
⩾18	. . .	. . .	3.34	−49
All	1.99	19	3.26	66

| | Black Females | | | |
| | 1959 | | 1969 | |
Years of Schooling	State & Local	% Differential with Private	State & Local	% Differential with Private
< 9	.44	−46	2.70	88
9–11	2.23	117	2.21	16
12	2.23	101	3.05	42
13–15	1.93	40	2.76	11
16	2.46	53	4.63	16
17	2.27	184	. . .	. . .
⩾18	2.23	−10	6.39	− 2
All	2.06	108	2.97	52

similar statement can be made concerning the relation of S–L earnings and those of all government workers. Among white females S–L earnings exceeded those in the private sector in both 1959 and 1969. The S–L advantage holds in all education classes during the former year, but there are two exceptions in the latter. S–L earnings for white females were slightly above the federal level at the bottom end of the educational ladder, but sharply below federal at the upper; this is true in both census years.

Black males generally received higher earnings in S–L than in the private sector in both 1959 and 1969. Unlike other groups, for black males the differential increased during the decade. The advantage of federal over *S–L* earnings was not great in either year, though it grew somewhat during the decade and was greater in both census years at the lower end of the education scale. The earnings of black females in *S–L* were generally above those in the private sector, though there are exceptions in some education classes in both years. The differentials reported in Table 6 shrank sharply during the 1960's. In both years black female earnings in *S–L* exceeded those in the federal government; in 1959 *S–L* earnings were higher than federal among the less educated, but lower at the upper end of the education scale. A decade later *S* and *L* earnings were greater in almost all schooling classes.

The aforementioned differentials are uncorrected for regional differences (see Fuchs, 1967). In effect, making these corrections adjusts earnings differentials by assigning to workers in different regions hourly earnings equal to the national average for workers of the same age, sex, color, and education. Thus computed, earnings differentials are adjusted, in a sense, for regional differences in earnings. The corrected percentage differentials are presented in Table 7.

Comparing Tables 4 and 7, we find the following:

White Males. For all education classes combined the "corrected" differential is substantially greater than the uncorrected in both years. However, within every education class in 1959 and in most of them in 1969 the corrected differential is positive, i.e., public-

TABLE 7. Public-Private Percentage Differentials in "Corrected" Average Hourly Earnings

Years of Schooling	White Males		White Females		Black Males		Black Females	
	1959	1969	1959	1969	1959	1969	1959	1969
< 9	2	1	0	0	3	4	2	3
9–11	5	5	3	2	6	3	7	− 2
12	4	5	3	2	13	6	7	3
13–15	5	7	4	3	11	8	3	5
16	2	−2	1	1	12	8	8	3
17	2	−1	4	3	7	3	238	−15
⩾18	1	2	3	1	−13	40	22	−19
All	14	17	26	25	19	19	53	34

sector hourly earnings exceed private. This means that within given regions for given years of schooling, public-sector earnings are slightly above private. Moreover, in contrast to the uncorrected differentials, the size of the corrected differentials is not associated with years of schooling.

White Females. The corrected differentials for all education classes combined are somewhat smaller than the uncorrected. By education class, the corrected differentials are very much smaller and uncorrelated with years of schooling. Within each education class, corrected public-sector earnings are still greater than private.

Black Males. The corrected differentials are not very different from the uncorrected. However, with one exception, they are all positive and almost all smaller in absolute size than their uncorrected counterparts. For given years of schooling the percent differentials among black males are generally larger than for whites.

Black Females. The corrected differentials are smaller than the uncorrected though substantially larger than the corrected differentials among any other age-sex category. Their reduction in the 1960's was featured by the emergence of an earnings advantage for private-sector employees in the two highest education classes.[47]

The corrections reduce the measured education-specific differentials and for white males alter their signs; they also virtually eliminate the association between the public-private earnings differential with years of shcooling. This means that the regional distributions of public- and private-sector workers are associated with their educational distributions.

It is important not to assume that quality is the same for workers with similar census characteristics but located in different regions; this is especially true of public employees. This similarity must be established independently of earnings data, and, until it is, the interpretation of "corrected" earnings will be difficult.

---

[47] Highly educated blacks were so few in number as to cast doubt on the sampling reliability of the observations. This applies not only here but everywhere in this Appendix.

COMMENTS

ALVIN K. KLEVORICK

Professor Reder prefaced his presentation by saying that he had been asked to write a broad, speculative "think piece" on the question of employment and wages in government. I think he has succeeded admirably in performing that function. His paper is very interesting, as it provides both a general framework for examining the theory of labor in the public sector and a number of interesting observations about specific aspects of the functioning of this labor market. The paper is replete with theoretical conjectures that call out for empirical testing and with descriptive empirical observations that undoubtedly can be synthesized into a coherent picture with the help of his general model. Reder's paper stimulated me to think further about public-sector labor markets, and I am sure it will also prove thought-provoking for others doing both theoretical and empirical work in the area.

Since I am confident that the paper will provide a basis for further work, I would like to comment on its basic approach to the problem of employment and wages in the public sector. (Because the Appendix of tables is attached only for reference, I will not comment on it here.) I agree fully with the fundamental premise of the piece: "That normally political factors are important in determining government wage-employment decisions." Reder's focus on political elements is quite helpful in understanding a number of phenomena he discusses, for example, why the government provides some services itself rather than contracting them out to private firms and how nonproductive characteristics enter into the public hiring process and into some public wage-setting negotiations. My problem with his incorporation of political considerations is that his modeling effort focuses almost exclusively on political *elements* or political *factors* rather than on the political *process*. Reder's approach is almost totally outcome-oriented, as it leaves aside the question of how decisions

49

are made, and this leads him to omit a number of important features of the process determining public wages and employment. Interestingly enough, on the other hand, a number of his empirical "stories" do focus on the decision-making process itself.

The outcome- rather than process-orientation of Professor Reder's model is reflected in his basic assumption that the government's objective is to maximize its expected number of votes, measured as a percentage of eligible voters, subject to a budget constraint that is assumed to allow no deficits. This is not to say that the author ignores all other elements besides votes. On the contrary, Reder discusses the possibility that votes might be traded for dollars, and, more importantly, he includes ideological parameters in the government's utility function. He recognizes that "A government gets utility not only by adding to its votes, but also by avoiding (engaging in) certain types of actions that it considers ideologically offensive (attractive)." Furthermore, Reder also notes that specific characteristics of the electoral system—for example, that the party winning 50 percent of the popular vote takes all in a two-party election—may generate jumps in the value of an extra vote, and, "Such salta sometimes cause great sacrifices of ideology to get a few extra votes."

Discontinuities in the value of a vote, which are induced by particular characteristics of the voting system, affect the discussion of public employment and wage decisions in another, more basic way. Specifically, such discontinuities imply that some political decisions are nonmarginal in character. Not every decision, including every decision to hire or to fire, every decision to raise or to lower wages, entails a balancing act at the margin of votes gained and votes lost by the decision. If, for example, the municipality has a two-party system with a winner-take-all rule, one might expect to observe a mayor who has just won by a 51–49 margin behaving differently from one who has just won by a 75–25 margin. With an eye to re-election, each of these heads of city government will want to maintain his voting strength at a level of at least 51 percent, or somewhat higher if an error margin is desired. It seems clear, though, that the mayor who came into office with stronger support will have greater flexibility in making his policy decisions. He may well be more the utility-maximizer of the Ashenfelter-Ehrenberg type models than the vote-maximizer of the Reder model, and this suggests that the mayor riding the wave of voter support *may* be considerably less tolerant of inefficiency than Reder's paper suggests.

The once-and-for-all nature of the vote-maximizing decision process that Reder envisions also leads to the omission of factors that undoubtedly play an important role in decisions concerning labor in the public sector. The budgeting decision is in fact a dynamic process rather than a one-time optimization problem. The process leaves scope for additional appropriations as time passes, that is, scope for incremental budgeting. The budgeting procedure may leave enough room for the head of the city government to grant wage demands of public employees in response to the political pressure of municipal voters who are inconvenienced by disruptions of government services. To put it another way, the public-sector budgeting process is an integral part of the city government's coordination of claims by competing interest groups. The budgetary decision emerges not as the solution to a straightforward optimization problem, but rather as the result of the interplay among those groups. (See Wellington and Winter (1971).) One can interpret the magnitudes of the partial derivatives of Reder's vote function (2) as reflecting the relative voting strengths of the several interest groups. For example, one can interpret $\partial V/\partial Q_1$ as reflecting the strength of the consumers of public service 1 and use $\partial V/\partial w_2$ and $\partial V/\partial X_2$ as measures of the strength of the suppliers of type 2 labor. But this does not adequately capture the forces that affect the outcome of public wage and employment decisions. It seems that the theory of public-sector labor decisions is an area where our usual attempt to abstract from dynamic process considerations is particularly inappropriate.

Reder's formulation of the municipal government's resource constraint also glosses over some important features of the political environment that bear on the determination of public wages and employment. He is quite explicit about how the excessive aggregation of his statement of the budget constraint masks the separation between responsibility for raising funds and authority to spend them that occurs frequently in the public sector. One particularly important form this separation takes is the externalization of the costs of municipal public services to other levels of government. At least some of these costs may, via revenue sharing and the like, fall upon the state in which the city is located or even upon the nation as a whole rather than on the municipal constituency alone. This raises the question of whether the funds required to provide government services will actually have a perceptible tax impact on the municipal voters. Add to this the complexity of municipal budgets and the difficulty constituents would face in trying to trace through the effect of a current wage and employment decision on a future tax bill (see Wellington and Winter (1971)), and one must question the stringency that Reder's budget constraint imposes on his model municipality. Neither every overly generous wage offer nor every overly generous employment offer need cost the politico votes as the result of perceived concomitant tax increases.

I would also like to make two observations about the applicability of Reder's model. On the one hand, in terms of the kind of workers to whom it is meant to apply, the model seems too general. At times Reder speaks as if it is a model for firefighters, sanitation men, or teachers, while at other points the paper seems addressed to the employment of staff assistants and high-level politicos. There are obviously significant differences in "market structure" for the kinds of services these two types of government employees provide, and these differences would seem to suggest the need for a different model to analyze the wage and employment decisions affecting each of them. In particular, constructing distinct models for these two types of workers might help to focus attention more clearly on the role of public-sector unions and their roots, in part, in the economies of scale that exist in the production of political influence.

At the same time the model Reder proposes seems too specific in terms of the kind of city government to which it can be applied. The model is applicable primarily to a single-party government in which the mayor and the city council or other legislative body not only belong to the same party but are also fully of one mind with regard to all policies. Casual empiricism suggests that the set of actual cases of sizable cities to which this description could apply is small, if not empty. As mentioned earlier, the author does recognize the excessive aggregation of the vote function and resource constraint he uses. But it seems critical to ask how we ought to model the more typical municipal governmental situation where conflicts of interest abound within the government, whether they are due to party differences, differences in individual political ambitions, or differences simply with regard to what the best policy is. Consider, for example, Herbert Kaufman's description of New York City (quoted in Polsby, 1963, pp. 127–128):

> Decisions of the municipal government emanate from no single source, but from many centers; conflicts and clashes are referred to no single authority, but are settled at many levels and at many points in the system: no single group can guarantee the success of any proposal it supports, the defeat of every idea it objects to. Not even the central governmental organs of the city—the Mayor, the Board of Estimate, the Council—individually or in combination, even approach mastery in this sense.
>
> Each separate decision center consists of a cluster of interested contestants, with a "core group" in the middle, invested by the rules with the formal authority to legitimize decisions (that is to promulgate them in binding form) and a constellation of related "satellite groups" seeking to influence the authoritative issuances of the core group.

The difficulty in applying Reder's model to this situation should be clear. For a start, one must ask how the vote-maximization goal he posits trickles down and through this intertwined, layered decision-making mechanism. One should also note that Reder's model also seems inapplicable at the other end of the municipal organizational spectrum. It provides little insight into the functioning of municipal governments that follow the city-manager model. Perhaps in the case of the city-manager form, the utility-maximizing models of Ehrenberg and others are the appropriate ones to use.

Let me close with a brief comment about the empirical testability of Professor Reder's model. Some of the predictions of his model (for example, those concerning which services governments will provide directly) could be examined by direct observation without complicated serious econometric work. Any test of the entire theoretical structure and its predictions will, however, require careful econometric examination. Data should be readily available on most of the variables entering his model, and he has already made some suggestions concerning aspects of the hypothesized structure, for example, short time lags to correspond to the weak voter memories he posits. There is, however, a rather major complication associated with a full test of Reder's model, because what one is actually testing is the sensitivity of voters' responses to a variety of variables. For that purpose one must surely look beyond the variables concerning government services and taxes which constitute the full set of factors his model includes. A test of Reder's model would provide an interesting local-government analogue to empirical tests of the theory of the rational voter performed by Kramer (1971), Stigler (1973), and others using macrovariables such as unemployment rates, inflation rates, income levels, and the rates of change of these variables.

To repeat my opening comment, I found Professor Reder's paper quite stimulating, and I am sure all those doing research on questions of public employment will benefit from reading it. Professor Reder has urged us to take "greater care in constructing models of public decision making." I would add to his call that we need to be more sensitive to the institutional features of that decision making, particularly to its process elements, when constructing such models.

ORLEY C. ASHENFELTER AND
RONALD G. EHRENBERG

The Demand for Labor in the Public Sector

Increased interest in the determinants of the demand for labor in the state and local sector has followed on the heels of the dramatic growth in government employment in this sector during the postwar period from around 8 percent to almost 15 percent of total payrolls. Simultaneously has come interest in both the problems and the special programs geared to these problems in the state and local sector. For example, the Emergency Employment Act of 1971 sets up a specific framework of federal grants-in-aid to state and local governments for the purpose of increasing employment in this sector. Aside from the general question of the impact of such legislation on aggregate employment or output, it is important to determine the extent to which these grants increase the demand for labor in the state and local sector over what would have occurred in their absence. This requires an explicit behavioral model of employment determination in this sector.

The rapid growth of collective bargaining in the state and local sector has produced substantial controversy over the legal treatment of unions and collective negotiations in the sector. A part of the controversy revolves around the relative magnitudes of the wage elasticities of demand for labor in the public and private sectors. If the public sector has a lower elasticity, unionists there face a smaller potential decrease in employment from a given wage increase than do unionists in the private sector, and market forces consequently impose a smaller constraint on unions negotiating in the public sector. (See Hamermesh in this volume for

Note: We are deeply indebted to David A. Smith for his extensive assistance. We are also grateful to Burton Weisbrod and Hirschel Kasper for their comments on an earlier version of the paper.

55

an extended discussion of this point.) In this case a theoretical framework is required both to define formally the "wage elasticity of demand for labor in the public sector" and to provide estimates of it for comparison with the private sector. Finally, predictions of the effects of both general and special revenue sharing schemes on the expansion of employment in the public sector may require information on the effect of changes in both income and relative prices on public-sector employment, depending on the formula that describes the scheme.

Our purpose in this paper is the *exposition* of the empirical implications of a theory of the demand for labor by state and local governments based on the classical theory of consumer choice.[1] Since we are primarily interested in empirical tests of the usefulness of this theory, we emphasize the full set of restrictions within and across the labor demand functions in the public sector that are implied by classical theory. We also report extensive tests of the degree to which these empirical predictions are consistent with data for U.S. states. Finally, we show how the empirical estimates and theoretical framework can be used to shed some light on a number of problems in public policy.

I. Theoretical Framework

The basic building blocks in our analysis of the demand for public sector workers are: (1) a well-behaved utility function that orders the satisfaction received by some "effective" decision maker from the services of workers employed in the various functional categories of the nonfederal *public* sector and from the quantities of goods and services purchased from the *private* sector; and (2) the budget constraint on total resources faced by this effective decision maker. The assumption that our effective decision maker chooses both employment levels in each governmental category and quantities of each privately purchased good to maximize his satisfaction, given the constraint imposed by the wage rates, prices, and income that he faces, leads immediately to an extensive set of familiar implications about the effects of ex-

---

[1] A more formal discussion of the system of demand equations we estimate is presented in the Appendix.

ogenous changes in the latter on the optimum quantities of the former. Set up in this way, the problem is a straightforward application of the classical theory of consumer choice to a case where the inputs of labor to the public sector are also subjects for decision. With one additional maintained hypothesis it is precisely these implications that we attempt to test.

Unfortunately, the interpretation of the demand functions for labor that we derive from the above assumptions remains cloudy until three further issues are resolved. First, since the choices that we describe in the public sector require a collective decision, it is appropriate to ask whose preferences are described by the utility function that it is presumed to be maximized. As is well known, there are plausible conditions under which we may be assured that an open, democratic political system will make the preferences of the median voter on an issue into those of the effective decision maker.[2] Under these conditions, the effective decision maker *is* the "typical" voter, whose wishes are carried out by elected officials chosen because their positions coincide with those of the typical voter. Although this description of the process of collective choice seems more realistic than others, it should be clear that successful empirical tests of the hypotheses we set out below do not constitute strong evidence of the existence of such a process if there are other contenders that give rise to a stable, well-behaved utility function.

Second, we must consider the rationale for including the services of labor, rather than the quantity of the public service produced and then consumed, as subject to choice in the public sector. Although public services rendered are no doubt what provide satisfaction to the typical consumer, it is often impossible to measure the quantity of public services, and it is generally impossible for the decision maker to change the quantity produced without changing the quantity of factor inputs set aside for their provision. Consequently, we may deal interchangeably with the satisfaction from the quantity of a municipal service produced and, so long as there exists a stable relationship between factor inputs and the quantity of service produced, the satisfaction from

[2] See Downs (1957) and Tullock (1967). These conditions have recently been spelled out in detail by Bergstrom and Goodman (1973).

the services provided by the inputs set aside to produce a particular municipal service.[3] In addition, we are forced by data limitations to assume that for the period of our analysis the per capita stock of factor inputs other than labor is fixed, so that changes in the per capita quantity of labor input are the only *short-run* method for changing the quantity of public services.[4] Since we take the year as our period of analysis, we are therefore assuming that the *year-to-year* change in the service flow received by the individual from a particular public service is a function only of the change in the per capita employment level. The change in the price of a unit of each public service is a function only of the change in the wage.

Finally, we must note that, in addition to the direct production of public services, governments have the option of purchasing services from the private sector. It is the sum of the public services provided in both manners that should enter our representative consumer's utility function. To the extent that the proportion of a public service provided by each method varies either across states or over time (other than by a trend factor), our

[3] It may be useful to make this point more concrete by putting it in symbols. Suppose that utility is a function of the quantities of public and private services consumed, X_1 and X_2, so that $U = U(X_1, X_2)$. If X_1 is produced with labor and capital, L and K, then $X_1 = f(L,K)$. Consequently, we may write the reduced utility function $U = U(f(L,K), X_2) = V(L,K,X_2)$, which contains all the information required to maximize utility given the budget constraint. That is, we may choose X_1 and X_2 so as to maximize U, or we may choose the quantities of inputs L, K and X_2 that maximize V. Either procedure leads to the same choices for X_1 and X_2. The alternative procedure to our own would require calculation of the values of L and K that minimize the costs of producing any fixed level of X_1, given the prices of L and K, and then the maximization of U treating the implied marginal cost of X_1 as the price of X_1. Of course, this second approach does require knowledge of the functional form of $X_1 = f(L,K)$, which is a disadvantage if X_1 cannot be measured even in principle. This second approach is followed by Borcherding and Deacon (1972).

[4] An alternative assumption, similar to the block-additivity in utility assumed between the inputs of labor services to the public sector and the quantities of private goods consumed, and set out below, will suffice here also. In particular, we can require that utility be block additive in the three blocks—labor services to the public sector, capital services to the public sector, and commodities purchased in the private sector.

parameter estimates of the demand for state and local government *employees* may be biased.

A. General Empirical Implications

With the stage set in this way, we may turn to the process whereby the optimum quantities of labor services for the public sector and the optimum quantities of commodities purchased from the private sector are chosen by the typical consumer. In general, the consumer will maximize his satisfaction, given his income and the prices of private and public services, by expanding the consumption of any commodity or service up to the point where the marginal utility of that service just equals the price of the service multiplied by the marginal utility of income. Given consumer's income and prices of public and private services, the $n + K$ marginal conditions (for the n functional types of public services and the K private-sector commodities) may be solved to determine the $n + K$ optimal choices of values for the public- and private-sector purchases as functions of the $n + K$ prices and consumer's income. These $n + K$ rules are, of course, the n demand functions for labor services in the public sector and the K demand functions for private-sector commodities. They describe how the consumer's choices of public- and private-sector purchases would change as income and prices change if the consumer were maximizing his satisfaction. The power of neoclassical utility theory applied to this problem resides in its implications for the predicted effect of price changes on the quantities of public- and private-sector services demanded.

The most fundamental of these implications is based on a breakdown of the effect of a change in the price of the jth commodity on the demand for the quantity of the ith commodity into substitution and income effects. The way we state this breakdown explicitly recognizes that the change in *any* price will effect the demand for *all* commodities. In particular, the income effect of the change in the jth price is the part of the change in the demand for the ith commodity that results from the fact that at the old equilibrium level of purchases the consumer's income has been effectively changed in the opposite direction from that of the change in the jth price. This change in income will have the same effect on the demand for the ith commodity as any other income change. The remaining part of the change in the demand for the ith commodity is the substitution effect of the jth price change. It is the same change in the demand for the ith good that would result from a change in the jth price if the consumer were simultaneously compensated with income to keep him at the same level of overall satisfaction as he attained before the price change.

Using this breakdown, we first have the result that the "own" substitution effect of a price change is negative. This means that an income-compensated increase in the wage rate for any municipal category must result in a decrease in the demand for labor in this category, just as an income-compensated increase in the price of a private-sector commodity must result in a decrease in the demand for this commodity. This is a powerful result, for it means that, if municipal services are not inferior goods, the labor-demand functions for municipal services must be downward sloping. Second, if we increase income, all private-sector prices, and all public-sector wages by the same proportion, both demand for labor in each category of municipal service and demand for each private-sector commodity must remain unchanged. This result on the homogeneity of the demand functions implies that there is no money illusion in the allocation of real resources; if the unit of account for wages, prices, and income were suddenly doubled (or halved), there would be no effect on the demand for real quantities. Finally, we have the result that the substitution effect on the ith commodity resulting from a change in the jth price must be the same as the substitution effect on the jth commodity resulting from a change in the ith price. This equality of cross-substitution effects means that, if we observe from the labor demand function for the ith municipal service that the ith and jth municipal services are substitutes (complements),[5] then we must also observe from the labor demand function for the jth municipal service that the ith and jth municipal services are substitutes (complements). In a sense, the equality of cross-substitution effects requires that the various labor-demand functions provide

---

[5]That is, that the income-compensated effect of a change in the jth wage on the demand for the ith type of labor service is positive.

consistent information on the substitution and complementarity among the various public services.

Although each of these empirical implications for the observable effects of public-sector wage changes and private-sector price changes on the demand for labor in municipal services might be put to a test, as a practical matter this would pose enormous difficulties. The theoretical structure we have laid out implies that changes in all public sector wages *and* private sector prices will have some effect on the demand for labor for each of the municipal services. As a sheer estimation problem, this places severe limitations on any empirical tests. The data requirements for empirical tests under these conditions are also more demanding than current sources can support. Under these conditions we must search for further assumptions to reduce the number of prices or wages that we must consider in constructing empirical implications of utility maximization for the labor demand functions in the public sector alone. As it turns out, the additional assumption we choose may also provide a more "realistic" description of the process of collective choice in the state and local sector.

B. Specific Empirical Implications

Our description of a typical consumer acting rationally when confronted with a bewildering array of both public- and private-sector choices strains at credibility. A more plausible description of the choice process has decisions made in two steps. We imagine that the typical consumer first budgets for broad categories of expenditure, such as food, shelter, clothing, and public services; then, given the budgets for each category, our consumer makes choices on the quantities of the various services purchased within each category. In the first step of the process the consumer must consider as constraints his income and a price index for each of the broad categories of services. Given his income and knowledge of these aggregate price indexes, choices regarding the most satisfactory expenditure levels for the broad categories are made. In the second step of the process the consumer must consider only the budgeted expenditure for a category and the prices of the detailed commodities within the category as constraints. Given the budgeted expenditure for a category, choices are made regarding the most satisfactory purchases for the detailed commodities.

Although this description of the consumer's budgeting process seems generally plausible, it has special appeal for the problem of allocation within and to the public sector. In this decentralized budget process, there is no reason why the detailed choices of purchases within a broad category need be made by the consumer at all. All that is required is that whoever makes the detailed decisions on purchases within an aggregate category should have knowledge of the consumer's desired aggregate budget for the category as well as the consumer's preferences among public services. These are, however, precisely the types of information that elected officials are expected to have; indeed, it is presumably the reason for their election. The framework we set out for economic choices is thus consistent with the existence of a role for the political process.

In view of the attractive nature of the decentralized budgeting process as a description for allocation of labor services in the public sector, it is natural to examine the conditions under which such a process is consistent with the utility-maximization hypothesis with which we started our discussion. It turns out that the answer to this question is not an entirely simple matter, but the implications of the two processes are consistent if the satisfaction received from *additional* public-sector goods does not depend systematically on the quantities of private-sector goods that the consumer already purchases. Stated differently, we require that public- and private-sector goods satisfy different (or independent) wants. Although this condition is undoubtedly not completely satisfied in practice, it serves as a useful approximation and may not lead us too far amiss in empirical matters. In any event, some such assumption is clearly required in order to reduce the problem of empirical estimation to manageable proportions, and we shall use this one in what follows.[6]

[6] Implicitly, we have also assumed that the wants satisfied by federal expenditures are independent of the wants satisfied by state and local government employment. To a large extent the services provided by federal and nonfederal government employees do not overlap, so that this may not be too unrealistic.

With this additional assumption in hand we can now state the specific empirical predictions of the utility-maximization hypothesis applied to the demand for labor in the public sector. With only slight changes, these parallel in substance and form the general implications of utility maximization that have already been stated. First, if, holding the real employment budget in the public sector constant, we observe a negative effect of a change in the ith wage on the change in the demand for the labor services in the ith (or own) category, then we can be assured that the income-compensated demand curve for labor in the ith category is downward sloping.[7] Since the latter prediction is a general implication of utility maximization, empirical verification of the former is tantamount to empirical verification of the latter. We will consequently call this the "negativity of own substitution effects" hypothesis. Second, if we hold the real public-sector employment budget constant and change the wages of all categories of public-service employees proportionately, then the demand for each category of public-sector employee should remain unchanged. We will call this the "homogeneity" hypothesis, since it follows directly from the general implication that the labor demand functions must be homogeneous of degree zero. Finally, if we hold the real employment budget constant, the effect of a change in the jth wage rate on the demand for the ith category of labor must be the same as the effect of a change in the ith wage rate on the demand for the jth category of labor. Alternatively stated, this implies that two categories of labor services estimated to be substitutes (complements) in the ith demand function should also be estimated to be substitutes (complements) in the jth demand function. In what follows we will call this the "symmetry" hypothesis.

II. Empirical Results

Our basic data source is a set of annual first differences of employment, wage rates, and income for individual states over the

[7]Strictly speaking, this statement is only correct if the aggregate of all public services and the aggregate of all public commodities are not inferior goods.

ORLEY C. ASHENFELTER & RONALD G. EHRENBERG

years 1958–1969 excluding 1964.[8]   Before we can turn to estimation, however, a number of preliminary considerations must be
examined.   In most investigations of the demand for public services, a large number of variables in addition to those reflecting
income and prices that we have discussed thus far are examined
for their explanatory power. These additional variables are generally taken to measure differences or variations in "tastes" for

TABLE 1. Elasticities of Demand for Labor Holding the Real
          Employment Budget Constant[a]

Category of Labor Services:	High Density States	Low Density States
1) Streets and Highway	−.018	−.099
	(.2)	(1.3)
2) Public Welfare	−.279	−.371
	(2.7)	(4.8)
3) Hospitals	−.291	.194
	(7.7)	(5.6)
4) Public Health	−.100	−.440
	(2.1)	(2.4)
5) Police Protection	−.218	−.255
	(3.2)	(3.2)
6) Fire Protection	−.665	−.700
	(5.1)	(6.5)
7) Sanitation and Sewerage	−.247	−.460
	(2.8)	(3.4)
8) Natural Resources	−.353	−.424
	(4.2)	(4.3)
9) General Control and Financial Administration	−.189	−.161
	(2.6)	(2.2)
10) Other Noneducational Services	−.468	−.317
	(8.9)	(3.5)

[a]Absolute value of t-statistics in parentheses.

[8]These data have been described in detail in Ehrenberg (1972,
Chapter 3).   They are time series of ten observations for each of fifty
states, though sporadic errors in the published Bureau of the Census sources
reduce the total number of data points to slightly less than 500. Employment is for full-time equivalent workers, and the wage rate is average
monthly payroll costs per man, obtained as the ratio of total monthly payroll to full-time equivalent employment.   All employment and income
data are expressed in per capita terms.

64

various types of public services. The most natural procedure for integrating such variables into the classical demand theory framework is to assume that satisfaction is derived from the quantity consumed per capita and to allow the weights in the population deflator to differ and thus reflect the age distribution of the population, the urban-rural location of the population, etc. The difficulty with this procedure is that it does not simply imply that the indicated variables should enter the demand functions as additional variables, but rather that the size of all of the income and price elasticities of demand should depend systematically on these variables. Of course, if all of these variables remained constant through time, demand functions for individual states could be estimated over time. Unfortunately, however, the time series for individual states are far too small to follow this procedure; we will be forced to pool our time series for the various states. In view of this we have tried to increase the homogeneity of the sample by arbitrarily splitting it into two subsamples according to whether or not a state was one of the twenty-five states with the highest density (in persons per square mile).[9]   As a practical

[9]The twenty-five high-density states (ranked in order of density from highest to lowest) are:

1. Rhode Island	10. Illinois	18. Tennessee
2. New Jersey	11. Michigan	19. South Carolina
3. Massachusetts	12. Indiana	20. West Virginia
4. Connecticut	13. Virginia	21. Kentucky
5. New York	14. California	22. Wisconsin
6. Maryland	15. Hawaii	23. Louisiana
7. Pennsylvania	16. North Carolina	24. Georgia
8. Ohio	17. Florida	25. New Hampshire
9. Delaware		

The twenty-five low-density states (ranked in order of density from highest to lowest) are:

1. Alabama	10. Arkansas	18. South Dakota
2. Missouri	11. Maine	19. North Dakota
3. Iowa	12. Kansas	20. Idaho
4. Mississippi	13. Nebraska	21. New Mexico
5. Minnesota	14. Oregon	22. Montana
6. Washington	15. Colorado	23. Nevada
7. Vermont	16. Arizona	24. Wyoming
8. Texas	17. Utah	25. Alaska
9. Oklahoma		

matter, the high-density states also tend to be the most urbanized and are concentrated in the northeast region of the United States. Though it is crude, this procedure does allow us to test whether there are systematic differences in the behavioral responses to wage and income changes according to one plausible criterion.

Unless the supply of labor to a given functional category in a state is very elastic, we will have a biased estimator for our demand functions if we use the conventional least-squares estimation procedures. In essence, we may confuse part of the effects of changes in wage rates on the supply of labor with the effects of changes in wage rates on the demand for labor. Although the small amount of evidence available does suggest that the relative supply of workers to the public sector is very elastic, we have simply adopted this assumption without further testing in what follows.[10]

We are faced with some decision about our assumptions on the breakdown of public-service labor categories. Our basic data cover the ten non-educational categories listed in Table 1 plus an eleventh category covering all educational workers. Since the educational expenditures constitute around one-half of the total payrolls for state and local governments, and since it seems at least plausible that educational services satisfy wants independent of non-educational services, we have treated the ten non-educational categories as a block separate from the educational category. This implies that we must estimate first the ten microeconomic demand equations for the allocation of the non-educational employment budget among its competing uses, and then the two aggregate demand equations for the real educational and non-educational employment budgets.[11]

---

[10] See Ashenfelter (1972a).

[11] As we show formally in the Appendix, it is necessary to estimate the micro demand equations first because the appropriate aggregate non-educational employees' price index entering the aggregate employment budget equations is a function of the marginal value shares of the micro categories. The latter are estimated in the micro demand equations.

A. Hypothesis Tests

Our most fundamental empirical results appear in Table 1.[12] We have tabulated here the estimated own price elasticity of demand for each category of labor (evaluated at the means), holding the real employment budget constant. These elasticities indicate the percentage change in employment in a category per percentage change in its wage rate, holding all other wages constant and making a simultaneous compensation that keeps the overall real employment budget constant. They thus represent substitution of labor among functional categories within a constant real employment budget. As we have already noted, if they are negative they imply that the compensated substitution effect of a wage change on employment demand is negative; this is the most fundamental implication of the utility maximization theory. As can be seen from Table 1, all of these demand elasticities are negative in the high-density sample of states, and they are significant at conventional test levels in all but one of the ten employment categories. The results for the low-density sample of states are slightly less favorable. While nine of the ten elasticities are negative and eight significantly so, it is disturbing that the elasticity for hospital employees in the low-density states not only has a positive sign, but a coefficient nearly six times its standard error. On balance, these results provide strong support for the utility-maximization theory from the data for the high-density states and weaker support from the data for the low-density states.

In the first line of Table 2 we report the results of our tests of the homogeneity hypothesis from the two samples. The test reported in Table 2 is a joint test of the ten homogeneity conditions for the ten demand functions. This is a test of the hypothesis that, if we change all ten category wage rates by the same proportion, holding the real employment budget constant, none of the ten employment levels will change. Table 3 contains more detail by providing a separate test statistic for each of the ten demand

---

[12] Though we do not go into the details in the text, our estimation scheme is a variant on the so-called "Rotterdam" model for estimating complete systems of demand functions. See Barten (1968) and Theil (1967, esp. pp. 233–237), and the Appendix.

ORLEY C. ASHENFELTER & RONALD G. EHRENBERG

TABLE 2. Test Statistics for Rejection of the Null Hypotheses that the
Labor Demand Functions Satisfy the Homogeneity and
Symmetry Restrictions

	F-Ratio for:	
	High Density States	Low Density States
Restriction Tested:		
Homogeneity	.112[a]	2.726[a]
Symmetry (and Homogeneity)	.743[b]	12.80[b]

[a]To be compared with a tabulated critical level of 1.86 for a .05 level test with 10 and 2106 degrees of freedom in the high density states, and 10 and 2169 degrees of freedom in the low density states.

[b]To be compared with a tabulated critical level of 1.40 for a .05 level test with 36 and 2106 degrees of freedom in the high density states, and 36 and 2169 degrees of freedom in the low density states.

functions. As can be seen from Table 2, the joint homogeneity hypothesis cannot be rejected for the high-density sample of states, but it is rejected for the low-density sample of states. Moreover, examining the detailed tests in Table 3, we see that homogeneity can be rejected in no more than three of the cate-

TABLE 3. t-Statistics for Rejection of the Null Hypothesis that the
Labor Demand Functions are Homogeneous of Degree Zero[a]

Category of Labor Services:	High Density States	Low Density States
Streets and Highways	.791	1.130
Public Welfare	1.413	4.132*
Hospitals	0.000	5.914*
Public Health	.714	2.340*
Police Protection	2.636*	7.116*
Fire Protection	2.210*	0.000
Sanitation and Sewerage	1.786	2.236*
Natural Resources	1.987*	2.116*
General Control and Financial Administration	.974	5.167*
Other Noneducational Services	.662	1.794

[a]Degrees of freedom for high density states = 229, and for low density states = 236. The critical level of t for the appropriate two-tailed test at the .05 significance level is 1.986. An asterisk indicates rejection of the homogeneity hypothesis.

68

gories for the high-density states, while homogeneity can be rejected in seven of the categories for the low-density states. In sum, the homogeneity hypothesis is supported by the results for the high-density states but rejected by the results for the low-density states.

In the second line of Table 2 we have gathered the statistics for a test of the symmetry hypothesis. This is a test of the hypothesis that, when we observe that the ith and jth labor services are substitutes (complements) in the ith labor demand function, we also observe that the ith and jth labor services are substitutes (complements) in the jth labor-demand function. Quantitatively this requires that, holding the real employment budget constant, the effect of a change in category j's wage on employment demand for category i be identical to the effect of a change in category i's wage on employment of category j. The stringency of this condition should not be underestimated. In our case it involves a joint test of the existence of nearly 40 linear restrictions on the 100 free coefficients in the complete set of ten labor demand functions. As can be seen from Table 2, the symmetry hypothesis *cannot* be rejected for the results from the high-density states, but it is clearly rejected for the results from the low-density states. The data again provide strong support for the utility-maximization framework in the high-density states and evidence against it in the low-density states.

We can only speculate at this point about the reasons for the different empirical results in the high- and low-density states. Clearly, more analysis that explicitly incorporates demographic and other factors into the analytical framework would be fruitful. At this point we are inclined to ascribe the difference to the much more homogeneous character of the high-density states compared to the low-density states.[13] Even so, perhaps we need not be too disturbed for the accuracy of the results that follow, since over 75 percent of all state and local government employment is in

[13] An alternative hypothesis suggested to us by Hirschel Kasper is that in the high-density states there is more political competition that forces decision-makers in these states to conform more closely to the preferences of the median voter than do decision-makers elsewhere. For an alternative test of this hypothesis see Kasper (1971a).

TABLE 4. Estimates of the Marginal Expenditures on Labor Services from an Increase in the Real Employment Budget[a]

Category of Labor Services:	High Density States	Low Density States
Streets and Highways	.120	.347
	(34.5)	(14.7)
Public Welfare	.018	.015
	(15.4)	(4.4)
Hospitals	.125	.171
	(37.5)	(10.9)
Public Health	.046	−.007
	(36.1)	(1.2)
Police Protection	.092	.032
	(55.7)	(7.3)
Fire Protection	.060	.021
	(32.2)	(3.0)
Sanitation and Sewerage	.042	.015
	(28.3)	(4.1)
Natural Resources	.076	.065
	(44.4)	(6.7)
General Control and Financial Administration	.174	.170
	(63.4)	(14.7)
Other Noneducational Services	.247	.170
	(59.5)	(8.2)

[a]Absolute values of t-statistics in parentheses.

the high-density group of states. Nevertheless, in order to see what additional light we can shed on this issue, we have tabulated in Table 4 our estimates of the marginal expenditures on labor services resulting from an increase in the real employment budget for the ten categories of labor services in the two samples. As can be seen from the table, the main differences are substantially smaller marginal expenditure shares for streets and highways in the high-density states and substantially higher shares for public health, police and fire protection, sanitation, and other non-educational services (e.g., libraries) in them. The latter services tend to be more important in urban or dense areas than the former, and these results seem plausible enough. Nevertheless, in the results that follow we will concentrate our attention on the parameter estimates derived from the data for the high-density group of states, since we have rejected the implications of the utility-maximization framework for the low-density group.

B. Parameter Estimates

Rows 1 and 3 of Table 5 contain our estimates of the basic income and wage elasticities for the two aggregate education and non-education employment groups using the data for the high-density states. As can be seen from the table, both the relative precision and the size of these elasticities are larger for employment in education than for employment in the non-educational categories. For the non-educational aggregate, we find that employment is inelastic with respect to both the wage rate and income, with the former elasticity around −.38 and the latter at around .37. For the educational aggregate we find that employment is nearly unit elastic with respect to the wage rate and income; the former elasticity is around −1.16, the latter 1.14. It is important to remember that our educational employment category includes elementary, secondary, *and* post-secondary public institutions. The inclusion of college and university employees may account in part for the difference in our results between the two aggregate employment groups.

TABLE 5. Estimates of Income and Substitution Elasticities in the Aggregate Demand Functions for Labor Services[a]

Aggregate Category of Labor Services	Own Wage Substitution Elasticity	Total Own Wage Demand Elasticity	Income Elasticity	Marginal Expenditure per Increase in Income	Differential Marginal Expenditure per Increase in Federal Grants
Noneducational Public Services	−.367 (1.3)	−.380	.367	.013 (1.4)	
Noneducational Public Services	−.368 (1.3)	−.381	.373	.013 (1.3)	−.006 (.04)
Educational Public Services	−1.018 (3.4)	−1.062	1.141	.044 (2.6)	
Educational Public Services	−1.018 (3.4)	−1.062	1.141	.044 (2.3)	.0006 (.002)

[a]Absolute values of *t*-statistics in parentheses.

TABLE 6. Estimates of Income and Substitution Elasticities in the
Noneducational Demand Functions for Labor Services

Category of Labor Services for:	Own Wage Substitution Elasticity	Total Own Wage Demand Elasticity	Income Elasticity
Streets and Highways	−.090	−.092	.271
Public Welfare	−.314	−.315	.153
Hospitals	−.302	−.304	.289
Public Health	−.118	−.119	.545
Police Protection	−.288	−.239	.297
Fire Protection	−.530	−.531	.371
Sanitation and Sewerage	−.230	−.230	.354
Natural Resources	−.385	−.386	.635
General Control and Financial Administration	−.277	−.279	.578
Other Noneducational Services	−.562	−.565	.385

In Table 6 we have brought together our results from Table 5 and the results based on the fully constrained estimation of the parameters analogous to those listed in Table 1. These are used to compute the complete set of wage and income elasticities of demand for each of the non-educational employment categories. Although the wage rate elasticities listed here vary from −.09 to a high of −.57, they vary rather closely around the aggregate elasticity in the first row of Table 5. Although the income elasticities listed vary from .15 to .64, they, too, hover closely around the aggregate elasticity in Table 5. We now proceed to show how the results in Tables 5 and 6 can be used for a simple examination of some important issues of public policy.

III. Implications

Let us begin by considering an analysis of an increase in federal grants-in-aid made to state and local governments. This is an old issue for empirical analysis, and we certainly do not intend to resolve it here.[14] Nevertheless, it is a straightforward matter to

[14] See Gramlich (1969) for a survey of the empirical work on this issue.

show how our analysis can be used to examine this issue. Let us assume to begin with that the size of federal grants is not tied to state revenues or expenditures. Under these conditions federal grants to state and local governments in the framework we have used are nothing more than an increase in the disposable income available to the community, as long as the grants are not financed by a corresponding increase in taxes. (Of course, if the grants are financed by a fully offsetting increase in federal taxes, we have no change in disposable income and hence no change in employment would be predicted.) As a practical matter, one may expect the actual situation to differ in the different states, so that in some states disposable income may increase while in others it may decrease. Presumably the aggregate result would reflect the average situation.

It is possible to test the hypothesis that untied federal grants on average only have income effects on the demand for labor services in the public sector if one is willing to assume that the historical pattern of changes in grants-in-aid may reasonably be considered as changes in untied lump-sum transfers.[15] To do this we add the change in federal grants as an additional variable in the aggregate demand functions of Table 5. Since the income variable in these demand functions reflects changes in personal and not disposable income, the income effect of changes in grants should already have been reflected in the marginal expenditure (or income elasticity) coefficients listed in rows 1 and 3 of Table 5. Hence, the hypothesis that federal grants-in-aid have had only income effects on the demand for labor services implies that the coefficients listed in the last column of rows 2 and 4 in Table 5 should be zero. As can be seen from the table, this is essentially the result we obtain. Taken at face value these results imply that in the absence of a compensating tax increase, a one dollar increase in federal grants leads to only about a six-cent increase in state and local expenditures on labor services. About one-fourth of the increase is allocated to non-educational public services and the re-

---

[15] Gramlich and Galper (1973) provide evidence that this may not be a reasonable assumption.

mainder allocated to educational services.[16] Alternatively, these results imply that a one-dollar increase in federal grants in the presence of a compensating tax increase would lead to no change in state and local expenditures on labor services.

Let us consider some of the recent proposals for revenue sharing by the federal government with state and local governments. One aspect of most of the formulae that characterize these schemes is that a state's share of grants is larger, the larger are the expenditures financed directly by the state. In the framework we have discussed, this is equivalent to a reduction in the price of labor services faced by state and local governments. To demonstrate how the effects of these wage changes may be estimated we use some calculations by Johnson and Mohan (1971). They estimate that a five billion dollar block grant distributed according to the 1970 Nixon Administration's revenue sharing proposal would have reduced the revenue costs of additional public services in 1969 by about 5.5 percent to a typical state. The weighted average of the educational and non-educational wage rate elasticities in Table 5 is about $-.7$, so that we would expect expenditures on labor services to increase by about 3.8 $(= -.055(-.7))$ percent in the typical state as a result of such a grant.

Finally, as an illustration, we may compare our estimated demand elasticities for labor in the public sector with plausible estimates of demand elasticities for labor in the private sector in order to determine whether market forces have a stronger or weaker effect on bargaining in the public sector than in the private sector. Unfortunately, there seem to be even fewer estimates of labor-demand elasticities (as opposed to marginal productivity relations) for the private sector than there are for the public sector. It is possible, however, to make some plausible, rough estimates for labor demand elasticities in the typical industry (which we take to be the bargaining unit) by using the classical Hicksian formula for the elasticity of derived demand.[17] Our calculations

[16]Since this result is substantially lower than those produced previously by both ourselves and others, it probably ought not to be taken at face value. See Ashenfelter (1972a), Ehrenberg (1972), and Gramlich (1969).

[17]For the case where the supply of capital to an industry is taken to be perfectly elastic, the elasticity of demand for labor is a weighted average

lead to the conclusion that private-sector demand elasticities are in the neighborhood of −.5 to −1.0, though perhaps as large as −1.5 for some durable goods.[18] The estimates of the comparable demand elasticities from Table 5 are −.4 for non-educational labor. Although there is more variability in the plausible values one might attach to labor demand elasticities in the private sector than we are comfortable with, it does not seem likely that comparable demand elasticities in the private sector are as much as twice the aggregate values observed in the public sector. Even if we take this extreme assumption and suppose 10 percent to be a reasonable estimate for the average union/nonunion wage differential in the private economy,[19] it would take only a 20 percent union/nonunion wage differential to produce the same disemployment effects in the public sector as the existing union/nonunion wage differential might produce in the private sector. More plausible estimates of private-sector elasticities imply union/nonunion wage differentials in the public sector that are even lower. To carry this line of reasoning much further, however, would require an explicit model of union behavior.

IV. Concluding Comments

In this paper we have developed the empirical implications of a theory of the demand for labor by state and local governments

---

of the elasticity of demand for the product and the elasticity of substitution between capital and labor. The weights equal the share of labor in the value of output and one minus that share. (See Hicks (1966, p. 244).) Our impression is that the elasticity of substitution is often estimated at near or below unity in most industries. With labor's share between .5 and .7 and most estimated product demand functions taken to be inelastic, this implies labor demand elasticities between −.5 and −1.0, though perhaps as high (in absolute value) as −1.5 for some durable goods where product demand functions may be elastic.

[18] Waud (1968) directly estimated wage elasticities of demand for various two-digit manufacturing industries and obtained mean elasticities of −.405 and −1.507 respectively for the nondurable and durable industries. His estimates, however, were obtained holding real GNP constant and consequently are biased towards zero.

[19] Ashenfelter (1972b) estimates an average union/nonunion wage differential in the private sector of 10 percent for 1967.

based on the classical theory of consumer choice. On the one hand, using a pooled cross-section of annual first differences in employment, wage rates, and income over the period 1958–1969, we have found substantial support for the extensive implications of this theory among the 25 highest-density states. On the other hand, for the 25 lowest-density states we must reject the implications of the utility-maximization framework, either because the sample is not homogeneous or because the logical structure we have used is inappropriate. Clearly, far more analysis will be required before our numerical estimates can be taken as anything more than preliminary guides in the analysis of the practical problems we have examined.

APPENDIX

Under the conditions we describe in the text, it can be shown that the following equations capture the full content of the utility-maximization hypothesis. For each of the ten non-educational employment categories we have:

$$(1) \quad w_i d \ln X_i = \sum_j \pi_{ij} d \ln p_j + [\mu_i/\mu_s] \cdot$$
$$\left[\sum w_j d \ln X_j\right] \quad i,j = 1, \ldots, 10;$$

where p_i and X_i equal the wage rate (price) and employment (quantity) per capita in each of the ten employment categories, y is income per capita, and $w_i = p_i X_i/y$ is the fraction of income spent on employment in the ith category. In equation (1) the π_{ij} and μ_i/μ_s are treated as parameters. The term μ_i is the change in expenditure on category i per dollar increase in income, and the term μ_s is the sum of the μ_i over the ten non-educational categories. Thus, μ_s is the change in expenditure on the total of the ten non-educational employment categories per dollar increase in income. It follows immediately that $\Sigma_i \mu_i/\mu_s = 1$. The estimated values of the μ_i/μ_s are contained in Table 4 of the text, and it can readily be verified that they satisfy this restriction. The utility-maximization hypothesis implies $\pi_{ij} = \pi_{ji}$ (symmetry) and $\Sigma_j \pi_{ij} = 0$ for $i = 1, \ldots, 10$ (homogeneity). The practical convenience of equations (1) lies in the fact that these restrictions take the form of linear restrictions on the parameters of (1) and thus are readily amenable to test or imposition onto the data by conventional linear regression.

The aggregate equation for non-educational employment is:

$$(2) \quad \sum w_i d \ln X_i = \mu_s \left[d \ln y - \sum_k w_k d \ln p_k\right]$$
$$+ \phi \mu_s \left[\sum [\mu_i/\mu_s] \, d \ln p_i - \sum \mu_k \, d \ln p_k\right];$$

where the summation over k on the right hand side is over the ten non-educational categories, the educational category, and all private sector goods as well. A similar equation for the educa-

ORLEY C. ASHENFELTER & RONALD G. EHRENBERG

tional category is

$$(3) \quad w_E \, d \ln p_E = \mu_E \left[d \ln y - \sum w_k \, d \ln p_k \right]$$
$$+ \phi\mu_E \left[\sum \mu_E \, d \ln p_E - \sum \mu_k \, d \ln p_k \right]$$

There are three points to notice about equations (2) and (3). First, the term $d \ln y - \Sigma w_k \, d \ln p_k$ is essentially the change in the logarithm of an index of real income. Hence, when $d \ln y - \Sigma w_k \, d \ln p_k = 0$, real income is unchanged. Second, the term $\Sigma [\mu_i/\mu_s] \, d \ln p_i - \Sigma \mu_k \, d \ln p_k$ is essentially the change in the logarithm of an index of the price of non-educational labor relative to all goods. Finally, the parameter ϕ, sometimes called the inverse of the income flexibility, is common to both (2) and (3), so that if we assume that the four bracketed terms in these equations are known, there are only 3 independent parameters to estimate. The results of fitting equations (2) and (3) are reported in Table 5 of the text.

In the system of equations (1), (2), (3) neither the compensated or uncompensated wage elasticities of demand are constants; nor are the income elasticities of demand. Nevertheless, these elasticities are easy to derive. First, setting all $d \ln p_i = 0$ in (2) and substituting in (1) we have $\partial \ln X_i / \partial \ln y = \mu_i/w_i$ for the ith income elasticity. The estimated values of these income elasticities (computed at the mean sample values of the w_i) are contained in the last column of Table 6. Likewise, setting all $d \ln p$'s but $d \ln p_i$ equal to zero in (2), setting $d \ln y - \Sigma w_k \, d \ln p_k = 0$ in (2), and substituting the result into (1) gives:

$$(\partial \ln X_i / \partial \ln p_i)^c = [\phi\mu_i^2 [1 - \mu_s]/\mu_s + \pi_{ii}]/w_i;$$

for the income-compensated wage-rate elasticity of demand. Likewise:

$$\partial \ln X_i / \partial \ln p_i = (\partial \ln X_i / \partial \ln p_i)^c - \mu_i;$$

gives the uncompensated wage rate elasticity of demand.

Finally, in estimation it is necessary to replace the infinitesimal changes in (1), (2), and (3) by their corresponding discrete year-to-year changes, which makes the fitted equations only approximations to (1), (2), and (3).

78

COMMENTS

BURTON A. WEISBROD

This is a bold, ambitious research conception. Orley Ashenfelter and Ronald Ehrenberg (A and E) have posed a problem—to build a predictive model of the demand for labor in the state and local government sector. They have constructed such a model, and they have tested it. They are moderately encouraged by their findings, but they emphasize the need for "more analysis" before their "numerical estimates can be taken as anything more than preliminary guides . . . ."

My comments apply primarily not to their numerical estimates but to their model, that is, to the likelihood that this model or a small modification of it is likely to be fruitful in helping us to predict the demand for labor in the state and local government sector.

There is, to begin, an important definitional matter. What, exactly, are A and E interested in when they talk about "employment in the public sector"? If, for example, a government decides to go into direct production of a good that it has previously been purchasing, do we want to say that employment in the public sector has increased? Perhaps so; it all depends on precisely what one is interested in, but the issue is not academic. Not only do choices between governmental production and outside purchase change over time, but they also vary across governmental units and, hence, influence the demand estimates of an A and E-type model. I do not fault A and E for their failure to develop a theory of governmental choice between production and purchase, a theory that is absent in our public finance literature today, but I do want to identify such a theory as one that is logically essential to the development of a structural model of actual governmental employment. When I said at the onset of my remarks that A and E have an "ambitious" paper, I meant that there exists a number of currently unresolved theoretical problems that A and E have boldly attempted to bypass in moving directly to a model of employment. The choice between government production, and hence employment, and government purchase, and hence non-employment, is but one of these problems. By ignoring it, A and E have biased their estimates in an unknown way.

Whether it is or is not "important" to distinguish the cases of governmental production and purchase is a matter to which neither A and E nor other economists have directed attention, but the issue is a real one, as is the distinction between governmental production and purchase, on one hand, and governmental regulation and subsidization on the other. If a government is willing to subsidize a "private" aircraft producer such as Lockheed, for example, is it or is it not useful to define Lockheed employment as *non*-governmental?

Before leaving this point involving definition of the issue, I would like to cite two examples of services that, while often provided by state and local government employees, are also often provided by private producers under contract with these governments. One example is trash collection and disposal; another is hospital services. Publicly financed hospital services are not always provided through public hospitals where much of the expenditure would appear as public employment. In 1970, 1.5 percent of all state-government direct expenditures on hospitals were made to nongovernmental hospitals, but it was 4.5 percent in California, 13.3 percent in Connecticut and Alaska, and 16.4 percent in Delaware.[1] Cross-section estimates of demand for *workers* in the governmental hospital sector will as a result give a misleading picture of the determinants of public-sector demand for hospital *services*.

I have been led to consideration of the demand for public-sector provision of goods and services, whether that provision is via government production or through other means. Although the A and E paper has a title dealing with the demand for *labor* in the public sector, it is, I believe, directed toward the demand for *output* in the public sector, for A and E state that they assume that the demand for labor is derived from the demand for output.

[1] Calculated from U.S. Bureau of the Census, *State Government Finances in 1970*, Series GF70-No. 3, U.S.G.P.O., 1971, p. 32.

I thus turn to a consideration of demand for public output, a second area where A and E have been ambitious. Having defined the problem of determining labor demand in the state-local sector, they have found it necessary to model the forces determining the amount of state and local government *output* vis-à-vis output in the remainder of the economy. To do this requires understanding consumer preferences as between individual-type goods, which private markets presumably provide, and collective-type goods, which private markets are likely to underprovide, so that consumer-voters demand public-sector supplementation (either via government production or stimulation of private markets through tax-subsidy mechanisms). It also requires understanding the forces that determine whether the private-market failures will be seen as requiring action by state and local governments, or by the federal government. This choice, in turn, would seem to hinge partly on technological, production function issues (on whether there exist means for satisfying consumer preferences via national-type collective goods as well as via state-and-local-type collective goods), and partly on the degree of homogeneity of consumer preferences across states and localities. The greater the degree of homogeneity of consumers' preferences for public-sector supplementation, the greater the likelihood, I believe, that the *federal* government will respond. Thus, homogeneity of preferences needs to be known before we can predict which level of government is likely to respond to consumer demands. Since A and E focus on state and local government, they assume, at least implicitly, the homogeneity of consumer preferences and their stability over time, i.e., the demand for state and local government services is independent of the level of provision of federal services.

Further theoretical problems confront any researchers who try to predict state and local government employment. The neat conceptual distinction between private goods and collective goods is not so sharp in reality, and it is the demand for the latter that determines in the A and E model the demand for public-sector output. There exist goods in the public and private sectors that are substitutes for each other (though not, in general, perfect substitutes). The collective good, lighthouse, for example, has a private-good substitute, shipboard radar; the collective good, standby fire department, has a private-good substitute, sprinkler systems; and the collective good, police department, has private-good substitutes that include alarms, locks, guards, and dogs. (For further discussion see Weisbrod, 1975). To understand the demand for public-sector output we must either know or make some assumptions about the availability of these substitutes and consumers' marginal rates of substitution for them. Through time, when research can alter the constellation of goods, we need to understand more fully than we do the processes by which new goods are developed and the balance between demands for public-sector and private-sector outputs is changed (Weisbrod, 1975).

Even if all of these weak links in our chain of knowledge were substantially stronger, there would remain another serious problem for A and E: we would not know the demand for *labor* unless we had some reasonable knowledge about the production function for those goods and services.

A and E recognize this factor-substitution issue and, indeed, recognize a number of the problems I have noted above. In their empirical work they have at many points made it quite clear to the reader what simplifying assumption they made. I applaud their clarity and honesty, but I must question several of these assumptions. (1) It is difficult to accept that the number of units of labor input into any public service is a reasonable proxy for quantity of output, and it is difficult to accept the assumption that "The per-capita stock of factor inputs other than labor is fixed, so that changes in the per-capita quantity of labor input are the only *short-run* method for changing the quantity of public services." It is, of course, essentially true by definition of "short-run" that only labor inputs can be changed; the data used by A and E to estimate demand, however, cover a 12-year period, a period that surely saw a great deal of change in the capital inputs into state and local government output. If the capital stock were fixed, then output would not be proportional to labor inputs. If the stock were not fixed, then it would be necessary to take account of the varying capital-labor ratio over time.

(2) In their empirical treatment, A and E scarcely deal with the existence of a federal government, and they do not consider at all the likelihood, to which I referred above, that consumers make choices between the satisfaction of their collective-good and other nonprivate demands at the federal vs. lower levels of government.

(3) The notion, presented by A and E, that consumers make budgetary allocations in two steps, first among broad categories of expenditure, of which "public services" is one and food and shelter are others, is an interesting one. My own assumption would be different: that there is no separate budget for *publicly* provided services and certainly no separate budget for state and local government services; rather, that consumers have demands for satisfying wants that are largely independent of whether those wants are provided publicly or privately. But my guess is no better than A's and E's, and it would be useful and certainly simplifying for predictive purposes if we could describe consumer behavior in such a sequential manner. Thus it would be worthwhile to test the A and E hypothesis. As they have presented it, however, I believe it is not yet defined well enough to be testable; for when A and E say that, "In the first step . . . the consumer must consider his income and a price index for each of the broad categories of services . . . ," they do not tell us how that price index is derived. Depending on that derivation process, the two-stage budget allocation process may collapse into a one-stage process.

(4) Another assumption made in A's and E's empirical estimation of their reduced-form system is that, "public- and private-sector goods satisfy different (or independent) wants." As I have suggested above, however, this assumption must certainly be questioned when one recognizes the widespread existence of public and private sector goods that seem to be reasonably good substitutes.

Even if A and E are approximately correct in assuming that there are distinct public and private wants, however, a question must surely be raised about their treatment of "public services" as services that meet an essentially homogeneous want. It is not at all clear to me that public libraries, hospitals, and police departments, for example, constitute one similar consumer want,

83

while the private-sector counterparts for these services each constitute a *different* want.

In the literature of public finance one of the older traditional questions is: what forces determine the size of the public sector? I share A's and E's view that focusing on consumer demands and on income and price elasticities will help us to gain a better understanding of those forces. However, as I have noted, there are many difficult problems to be resolved before we can expect to construct very satisfying models to predict not only aggregate government employment, but employment by service function and level of government.

RICHARD B. FREEMAN

Demand for Labor in a Nonprofit
Market: University Faculty

The allocation of resources and setting of wages in markets where
employers are nonprofit institutions has received considerable
professional and public attention. In what ways do nonprofit
factor demands and wage policies differ from those of for-profit
enterprises? How do "nonprofit labor markets" compare to for-
profit markets? This paper investigates these issues, with special
reference to the college and university system. Section I is a theoretical analysis of nonprofit demand for labor (or other inputs)
in which administrators make the key budgetary and employment
decisions and sell at least some outputs in the market. The analysis is applicable to a wide variety of nonprofit market settings in
addition to that for university faculty.[1] Section II deals more
narrowly with the college and university system, particularly the
importance of quality, internal compensation and employment
rules, and the capital goods and demographic features of the
academic marketplace. Section III develops a small econometric
model of the demand for faculty and uses it to analyze faculty
income and employment from 1920 to 1970.

I. Factor Demands under the Zero-Profit Constraint

The most general and distinctive feature of nonprofit enterprises is that they operate under the *budget constraint* that

Note: This paper benefited greatly from the critical comments of M.
Nerlove, J. T. Dunlop, and M. Segal. Discussions with K. Arrow, P.
Doeringer, S. Rosen, E. Leamer, Z. Griliches, M. Feldstein, E. Toder, M.
Rothschild, among others, and H. G. Lewis' lectures on factor demand also
helped significantly.
[1]To the extent that hospitals behave as workers' management coopera-
tives with doctors making the important decisions, the analysis is not

85

profits be zero. Unlike profit-seeking firms, which remit profits to owners, nonprofit enterprises must spend potential excesses of receipts, including *endowment or subsidy income*, over expenditures in their operations. Presumably, they *maximize a utility function* set by complex bargaining among social groups.[2] The *formation of new nonprofit enterprises* will be motivated by the desire of subsidizers or purchasers to obtain nonprofit outputs at the lowest possible cost, rather than by profit-seeking behavior.

This section examines the way in which the zero-profit and related features of nonprofit enterprises differentiate their demand for labor from that of otherwise identical competitive firms. Comparisons are limited to nonprofit and for-profit enterprises with the same production functions, market prices, and operating efficiency, and to markets where all firms are of one form or the other. Differences between nonprofit and for-profit enterprises that result from the concentration of the former in particular kinds of market settings are ignored. The analysis thus highlights the distinct aspects of nonprofit behavior that result from the zero-profit constraint at the expense of neglecting those due to their particular utility goals and the reasons for the organizational form itself.

The principal results of the analysis, to be developed in detail, can be summarized briefly: nonprofit demand for labor tends to be more elastic with respect to wages and output in the short-run than for-profit demand because of the zero-profit constraint; wages and employment respond differently to exogenous developments in nonprofit than in profit markets; the nonprofit mix of goods also differs from that of comparable profit-seeking firms, in accord with nonprofit income elasticities of demand and "potential profits" (defined as the excess of nonprofit receipts over

---

directly relevant to nonprofit hospitals. See Ward (1958) for the basic workers' management model, and Pauly and Redisch (1973) for an application to the medical case.

[2] The difficulty is in forming a group utility function when interests diverge greatly. Absence of a general game-theoretical analysis of bargaining and of empirical measures of bargaining strength complicates the investigation of social utility functions of nonprofit enterprises.

expenditures at the profit-maximizing point); formation of new nonprofit enterprises by subsidizers or purchasers to obtain non-profit output efficiently leads to long-run entry conditions and factor demands identical to those in for-profit markets.

A. *The Single-Output Model*

Consider first a nonprofit enterprise combining two factors, faculty (F) and other resources (R), to produce a single good (G), and obtaining all income from market sales. It operates under the budget constraint:

$$(1) \qquad\qquad p_G G = wF + p_R R;$$

where p_G, w, and p_R are the relevant prices. The assumption of a single good makes output and utility maximization identical, sidestepping specification of the nonprofit utility function and consideration of the mix of goods. The assumption that all in-come is earned in the market facilitates comparison with for-profit enterprises. Both assumptions are relaxed in the ensuing analysis.

Adherence to (1) requires particular production and employ-ment decisions by nonprofit firms that differentiate their demand for labor from that of comparable profit seekers. In particular, the absence of profits implies that *in the short run*: 1. nonprofit output and employment exceeds that of for-profit enterprises; 2. nonprofit supply schedules are determined by average rather than marginal cost conditions; 3. factor demand schedules are more elastic with respect to wages and shifts in output; 4. nonprofit prices are more responsive to changes in costs and less responsive to changes in demand than profit-market prices; 5. shifts in the supply of workers and demand for output have greater effects on wages and employment in the nonprofit case.

Proposition 1 follows directly from the requirement that non-profit enterprises spend potential "normal" or extraordinary profits on producing G. As Figure 1 shows, with no required entrepreneurial return the nonprofit cost curve AC' lies below the profit cost curve, AC, so that at any price—say p_0—output is higher $Q_2 > Q_0$. Even when nonprofit enterprises require a "normal return," output exceeds for-profit output in the region

FIGURE 1. Production Under the Zero-Profit Constraint

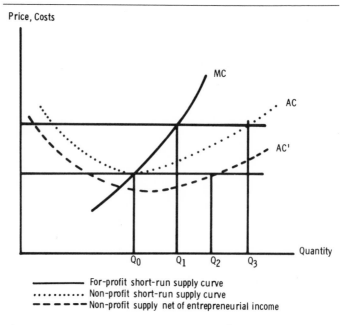

$p > p_0$, due to the absence of extra profits.[3] At p_1, for example, the for-profit firm produces Q_1, earning $Q_1 \cdot [p_1 - AC_1]$ excess profits. The nonprofit firm, by contrast, produces Q_3 and has zero profits.

Differences in the response of nonprofit and profit enterprises to short-run changes in prices, proposition 2, can also be demonstrated graphically. While for-profit firms produce so that $MC = p$, nonprofit firms, obeying the zero-profit constraint, operate

---

[3] It is unclear whether the normal entrepreneurial return is to be included as a cost of the for-profit firm, making its operation more expensive than that of the nonprofit enterprises. If entrepreneurial return is only a reward for risk-holding and risks average out in an industry, we would *not* want to include it. If, on the other hand, the entrepreneurial return is a reward for founding an enterprise requiring future monitoring, the "free" founding of nonprofit institutions by donors and *gratis* trusteeship reduce the cost of nonprofits. They face a lower price of entrepreneurship in the market as a result of their nonprofit status.

along the average cost curve in regions of potentially positive profits. Assuming loss minimization, they move along the marginal curve when profits are negative.

If initial output is at the minimum on the same or parallel cost schedules $(AC$ or $AC')$, the fact that the marginal curve increases more than the average to the right of the minimum point implies *greater* nonprofit responsiveness to price changes. More generally, with a U-shaped cost curve having returns to scale, θ, above 1 when $MC < AC$; 1 at minimum average cost; and below 1 when $MC > AC$, the elasticity of the marginal cost curve, ϵ_M, will exceed that of the average cost curve, ϵ_A, by the absolute value of the scale elasticity.[4] Since the supply elasticity is the inverse of the cost elasticity, output and employment responses to short-run changes in price will be greater in nonprofit than profit enterprises, as asserted in proposition 3.

In the short run with the number of firms fixed, nonprofit average-cost supply behavior will lead to distinctive market adjustments to exogenous demand or supply shifts. Assume for simplicity that factor ratios are not affected by levels of output.[5] Cost and price changes are thus set by changes in wages or output according to:

(2a) $$\dot{p} = \dot{C} = a\dot{w} + \epsilon\dot{G},$$

where dots above variables refer to logarithmic derivatives, and the previously undefined parameters are a, the share of the input F in cost; and ϵ, the elasticity of costs with respect to output $[\dot{C}/\dot{G}]$. This equals ϵ_A, the elasticity of the average cost schedule, in the nonprofit case, or ϵ_M, the elasticity of marginal costs, in the for-profit case. Let the change in demand be represented by a percentage shift, $\dot{D}$, in a demand schedule with elasticity η:

(2b) $$\dot{G} = \dot{D} - \eta\dot{p}.$$

Finally, demand for the input F depends on the level of output and substitution with other resources, given the elasticity of sub-

---

[4] Formally, $\epsilon_A = \epsilon_M + \epsilon_\theta$, so that with $\epsilon_\theta < 0$ because of the U-shape of the cost curve, $\epsilon_A < \epsilon_M$.

[5] The basic analysis is *not* affected by the lack of homotheticity.

RICHARD B. FREEMAN

stitution, σ:

(2c) $$\dot{F} = [1/\theta]\ \dot{G} - [1 - a]\ \sigma\dot{w}.$$

Solving the system (2a–2c) yields:

(3a) $$\dot{F} = \frac{1}{\theta\ [1 + \epsilon\eta]}\ \dot{D} - \left[\frac{a\eta}{\theta\ [1 + \epsilon\eta]} + [1 - a]\ \sigma\right]\dot{w};$$

(3b) $$\dot{G} = \frac{1}{1 + \epsilon\eta}\ \dot{D} - \frac{a\eta}{1 + \epsilon\eta}\ \dot{w};$$

(3c) $$\dot{p} = \frac{\epsilon}{1 + \epsilon\eta}\ \dot{D} + \frac{a}{1 + \epsilon\eta}\ \dot{w}.$$

The smaller elasticity of cost in nonprofit than for-profit markets ($\epsilon_A < \epsilon_M$) implies that the coefficients on $\dot{D}$ and $\dot{w}$ in (3a) and (3b) are larger in the former case and thus that factor demands are more responsive to wages and outputs (proposition 3). In (3c), moreover, the coefficient on $\dot{D}$ is smaller and that on $\dot{w}$ larger in the nonprofit market, implying greater sensitivity of short-run prices to costs and less sensitivity to demand shifts (proposition 4).[6]

We now make wages endogenous by adding a faculty supply relation shifting at a rate $\dot{S}$, with elasticity ϕ:

(4) $$\dot{F} = \dot{S} + \phi\dot{w}\ .$$

The equilibrium changes for the faculty input are:

(5) $$\dot{w} = [\eta_D\ \dot{D} - \dot{S}]/[\eta_E + \phi]\ ;$$

and

(5') $$\dot{F} = [\eta_D\ \phi\dot{D} + \eta_E\ \dot{S}]/[\eta_E + \phi]$$

where

$$\eta_D = \frac{1}{\theta}\ [1 + \epsilon\eta],$$

---

[6] To prove propositions (3) and (4) we examine the derivative of the coefficients with respect to ϵ in (3c). $\epsilon/[1 + \epsilon\eta]$ rises, implying greater for-profit responsiveness to $\dot{D}$, while $\alpha/[1 + \epsilon\eta]$ falls as ϵ rises, implying greater nonprofit responsiveness to $\dot{w}$.

90

and

$$\eta_E = a\eta\eta_D + [1-a]\sigma$$

are greater for nonprofit than profit enterprises. The consequences are that employment in nonprofit markets will be more responsive to shifts in short-run supply or demand than in profit markets, while wages will be relatively more responsive to demand shifts and less to supply shifts (proposition 5).[7] Moreover, both $\dot{S}$ and $\dot{D}$ produce greater changes in output and prices in the nonprofit case.

B. Multiple Outputs and Two-Stage Maximization

When more than one good is produced, nonprofit utility maximands and the interrelations among goods in utility and production functions must be analyzed explicitly. We develop a two-output model of the nonprofit enterprise that highlights the "profit-expenditure decision" resulting from the zero-profit constraint and then consider problems created by additional outputs. To focus on the distinctive behavior of the enterprises the usual utility-maximization process is decomposed into two stages: 1. an initial stage of "profit maximization," in which the nonprofits behave like competitive firms; and 2. a second stage of profit expenditure to maximize utility.

Our nonprofit firm has a utility function dependent on outputs G and Q, sold at p_Q and p_G, respectively, and produced jointly according to the production functions $Q(F,R)$ and $G(F,R)$.[8] Maximization of $V[G,Q]$ subject to the production and budget $[p_G G + p_Q Q = wF + p_R R]$ constraints yields the following condition with respect to marginal changes in F:

(6) $$w = p_G G_1 + p_Q Q_1 + \frac{V_1 G_1}{\lambda} + \frac{V_2 G_1}{\lambda},$$

where G_1, Q_1, V_1, V_2 are partial derivatives of the production

[7] The proof follows from examination of the derivatives of the coefficients with respect to η_D and η_E, as before.

[8] If the outputs are produced separately rather than jointly, we add subscripts to the inputs F and R and carry out the analysis as in the text. The implications are the same, but the algebra is slightly more complex.

and utility functions respectively, and λ is the marginal utility of "profits" derived from the budget constraint. Equation (6) can be compared to the equilibrium profit-maximizing condition:

$$(6') \qquad w = p_G G_1 + p_Q Q_1.$$

Equation (6') lacks terms relating inputs to utility; as a result of their positive sign, this leads to lower output and employment, as stated in proposition 1.

The difference between (6) and (6') can be examined further by decomposing nonprofit utility maximization into stage I, in which the enterprise maximizes profits like a competitive firm, and stage II, when profits are expended according to the utility function. Any utility maximization can be so decomposed, with stage I yielding an initial profit-maximizing vector $(\pi^*, G^*, Q^*, F^*, R^*)$, and stage II yielding additional outputs and inputs from maximizing:

$$V(G^* + \Delta G, Q^* + \Delta Q) = \overline{V}(\Delta G, \Delta Q),$$

subject to the profit constraint:

$$\pi^* = p_G \Delta G + p_Q \Delta Q - w\Delta F - p_R \Delta R;$$

and production relations:

$$G = G^* + G(F^* + \Delta F, R^* + \Delta R);$$

and

$$A = A^* + A(F^* + \Delta F, R^* + \Delta R),$$

where (*) refers to first-stage values and Δ to increments from these values.[9]

The decomposition pinpoints the distinctive behavior of nonprofit enterprises in their expenditure of potential profits in production and shows that, in one sense, they are as concerned as competitive firms in maximizing such funds. Since stage II behavior is contingent on positive potential profits $(\pi^* > 0)$, non-

[9]Note that the Δ's can be positive or negative, permitting decreases in "inferior" outputs; this is what makes the analysis valid.

profit firms can be expected to operate differently from for-profit firms only if receipts exceed expenditures at the profit-maximizing point. When $\pi^* \leq 0$, the two organizations should operate similarly. Empirically, this suggests very different behavior by colleges and universities in periods of market boom (the 1960's) and in periods of market decline, as predicted for the late 1970's–1980's (Cartter, 1971).

Stage II behavior is determined by the evaluation of outputs in the nonprofit utility function and the income and price elasticities that underlie profit expenditure patterns. If, as seems likely, the utility function of the nonprofit enterprise differs from that of the representative consumer, the mix and quantity of output in nonprofit markets will be different from that in profit markets.[10] In the extreme case where the nonprofit maximand depends solely on an output Q that has no market value, the institution produces the market good G to obtain profits for the purchase of Q. As a result, it operates at the profit-maximizing point for G, just as the competitive firm, but it employs additional resources from profits to obtain Q. Production will seem inefficient, with input/output ratios above cost-minimizing levels; in fact, production is efficient, but choice of output is in some sense not.

Finally, how do the strong elasticity and responsiveness predictions (propositions 1–5) of the single-good model stand up in the two-good case? Barring peculiarities due to inferiority of goods in the utility function, the predicted differences between nonprofit and for-profit firms generalize readily. Take, for example, the expected difference in elasticities of demand for labor. When goods are jointly produced, changes in output guarantee greater nonprofit responsiveness, just as in the single-good case. When goods are produced separately, with different labor intensities, the relative price of the labor-intensive good and total

[10]If the nonprofit utility function is determined by some latent or actual voting procedure, it will depend on median preferences. The representative consumer, on the other hand, is clearly the mean of the population. For a discussion of other possible differences between nonprofit and consumer preferences see Nerlove (1972).

employment will change in the same direction as wages due to substitution in the university utility function.[11] Only when the labor-intensive good is inferior, and changes in its labor usage dominate adjustments, will the nonprofit firm be less responsive.

With three or more outputs and additional inputs, however, further conditions are needed for propositions 1–5, as complementaries among goods in production or consumption and diverse factor intensities create additional response possibilities. (See Nerlove, 1972.) Consider, for example, the difficulties that arise when the university maximand contains, in addition to outputs G and Q, the level of inputs (pleasure of large staff or buildings (Veblen, 1934)) and prices or wages (concern with needy students and worker well-being).[12] With prices and inputs in the utility

---

[11] Even when the majority of workers produce the good whose output falls in response to a wage increase (rises due to a decrease), the substitution effect will be negative and augment changes in employment due to profit-maximizing behavior. To see this let $F_1 > F_2$ be the number of workers producing Q_1 and Q_2 so that:

(a)
$$\dot{F} = [F_1/F]\dot{Q}_1 + [F_2/F]\dot{Q}_2.$$

By definition of the elasticity of substitution (σ) between Q_1 and Q_2 in the demand for these goods:

(b)
$$\dot{Q}_1 - \dot{Q}_2 = -\sigma[\alpha_1 - \alpha_2]\,\dot{w},$$

where $\dot{w}$ is the wage change, and $\alpha_1 > \alpha_2$ are the cost shares of labor in producing Q_1 and Q_2, respectively. Thus the price increases most for good one, causing substitution against it. With total output fixed we have:

(c)
$$\gamma_1\dot{Q}_1 + [1 - \gamma_1]\dot{Q}_2 = 0,$$

where γ_1 is the share of good one in the budget. Substitution of (b) and (c) into (a) to eliminate $\dot{Q}_1$ and $\dot{Q}_2$ yields:

$$\dot{F} = \sigma[\alpha_1 - \alpha_2]\,[\gamma_1 - F_1/F]\,\dot{w}/\gamma_1.$$

With $\gamma_1 > \gamma_2$ $\dot{F}$ is negative if and only if $\gamma_1 < F_1/F$; but $\gamma_1 > \gamma_2$ implies $F_1/p_1Q_1 > F_2/p_2Q_2$, where p_1 and p_2 are the prices of the goods; therefore $F_1/F_2 > \gamma_1/[1 - \gamma_1]$, which implies that $\gamma_1 < F_1/F$, as claimed. Hence substitution due to nonprofit purchase of outputs necessarily augments the demand curve.

[12] Feldstein (1971) has stressed the role of "philanthropic wage payments" by hospitals concerned with worker well-being. The rapid rise in hospital wages due to such attitudes represents expenditure of profits on this particular output in the context of our analysis.

function, input/output distinctions disappear and prices become endogenous. Complex interactions arise among variables such as number of faculty and wages, with increases in one altering the cost of the other along lines to be considered in Section II.

C. Subsidies and Endowments

Nonprofit enterprises, especially colleges and universities, receive much of their income in the form of subsidies, gifts, and endowments. This type of income can be divided broadly into two categories: funds awarded for particular nonprofit outputs or activities (such as students, curricula, salaries and buildings), which constitute the bulk of governmental and private support, and those received irrespective of institutional performance, notably endowments and some related gifts. The way these two forms of income affect nonprofit markets is examined next.

Subsidies awarded for particular outputs or activities establish a subsidy market where subsidizers and nonprofit firms trade dollars for goods. The supply of subsidies to the market is an upward-sloping curve linking dollars to outputs in accord with subsidizer demands for nonprofit goods. In this market, shadow prices are attached to particular outputs and become components of the overall price of the good, influencing employment and production decisions.[13] If, as seems to be the case, subsidy markets are segmented, for example with state aid going to public institutions for certain goods (number of students) and private aid to private colleges for other goods, subsidy prices will differ by source and institution. This may explain some output and behavior differences among institutions. Differential financing arrangements will, in any case, provide important clues to institutional activities and decisions. In the extreme situation of restricted or *tied monies* (donations for buildings, professorial chairs in American studies, etc.) there is a one-to-one correspondence of funds to inputs or outputs. If, as seems to be true, donors prefer tangible capital goods to less tangible purchases of student or faculty quality, the price of such capital will be low and buildings, stadia,

[13] In many cases subsidy prices are explicit, for instance when a state pays institutions in a per-student basis.

etc., excessive in terms of optimal (unrestricted) budget decision making. Physical plant may, accordingly be "under-utilized."

What is important about subsidy markets is that they make nonprofit receipts dependent on market transactions, not, as might appear to be the case, on exogenous funding; they thereby enhance the importance of stage I behavior. The empirical problem in using subsidy prices to explain phenomena is the absence of explicit price data and possible confounding of differences in prices and utility functions.[14]

Subsidy or endowment income received regardless of activity has, barring complicated interactions among variables (see Section II), a "pure" income effect on institutional decisions which can be used to infer the goods in the nonprofit maximand. Endowment should be positively correlated with goods that enter the utility function, all else the same. In the single-output model endowment-type subsidies can be viewed as affecting the slope of the cost curve. E dollars of subsidy income lower "effective" average costs by E/Q and shifts the minimum point to the right. This implies that increases in endowment and related lump-sum subsidies will increase the size of nonprofit enterprises and the elasticity of their effective costs, $AC - E/Q$.

Institutional factor demands and the response of market prices to parametric changes in costs are also affected by endowment-type receipts. If all receipts were exogenous, total spending would be fixed and input demands would be of the "wage fund" type, with unit elasticity given constant cost shares. If some receipts were variable, on the other hand, demand would be of the usual form, but market equilibrium would require significant changes in the prices associated with the receipts. Assume, for example, that university income consists of variable student fees paid for the single output G and fixed lump-sum subsidies in the proportion a_G to $1 - a_G$. Then a change in wages of $\dot{w}$ will, by the balanced-budget condition (1), lead to an increase in tuition of $\dot{p}_G = [a_F/a_T]\ \dot{w}$.[15] In the absence of subsidies, prices would

---

[14]While confounding could be important in comparing institutions at a point in time, time-series data on governmental funds can be used to infer changes in "subsidy prices" over time.

[15]Since only p_T changes, balancing the budget requires $\alpha_F \dot{p}_T = \alpha_F \dot{w}$.

change by a_F (less than a_F/a_T since $a_T < 1$). Thus fixed endowment or subsidy incomes create greater changes in nonprofit than for-profit prices in response to long- and short-run changes in costs. Moreover, if $a_F > a_T$, a 1 percent change in wages will produce changes in prices greater than 1 percent; this could not occur in unsubsidized profit markets.

D. Nonprofit Entry and Entrepreneurship

Long-run output, factor demands, and efficiency depend on exit and entry conditions. We argue that when the organizations subsidizing nonprofit operations perform the entrepreneurial function of forming new enterprises, nonprofit entry conditions mirror those of profit industries. In both cases, whenever costs rise above minimum average cost, new institutions will enter, driving costs back to the minimum point. As a result, the only source of efficiency differences between the two organizational forms will be in the quality and behavior of entrepreneurs and managers.

The argument for similar nonprofit and profit entry conditions is direct. Assume for simplicity that institutions produce a single output, G, that enters the subsidizers' utility function, and that subsidy and market income are the sole source of receipts. Subsidizers will maximize the net benefit of their support:

$$(9) \qquad V(G) - S = V(G) - [AC - p]\, G,$$

where S is total subsidy payments. (Since S/G, subsidy per unit output, necessarily equals average cost less market price, we can multiply S by G/G to derive (9).) Maximizing $V - S$ requires minimum costs of production; if possible, subsidizers will form new institutions when costs exceed minimum average cost $(\overline{AC})$. When $AC > \overline{AC}$, they obtain $[1/\overline{AC} - 1/AC]$ more output per dollar by reducing subsidies to existing institutions and using the funds to form new ones. Rational subsidy behavior guarantees an infinitely elastic supply of institutions at $AC = \overline{AC}$; $\overline{AC}$ is the long-run production point, just as in the competitive "free-entry" case.

The implications of such long-run market behavior for factor demand are clear: Substitution effects will depend on the elasticity of substitution at $\overline{AC}$, while "scale effects" will be a function of number, N, of firms rather than of the elasticity of cost schedules. Formally, the long-run demand is:

(10a) $\qquad \dot{F} = \dot{N} + \dot{G}_0 - [1 - a] \sigma \dot{w} = \dot{N} - [1 - a] \sigma \dot{w} ,$

where

$\qquad G_0 \qquad$ = fixed minimum cost output $(\dot{G}_0 = 0)$;
$\qquad [1 - a] \sigma \dot{w}$ = change in labor demanded per firm;
$\qquad$ and $\dot{N} \qquad$ = change in number of firms.

The change in price is set by:

(10b) $\qquad \dot{p} = \dot{C} = a\dot{w} + \epsilon \dot{G}_0 = a\dot{w}.$

Market clearing is set by:

(10c) $\qquad \dot{G} = \dot{N} + \dot{G}_0 = \dot{N} = \dot{D} - \eta\dot{p},$

with a total output of NG_0.

Solving (10a)–(10c) for factor demand and number of firms yields:

(11a) $\qquad \dot{L} = \dot{D} - [a\eta + [1 - \alpha] \sigma] \dot{w} ;$

(11b) $\qquad \dot{N} = \dot{D} - a\eta\dot{w}.$

Since the basic condition for long-run "constant-returns" factor demand is that firms' output be fixed at G_0, the analysis is readily generalized to the situation in which the supply of enterprises is infinitely elastic at some $AC > \overline{AC}$. It is thus applicable to inefficient as well as efficient markets; the only requirement is that there exist some price or cost which triggers entry. If, on the other hand, the supply of entrants is less than infinitely elastic, demand will be a weighted average of short- and long-run demands, with the weights functions of the elasticity of entrants in response to changes in cost.

While the model focuses on average cost as the motivating force, the particular way in which $AC > \overline{AC}$ influences behavior will depend on the institutional structure of the market. If, for example, tuition (p_t) is fixed, as in some state universities, shifts in the demand for education will not alter AC, but will change the number of applicants rejected by universities. The resultant "shortage" of places will then motivate entry in the same manner as excessive cost in the preceding discussion. Geographic transportation and residence costs, coalescing in demands for local colleges, offer another specific impetus for new colleges and universities. Detailed analysis of the actual formation of nonprofit institutions, which is beyond the scope of this study, would seem to have a significant research payoff.

E. Managerial Quality

The absence of normal entrepreneurial or abnormal profits can be expected to affect the quality and behavior of nonprofit managers. If we assume that the supply of "able" managers depends on their rewards, and that nonprofit institutions do not substitute salary or prestige for ownership income by enough to counterbalance the absence of the latter, nonprofits will be unable to attract high quality management talent.[16] Exceptionally able businessmen, adept at cost-minimization/profit-maximization, will concentrate in for-profit enterprises. In addition, equally able administrators will tend to operate less efficiently in nonprofit settings due to the absence of a link between efficiency and remuneration. Differences in entrepreneurial/managerial ability and incentives would, according to these arguments, be the prime cause of oft-alleged nonprofit "inefficiencies."

F. Summary and Provisos

The preceding analysis suggests that, as a result of the zero-profit constraint and nonprofit expenditures of potential profits on output, nonprofit factor demands, mix of goods, and market responses to exogenous development differ from those of for-profit enterprises in the short-run. The enterprises will, given the postulated entry conditions, behave similarly in the long run. A wide variety of testable implications was derived regarding nonprofit behavior, responses to subsidies, and so forth. The major shortcoming of the analysis is the assumption that nonprofit and

---

[16]The desire for equitable salaries (see n. 20, below) presumably places bounds on nonprofit rewards to managers.

for-profit enterprises are identical in all respects save the required absence of profits. As remarked at the outset, differences in behavior due to the particular factors leading to nonprofit predominance in certain kinds of markets could be more important than those examined here. In addition, detailed specification of utility functions and specific institutional goals, of the type examined in the following section, are needed for the analysis to be applied fruitfully to actual market phenomena.

II. Labor in the Higher Educational System

Education and research, the major products of colleges and universities, have several distinctive features that affect academic labor markets. The importance of quality in intellectual matters makes faculty quality a key market variable. Nonappropriability of knowledge, and educational and research interdependencies complicate interdisciplinary comparisons of outputs and create pressures for interfield wage parity. Specialization and collegiality lead to peer-group evaluation of potential faculty and the tenure system. Production of faculty by faculty, due to research and education complementarities (Nerlove, 1972), creates significant capital goods/acceleration interaction. Last, investments in education, which are more profitable to those with many years to reap benefits and low opportunity costs, tie the educational system critically to the population of young persons. The purpose of this section is to examine the effect of the above characteristics of higher education on the market for faculty and, to a lesser extent, to determine the underlying reasons for their especially great significance in academia.

A. Quality of Inputs and Outputs

Concern with the quality of educational inputs and outputs by institutions, students, faculty, and subsidizers can be analyzed with a factor-of-production variant of the Theil (1954)–Houthakker (1954) quality-of-goods model. This model, recently extended by Becker and Lewis (1973), focuses on the interaction between the quantity and average quality of goods that make the cost of quality (quantity) a function of quantity (quality). The interaction can yield "anomalous" market adjustments—reductions in employment in response to wage declines, increases in some university outputs when "profits" fall, etc. In addition, faculty concern with peer quality may drive a wedge between the marginal cost of employment and the wage rate.

To see how the quality-quantity interaction affects the labor market, consider a university that hires numbers of faculty (F) of average quality (Q_F) to produce graduates (G) and quality of education per graduate (Q). The market wage of a unit of "quality-quantity," w, is fixed, so that two workers of unit quality can be hired for the same cost as one employee with twice as much quality. The maximization problem is:

$$\text{(12)} \qquad \text{Max } V(G,Q),$$

$$\text{s.t. } G = G(F^1, Q_F^1, R^1);$$

$$Q = Q(F^2, Q_F^2, R^2);$$

and

$$Q p_Q + pG + E = wFQ_F + w_R R,$$

where

$$F = F^1 + F^2, Q_F = Q_F^1 + Q_F^2, \text{ and } R = R^1 + R^2.$$

The distinctive feature of (12) is the hyperbolic cost function (wFQ_F), which relates the cost of quality or quantity to the level of the other as well as to the market wage. Differentiating wFQ_F with respect to Q_F yields wF as the marginal cost of quality; it is an increasing function of F. (Analogous results hold for the marginal cost of F.) The relative cost of quality to quantity is F/Q_F, depending solely on the relative amounts purchased. One implication is that changes in Q_F or F due to changed purchases of outputs will alter the relative cost with "secondary price effects," possibly causing anomalous employment adjustments.[17] A scenario for anomalous demand behavior is: lower wages imply increased "profits" of universities imply a relative increase in the purchase of quality-intensive output, Q. This leads to additional

[17]Becker and Lewis (1973) consider this effect in great detail.

employment of Q_F relative to F, implying an increase via the quality-quantity interaction in the relative cost of quantity, leading finally to a reduction in faculty employment. Such a response pattern requires that the quality-intensive good be income-elastic, quality-quantity substitutions dominate employment adjustment, and quality and quantity costs depend solely on the joint term wFQ_F.[18] The quality of education or research is probably income-elastic and quality-intensive, and numbers and quality of faculty are reasonable substitutes; as independent adjustments in the cost of quantity relative to quality are presumably limited, perverse wage-employment patterns are not implausible, particularly in the short run. Within limits, declines in faculty wages relative to the price of output are likely to induce increases in the quality rather than in the number of appointments, and conversely.

Analysis of university employment and wage behavior in Feldstein's (1971) "philanthropic wage" situation, where wages or prices enter utility functions because of concern for worker well-being, follows similar lines of reasoning. The cost function is hyperbolic with the price of philanthropic wages dependent on the number of employees and the cost of employment a function of these wages.

Rationing of places in high-quality schools can be explained partly by concern with input qualities that drives a wedge between wages and marginal costs of employment. When, for example, faculty prefer working in institutions with high-quality persons, supply prices will vary in the market depending on the existing quality of faculty. Given the hyperbolic cost function of (12), and $w = w(Q_F)$, the marginal costs of Q_F and F will be:

(13a) $$\partial c/\partial Q_F = Fw + Q_F Fw' > 0;$$

(13b) $$\partial c/\partial F = wQ_F.$$

In (13), appointments lowering (raising) quality cost more (less) than the wage due to the induced change in supply price, which

[18]Precise conditions for this can be easily derived from the algebra, but in the absence of estimates of the relevant elasticities we do not pursue it here.

will lead to job rationing in institutions with high average quality, *ceteris paribus*. If, in addition, the supply price of the highly qualified is very high to lower-quality schools, offsetting the induced wage reduction, the more able will be concentrated in a small number of universities whose initial income permits quality accumulation.[19] When student concern for quality makes them willing to pay higher tuition to associate with the more able, a similar pattern in the student market is also likely. Place rationing and concentration of the more qualified in a limited number of institutions will be observed. The uncertainty of quality evaluations among persons and different perceptions of quality are also presumably important in accounting for rationing of places.

B. Internal Labor Market Policies

There are two distinctive features to the internal labor market policies of colleges and universities: desire for an "equitable" wage structure that rewards faculty roughly equally across specialties, and tenure, which effectively guarantees lifetime employment. That most colleges and universities would like to pay faculty of similar rank, experience, and academic ability but different specialization the same basic salary is evident from expressed salary goals. A 1973 Dartmouth College compensation committee, for example, stated, "Since institutions constitute essential communities of scholars, there is a general feeling of what may be termed academic equity—that differences of compensation among faculty members of equal experience and standing within their own special fields should be as small as is consistent with maintenance of high quality faculty in each department." National Education Association (1972) surveys show that nearly all institutions have explicit faculty salary

---

[19] Since there are relatively many lower quality faculty at poorer schools, it might appear that their change in wages would more than counterbalance the increased supply price of qualified faculty leading to dispersion of the more able. The number benefitting from high-quality colleagues may, however, be quite limited, and the benefits may be greater for others of similar talent, thus producing the concentration observed in academia.

schedules providing for minimum-maximum or average pay based on merit, rank, and experience *applying equally across fields*.

In essence, universities affirm an intellectual value structure that presupposes little or no inherent superiority to knowledge in various fields. According to this nonprofit "price scheme," faculty are judged by their intellectual quality and scholarly output, with differences in the market price of output (which are substantial between, say, economics and Hittite archeology) ignored as much as possible in determining wages. Underlying the rejection of market prices is the belief that valuation of knowledge involves considerable uncertainty, nonappropriability, externalities, and time horizons that may be inadequately handled by for-profit market prices.

Another factor leading to the equitable wage goal is the tendency for university administrators and members of faculty committees to come from various departments. The Dartmouth compensation committee, for example, included professors of economics, French, mathematics, and sociology among other fields. Explicit or implicit bargaining on such committees or in administrative decision making, with unclear standards of judgment, diverse evaluations and similar "bargaining power," is likely to produce symmetric treatment of fields, as some game theory models would predict (Rapaport, 1970). When faculties are divided by schools, on the other hand, as among law, business, medicine, and arts and sciences, pressure for wage equity across disciplines will be attenuated.

Whatever the cause, the desire for interfield equity in salaries exacts a cost on the university system when nonacademic opportunity wages differ. This cost must be traded off against other goals and expenditures in the decision process. The use of resources to purchase equity in salaries will produce: 1) a narrower interfield dispersion of salaries in academia than in industry; 2) shortages (surpluses) in specialities where opportunity wages are high (low); and 3) reliance on *compensatory nonmonetary remuneration schemes* to alleviate market problems by widening the *real* incentive structure despite the constraint on salaries. Such compensation policies would include differential work conditions (office space, secretarial aid), speeds of promotion, liberal outside time rules, provision of special professorial chairs, laboratories, etc., though equity pressures may also limit these options. As such rewards are possible in the absence of the "constraint" on salaries and substitute imperfectly for flexible salaries, they will only partly alleviate the manpower problems due to the equity goal. *Hiring standards* are, as a consequence, likely to be an extremely important adjustment tool, with lower quality faculty employed in "shortage" fields and higher quality faculty in "surplus" areas, where job rationing will prevail.

Comparisons of the interfield structure of academic and non-academic salaries in 13 scientific fields reporting to the National Science Foundation (1972) suggest an important role for the equity goal in the market. Academic salaries turn out to be much more narrowly dispersed across fields than are industrial or government salaries, ranging from $12,900 to $15,000 for Ph.D.'s in college and universities, a $2,100 difference, compared to an industrial range of $7,500. Similarly, among master's graduates, the interfield range is $1,200 in academia compared to $5,400 in industry. Overall, interfield coefficients of variation are far lower in academic than in industry or government pay structures, with young academics, assistant professors with 2-4 years experience, having the narrowest interfield structure.[20] A similar pattern is found in comparisons of percentage changes in salaries. From 1964 to 1970 the coefficient of variation in the change of academic salaries varied from .081 for professors to .115 for

[20] The evidence is summarized below:

Interfield Dispersion in Academic and Nonacademic Salary Structures

Levels, 1970	Coefficients of Variation		
	Academic	Industry	Government
Ph.D.	.054	.096	.091
Master's	.043	.114	.089
2-4 years experience	.060	.125	.091
20-24 years experience	.081	.123	.154
Assistant Professor	.041	. . .	. . .
Associate Professor	.050	. . .	. . .
Full Professor	.065	. . .	. . .

Source: National Science Foundation (1970).

assistant professors, while comparable industrial variations were on the order of .183. Recruitment also appears to be influenced by the interfield salary structure, as predicted by the analysis, with vacancy rates in universities, defined as the ratio of unfilled budgeted positions to newly filled and unfilled slots, substantially positively correlated $(r = 0.88)$ with the ratio of nonacademic to academic salaries in 1964 (Freeman, 1971). Vacancies, like high wages, are likely to attract additional specialists due to the increased probability of obtaining desirable jobs and are thus to some extent self-correcting.

Finally, a rigid "equitable salary" policy will alter elasticities of response to supply-demand imbalances in particular fields. Under a flexible wage regime, when a 1 percent change in wages clears the market in a specialty accounting for a percent of the faculty budget, average wages change by a percent. In a world of rigid wages among fields, the same adjustment requires that all salaries change by 1 percent, an adjustment $1/a$ times as great. Formally the constraint reduces the elasticity of demand or supply in a field from, say, η_d and η_s to $a\eta_d$ and $a\eta_s$ necessitating a greater response to attain equilibrium.

Tenure, which guarantees lifetime employment to the faculty except for reasons of institutional financial crisis or individual incompetence, is a much-criticized feature of the academic market. In some respects, though, it is quite similar to industrial seniority systems that also protect older workers from the vagaries of the market. Both tenure and seniority result, in part, from workers' desires for job security and their willingness to forego income for seniority, and both place the burden of market adjustments on the young.

What distinguishes tenured faculty from other senior employees is the *power to hire additional faculty* who do essentially the same work and could replace them on the job. It is this power that makes university departments similar to Yugoslav-type collectives, with average quality of departments rather than profits as the maximand and the quality of appointments, generally not the number, as the policy variable. In the absence of tenure, the operational problems involved in faculty hiring and firing would be immense, with each professor judging possible new colleagues as competitors who could replace him at the work place and electors deciding his future. The danger of collusive agreements, bargaining, and coalition formation seriously hampering education and research is substantial. Tenure effectively reduces such "nonproductive" behavior, making "partnership" viable in a market where profit-and-loss sanctions are relatively inoperative, at least in the short run.

The historical development of tenure in the United States lends some support to the postulated tenure-appointment power link, for the growing participation of faculty in the recruitment and selection of its own members and the shrinking of presidential competence in appointments occurred roughly simultaneously with the beginning of the tenure system. It "was one of the instruments whereby university and college professors gained a nearly exclusive power to determine who was entitled to membership in their ranks."[21]   A more formal test of the tenure-appointment power link would involve examination of employment in institutions lacking tenure. Deans or presidents would probably make hiring decisions in such educational enterprises.

Tenure, like other seniority arrangements, makes the age structure of employees and rates of expansion key parameters in market adjustments. When the higher educational system is expanding, the probability of tenure will increase above its steady-state level. To attract additional personnel many lower-quality faculty will be promoted and the income of those of tenure age increased relative to that of older faculty. While the *number* of tenure appointments increases, the proportion may remain constant or even fall due to rapid expansion. Despite the fixed employment of tenured people, there are no difficulties in adjusting the mix of faculty to educational or research demands, as expansion in fields in great demand is an adequate tool (Freeman, 1971). The 1960's were, in general, a period of this type because of the extraordinary demand for academic research and educational outputs.

At the opposite end of the spectrum is a period of market con-

---

[21] The developments are described in Metzger (1973, pp. 142–143).

traction in which tenure becomes a serious barrier to the adjustment process. In contracting markets, universities cannot readily retain young workers of high quality due to tenure commitments and have difficulty in altering the distribution of professors across disciplines to meet changing market demands. Some tools exist for removing less desirable tenured faculty, such as closing departments, reducing office space and related prerequisites, failing to award normal salary increases or cutting salaries, and ultimately "buying out" a position, but such activities are difficult in the university setting. For one thing, the academic job ladder is short, making it difficult to differentiate among permanent employes through promotion or assignment of tasks; the rank of professor is the top of the ladder in particular institutions. For another, the collegial pressures needed to push men out of jobs are presumably unpleasant, especially in declining markets, and require decisions of the type that tenure is designed to eliminate, those relating to the status of senior personnel.

Patterns of institutional mobility are also likely to be altered in a contracting market. In steady-state or expanding markets, it is frequent for high-quality junior faculty to "invest" several years in top institutions where they continue their education, and then move to other colleges and universities. Contraction creates great pressures against such institutional mobility patterns, largely on the part of junior faculty outside the top schools whose promotion is threatened by importing outsiders. The risk that immediate post-degree investments in training will not bear fruit causes more high-quality younger specialists to move outside major universities early rather than late in their careers.

When an expanding market suddenly contracts, adjustment problems are exacerbated, with younger tenured faculty and relatively small replacement demands for new appointments. Movement to a steady-state equilibrium will be extremely difficult and the entire ethos of the system unpleasant, producing, as Moynihan (1973) puts it, "A (Balzacian) society, where, if you want to be a professor, you wait until the man who is professor dies. Then the 15 of you who want the job compete in various ways. One of you gets it."

Finally, tenure probably reduces the efficiency of academics by removing the possibility of being fired for nonperformance. Those nearing retirement may be particularly affected, since "compensatory firing policies," failure to grant normal salary increases, or even salary cuts are likely to have a small effect due to the short future work life. The danger of loss of pension rights, which exists in industry, is eliminated by the vesting of academic retirement plans.

C. Capital Goods and Demographic Factors

The dependence of the demand for new faculty on changes in enrollments and the production of new faculty from graduate enrollments suggests application of capital-goods accelerator models to the faculty market.[22] These models highlight the dynamic adjustment problems of an industry producing and employing a long-lived capital resource and its potential for cyclic fluctuations. Consider a simple accelerator-type model, in which demand for faculty depends on numbers of undergraduate (U) and graduate (G) enrollments, on academic salaries (S). Supply of faculty is determined by Ph.D. graduates and last period's supply net of the outflow of workers due to retirement and mobility at depreciation rate δ. For simplicity, only graduate students and Ph.D.'s intending to teach are distinguished in the model; the decision to enroll in graduate studies is dependent on academic salaries and, once made, is assumed fixed. This eliminates several degrees of flexibility from the market in order to focus on the behavior of interest.

The model can be represented as follows:

$$(14) \quad F^D = aG + bU - cS \quad \text{(faculty demand)};$$

$$(15) \quad F^S = PhD + [1 - \delta] F_{-1} \quad \text{(faculty supply)};$$

$$(16) \quad PhD = G_{-1} = A + BS_{-1} \quad \text{(new faculty supply)},$$

where a, b are incremental faculty-student ratios for graduate and other students, and c and B are the coefficients of response to

[22] See Porter (1965), Stone (1965), and Tinbergen and Bos (1965), for fixed-coefficient models.

salaries by institutions and young persons. Alternative salaries are ignored in this formulation.

Given market clearing, equations (14)–(16) yield a second-order difference equation, which under plausible assumptions about parameters has complex roots producing damped cyclic fluctuations. The cycle will be longer than the classic cobweb cycle in the labor market because demand as well as supply is influenced by the enrollment decisions of students.[23] On the demand side, a typical scenario for the cycle would be high academic salaries lead to increased graduate enrollments, greater demand for faculty, and even higher salaries; this response pattern tends to explosive movements. On the supply side, high academic salaries lead to increased graduate enrollments, increased supply of new Ph.D.'s, increased supply of faculty, then decreases in academic salaries; this is the usual cobweb adjustment process. The demand-side cycle is attenuated when graduate students are used as teachers, for the demand-increasing effect of graduate enrollments is reduced and possibly reversed. Investigation of this aspect of the market requires analyses of the substitutability between faculty and graduate teaching assistants and consideration of their relative salaries or costs.[24]

The significance of the endogenous cyclic mechanism in the faculty market will differ across fields depending on the relative importance of faculty used to produce faculty. When undergraduate enrollment or graduate enrollments independent of the faculty market account for the bulk of academic demand, as in engineering, for example, fluctuations in the faculty market will be proportionally small. When, on the other hand, graduate students loom large in enrollments and tend primarily to become teachers, as in the more arcane subjects, fluctuations could be substantial until equilibrium is attained.

Nonacademic market developments, such as changes in research

[23] Plausible values for a, b, c and δ are .1; for B, .07. These coefficients are small due to the units of measurement; elasticities are on the order of one to two.

[24] Strotz has a model focusing on this aspect of the market (personal communication). Freeman (1971, Chapter 9) examines the effect of graduate students on faculty in engineering and the university as a whole.

and development spending that shift demand for faculty and initiate cyclic ups and downs in academia make the amplitude of faculty-market cycles especially great. In this case, enrollments by students intending to work in industry and government as well as academia vary the cobweb manner. The two-sector general equilibrium model of Harberger (1957) and Johnson (1972) provides an appropriate framework for analyzing such market interactions.

Finally, as George Johnson stresses in his discussion, the assumption of instantaneous market clearing used to solve (14)–(16) can be replaced by a salary-adjustment equation:

$$(17) \qquad \Delta S = \lambda [S^* - S_{-1}],$$

where S^* is the equilibrium salary and λ a partial adjustment coefficient. With salaries no longer clearing markets the model yields vacancies or job rationing, defined as differences between demand and supply at disequilibrium wages.

Since colleges and university enrollments consist largely of young persons, demand for higher education is potentially critically dependent on the age structure of the population. While in years past the proportion of a young cohort in college was sufficiently small to provide an important buffer to demographic fluctuations, recent increases in enrollment propensities substantially limit the possible effect of such adjustments to future demographic declines. As a result, instability in higher education due to changes in the age structure of the population is likely to be more important in the future than in the past and deserves serious attention in public policy.

III. Faculty Market Developments

The higher education system has undergone considerable change in the postwar and earlier periods and will, according to current forecasts (Cartter, 1971), experience an extraordinary demographic shock in the 1980's. This section examines past and likely future responses of the academic labor market to exogenous changes in market conditions using a small econometric model of employment and salary determination. While the

111

theoretical and institutional discussion of Sections I and II
provides a framework for interpreting developments and findings,
detailed empirical investigation of nonprofit demand and institutional features of academia lie beyond the scope of the paper.

A. Patterns of Change

The major demographic and economic forces that affect the
market for higher education and faculty employment and salaries
are examined in this section. The numbers reveal an extraordinary
expansion of the college and university system in the 1960's and,
to a lesser extent, the 1950's as well, an expansion that created
what may be termed a golden age for academics. Associated with
rapid growth were several noteworthy developments.

First is the extraordinary change in the number of college-age
(18–24 year old) persons, an increase of 8 million in the 1960–
1970 decade, and in the number of high school graduates (U.S.
Office of Education, 1971). The high school class of 1970 was 1
million persons larger than that of 1960; this is twice as great an
absolute but a similar percentage increase as in the preceding
decade. Though important, demographic developments do not
explain the bulk of increased college enrollments. During the
1950's, enrollment expanded by 57 percent despite a roughly
unchanged number of 18–24 year olds; during the 1960's only
40 percent of increased enrollments can be attributed to the
growth of the 18–24 year old population.[25] In both periods, the
increased propensity to graduate from high school and to choose
college was the dominant factor in expanding enrollments.

The income of higher education institutions also grew sizably in
the 1960's, tripling from 1960–1961 to 1968–1969, spearheaded
by state and local aid and tuition. (O'Neill, 1971, and Office of
Education, 1971). The federal contribution to current income
went up more moderately, though total federal aid, including
diverse direct student support, facilities, and equipment purchases, did rise rapidly for nonresearch purposes. The price of

[25] Estimates of the relative impact of decision and demographic factors
on increasing college enrollments are given in Amacher and Freeman
(1973).

112

education to students, in the form of gross tuition per full-time equivalent enrollment (unadjusted for student aid), spurted upward in the 1960's. The rate of increase in net tuition declined relative to that of the 1950's as the diminished rate of GI Bill financial support produced an exceptionally large rise in net tuition. Public tuition and fees increased more slowly than private charges, raising the ratio of private to public tuition from 4.0 in 1960 to 4.7 in 1970.

On the supply side, the major development was the enormous inflow of new Ph.D. and Master's degree graduates in the 1960's, which substantially augmented the population of potential faculty (NORC, 1965, and U.S. Office of Education, 1971). Between 1960 and 1970, the number of Ph.D. degree recipients tripled; the ratio of new Ph.D.'s to enrolled students rose 36 percent; and the total stock of Ph.D.'s increased by 80 percent. Concurrently, over 500 new educational institutions were formed, primarily by public bodies at the junior and community college level, and faculty employment increased by 227 percent.[26] Faculty salaries also responded to the booming market, advancing more rapidly than other wages and salaries from 1960 to 1970, after a decade of about average rates of change. The AAUP data show a jump in the ratio of professional salaries to annual compensation per full-time worker from 2.10 to 2.29; the NEA figures reveal an advance from 1.92 to 2.22 (U.S. Office of Education, 1971; U.S. Bureau of the Census, 1972; AAUP, 1950–1972; and NEA, 1958–1972).

Toward the end of the 1960's, however, many of the forces causing the higher educational boom began to level off or decline, with a consequent turnabout in the academic job market. The rate of growth of enrollments stabilized: between 1970 and 1972, enrollments increased by just 3.8 percent; first-year graduate students by 3.5 percent; and the proportion of white male high school graduates enrolled in college fell from 46 to 39 percent.

---

[26]Census data show smaller increases in faculty salaries. This is partly due to the changing composition of employment, with more faculty working in junior and community colleges and possibly inclusion of teaching assistants.

TABLE 1. Academic and Other Salaries, 1960-1973 (in 1958 dollars)[a]

	Levels				Changes		
	1960-61	1967-68	1969-70	1972-73	1961-67	1967-69	1969-72
Professors[b]							
1. Total Compensation	10757	13867	14242	14146	28.9	2.7	-0.7
2. Salaries	10033	12658	12841	12564	26.2	1.4	-2.2
universities	11554	13425	13750	13630	16.2	0.2	-0.9
public	—	13301	13414	13195	—	0.8	-1.6
private	—	15042	15007	14961	—	0.3	-0.3
junior colleges	8862	11433	11676	12195	29.0	2.1	4.4
3. Economics Departments	11591	15883	16075	15973	37.0	1.2	-0.6
4. Salaries (NEA)	8833	12139	12416	11575	37.4	2.3	-6.8
Assistant Professors							
1. Total Compensation	6858	8557	8982	8836	28.8	5.0	-0.6
2. Salaries	6475	7852	8140	7817	21.2	3.7	-4.0
universities	6961	8201	8249	8213[c]	17.8	0.6	-0.4
public	—	8199	8267	8169[c]	—	0.8	-1.2
private	—	8297	8258	8439[c]	—	-0.5	2.2
junior colleges	6944	7770	8228	8813[c]	11.9	5.9	7.1

3. Economics departments	6094	8787	9113	8658	44.2	3.7	-5.0
4. Salaries (NEA)	6044	7815	7906	7663	29.3	1.1	-3.1
Other Workers							
1. Annual Compensation Industry	4600	5140	5246	5473	11.7	2.1	4.3
2. Professional (Male) Incomes	6152	7328	7581	—	19.1	3.5	—
3. Mfg. Average Hourly	2.19	2.34	2.36	2.42	6.9	0.1	3.4

Source: American Association of University Professors (1960–1973); National Education Association, *Salaries in Higher Education*, various editions; U.S. Department of Commerce, *Survey of Current Business*, various July editions; U.S. Department of Labor (1972); U.S. Bureau of Census, *Current Population Reports*, various editions; University of Minnesota (1957–1972).

[a] Deflators were: 1960 = 103.1, 1967 = 121.2, 1969 = 135.3, 1972 = 157.2.

[b] All data from AAUP, except economics department and salaries (NEA).

[c] Estimated by using percent change in "class" or university data reported in 1971–1973.

115

Total graduate enrollments also dropped in areas such as physics (Freeman, 1973) and other physical sciences despite the increased number of bachelor's graduates from which to draw students. Federal support dried up for graduate training and research, and research and related Ph.D.-intensive activities declined in importance. While demand fell, the large classes of Ph.D. students drawn into the market in the 1960's graduated and sought work. Although some of the causes of the market turnaround (decline in federal aid, research spending, increased number of Ph.D.'s) may be treated as once-and-for-all changes in exogenous or predetermined factors, the forecasted decline in the youth population in the late. 1970's and 1980's promises even more dramatic contractions (Cartter, 1971). In the 1970's the number of 18–21 year olds is expected to increase by much smaller percentage (19 vs. 56 percent) and absolute numbers (2.6 million vs. 5 million) than in the 1960's. In the 1980's, this group is expected to decline by 2.5 million. Whatever assumptions are made about the proportion of cohorts choosing college, enrollments will almost certainly fall in the 1980's, with dire consequences for the faculty market.

The response of higher education to the turnaround provides important clues to the functioning of the faculty labor market and to potential adjustments to the forecasted crisis. What has been the effect of the turnaround on faculty salaries, employment, and conditions of work, and the supply of graduate students and future Ph.D.'s?

Table 1 presents evidence on the response of salaries; it shows that after substantial gains in the early and mid-sixties the rate of change in (deflated) academic salaries lessened from 1967 to 1969 and was negative from 1969 to 1973. Regardless of the source or type of data, a general pattern of falling real and, more strikingly, relative compensation emerges. In contrast to the rise in relative academic salaries from 1961 to 1967 the ratio of academic to industrial compensation stabilized at 2.70 between 1967 and 1969 and then dropped to 2.58 in 1969–1972. The responsiveness of real and relative faculty salaries to the market decline may have been facilitated by the inflation of the early

1970's. This permitted substantial monetary increases to accompany falling real and relative earnings.[27]

The turnaround in the market brought with it considerable change in the pattern of employment as well as in pecuniary rewards. A significant aging of the faculty occurred between 1969 and 1972, when the proportion under age thirty dropped from 16 to 7, and that under forty from 51 to 38, following a decade of decline in the median age. Similarly, the percentage of faculty at the professor or associate professor ranks increased by about 9 percentage points and the percentage tenured by 18 points. There was a large increase in the number of class hours taught, a rise in the percentage of faculty teaching 13+ hours from 23 to 31, and a decline in the percentage doing 8 or fewer hours (Bayer, 1973). Presumably this was partly in response to the cutback in research and development activities. Increasing the hours of work of academics reduces real income and costs of employment, but creates additional jobs only if the elasticity of demand exceeds unity. While new Ph.D.'s continued to be employed primarily in academia, the type of job held underwent considerable change, with fewer obtaining research positions, relatively many in post-doctorate nonfaculty slots, and increasing numbers accepting jobs in "lower-level" institutions. The proportion of new doctorates obtaining jobs outside of Cartter's "rated" universities dropped from less than one-half in 1967 to over two-thirds in 1971. The proportion in Level I or II universities was halved and, regardless of work activity, new Ph.D.'s were increasingly likely to end up in institutions of lower quality than that from which they obtained the degree (Nilon, 1973). This has the consequence of improving the quality of poorer schools at the cost of reducing nonpecuniary "prestige" income and potential learning from top faculty.

The market decline appears to have affected graduate enrollments substantially. In the areas most severely affected by the

---

[27] Thus one of the *potential* benefits of inflation is a more flexible wage structure. In the absence of theoretical and empirical analyses of the impact of inflation on the flexibility of the wage structure, however, the statement should be treated as a tentative generalization only.

turnaround, notably physics, enrollments fell at astounding rates. Between 1965 and 1972, first-year graduate enrollments in physics declined by 33 percent; in other physical sciences the decline in enrollments was more moderate but nonetheless striking in view of past trends and the growing number of baccalaureates. Many major universities embarked on policies to reduce graduate classes, with the consequence that the proportion of students trained in the top institutions also fell (NSF, 1972). All told, the salary, employment, and supply adjustments of the late 1960's and early 1970's have produced a market for faculty that differs drastically from that of the preceding golden age.

B. An Econometric Model

The response of the faculty market to the 1960's boom, the ensuing turnaround, and earlier economic conditions are analyzed in this section with a small econometric model of employment and salary determination. Unlike most education-sector models (Cartter, 1971; and Porter, 1965), which assume fixed faculty-student ratios, the model examines demand adjustments to changes in academic salaries and the interrelation between employment and salary determination. Its principal outputs are estimates of long-term elasticities of demand and of the responses of employment to exogenous market developments.

The model contains three equations for demand, salary adjustment, and supply. In its simplest form, with immediate market clearing, the demand and salary equations are identical save that the dependent variable is employment in the former and salaries in the latter. More generally, salaries and employment are expected to adjust differently to market developments, yielding interrelated but distinct price and quantity adjustment processes. The three equations are presented below in the form of immediate and partial adjustment relations:

(18a) $FAC = a_1 \, ENR - a_2 \, SAL + u_1;$

(18b) $FAC = [1 - \lambda_1] \, FAC_{-1} + \lambda_1 a_1 \, ENR - \lambda_1 a_2 \, SAL + v_1;$

(19a) $SAL = b_1 \, ENR - b_2 \, FAC + v_2;$

(19b) $SAL = [1 - \lambda_2] \, SAL_{-1} + \lambda_2 b_1 \, ENR - \lambda_2 b_2 \, FAC + v_2$;

(20) $FAC = c_1 \, STK + c_2 \, SAL - c_3 \, ASAL + u_3$;

where

FAC = number of faculty;
ENR = enrollment in higher education;
SAL = salary of faculty;
STK = stock of qualified workers, potential faculty;
$ASAL$ = alternative salaries available to faculty;

and u and v are disturbances, with the v's possibly autocorrelated due to the adjustment transformation.

All variables are in log form, constants are omitted for simplicity and lags are indicated by the subscript (-1). Equations (18a) and (19a) are simple demand relations, with quantity and price as the dependent variable. With enrollments fixed but the quality of education allowed to vary, however, the equations are not to be viewed as fixed-output relations yielding elasticities of substitution. The salary parameter in (18a), a_1, reflects factor substitution and, perhaps more importantly, changes in the output of quality in response to cost changes. Absence of data on the costs of other inputs dictates omission of substitute input prices.[28] Aside from cost incentives, if the faculty-student ratio tends to be fixed, the coefficient on enrollments will be about one in (18) due to the log form of the equations, while the coefficients on enrollments and employment will be approximately equal in (19). Solving the demand and salary relations for long-run elasticities yields bounds on the desired parameters, given errors in the employment or salary variable.

The adjustment versions of (18) and (19) are simple partial-adjustment equations, with employment or salaries moving toward desired levels at rates λ_1 and λ_2. In the following empirical computations, somewhat different adjustment lags are

[28] The impact of the costs of alternative inputs on demand will depend on the elasticity of final demand for academic outputs and on the substitution possibilities. Increases in the price of alternatives will induce negative scale and positive substitution effects that may roughly net out.

119

favored by the data. As our prime concern is with the long-run elasticities needed to evaluate future market probabilities, the adjustment process is not considered in detail.

Equation (19) relates the number of faculty supplied in the short run to the stock of available personnel, such as the number of Ph.D. and Master's degree graduates in the work force, and to academic and nonacademic salaries. The long-run supply of faculty, which depends primarily on Ph.D. graduates, has been examined elsewhere (Freeman, 1971, 1972, and 1973) and is not investigated here.

Tables 2 and 3 summarize regression estimates of the demand and salary equations from 1920 to 1970 using data described in detail in the source note to Table 2. The tables present ordinary

TABLE 2. Regression Estimates of Demand for Faculty, 1920–1970[a]

Regression	Constant	SAL[b]	ENR	SAL_{-1}	ENR_{-1}	FAC_{-1}	R^2	d.w.
(1)[c]	−.74	−.26	1.04				.996	1.00
		(2.6)	(34.7)					
(2)	−.29	−.24	.67	−.12	.40		.998	1.00
		(2.4)	(7.4)	(1.3)	(4.4)			
(3)[d]	.21	.01	.46	−.15	−.04	.62	.999	2.38
		(.1)	(7.7)	(3.0)	(.4)	(5.7)		
(4)[d]	−.46	−.13	.50			.53	.999	2.18
		(2.6)	(7.1)			(7.6)		
(5)[d]	−.20		.46	−.15		.58	.999	2.26
			(9.2)	(3.8)		(11.6)		

Source: FAC = total instructional staff, from U.S. Bureau of the Census, *Historical Statistics of the United States* and Office of Education (1971). ENR = total degree credit enrollment in institutions of higher education, from the same sources. SAL = salaries of professors, from Stigler (1950), linked with AAUP (1950–1972) salary data.

[a] The dependent variable is the number of faculty; absolute values of *t*-statistics are in parentheses; d.w. = Durbin-Watson statistic, and all variables are in log form. Observations for all even-numbered years, save 1942–1946, are used in the regressions.

[b] Salaries are in real units, deflated by the Consumer Price Index. A more appropriate but unavailable deflator would be the price of output of institutions, including subsidy prices.

[c] Two-stage regression estimates of the salary coefficient yielded −.29.

[d] Nonlinear estimates in which the autocorrelation parameter is also calculated do not change these findings measurably.

TABLE 3. Regression Estimates of Salary Adjustment Equation, 1920–1970[a]

Regression	Constant	FAC	FAC_{-1}	ENR	ENR_{-1}	SAL_{-1}	R^2	d.w.
(1)[b]	3.02	−.95 (2.6)		1.21 (3.3)			.850	1.07
(2)	1.92	−1.47 (4.1)		1.06 (3.4)	.65 (3.1)		.900	1.42
(3)	−.26	−1.01 (1.5)	−.45 (.8)	.88 (2.3)	.81 (1.0)		.903	1.23
(4)[c]	1.28	−.13 (.2)	−.95 (1.7)	.34 (.8)	.60 (2.1)	.43 (2.3)	.926	1.93
(5)	1.28	−1.03 (2.4)		.32 (.7)	.39 (1.5)	.31 (1.6)	.913	2.03
(6)	1.25		−.87 (3.1)	.40 (2.2)	.60 (2.2)	.41 (2.9)	.926	1.91

Source: Same as in Table 2.

[a]Dependent variable is the deflated salary of faculty.

[b]Two-stage least-squares estimate of the employment coefficient was −1.57.

[c]Two-stage estimates of the employment coefficient yielded −.29.

least-squares calculations. As pointed out in the table note, two-stage least-squares regressions and nonlinear regressions, each with first-order autocorrelation parameters estimated with the other parameters, yielded similar results.

The main finding in Table 2 is that the demand for faculty responds to changes in academic salaries with a small but reasonably well-specified elasticity. In regression (1), which estimates the "immediate-response" demand curve, the elasticity with respect to salaries is −.26. In regression (2), which adds lagged explanatory variables, it increases to −.36 (the sum of −.12 and −.24). In the lagged-adjustment calculations of regressions (3)–(5), the long-run elasticity estimate ranges from −.28 to −.37, with various time-response paths. In (3), addition of the lagged dependent variable reduces the impact of current salaries and past enrollments essentially to zero, making last period's salary and this period's enrollments the key explanatory variables. If past salaries and enrollments are omitted (regression 4) the usual lagged-adjustment model does quite well, though the evidence favors an additional lag on salaries, regression (5). Enrollments obtain a coefficient of about unity in all of the calculations, supporting the notion of a fixed faculty-student ratio, cost incentives held fixed. In short, the evidence indicates a long-term elasticity of demand with respect to salaries of -.35 to -.40, and of unity with respect to enrollments, and suggests an adjustment process in which demand responds to past salaries and current enrollments with a partial adjustment parameter of about .45.

A similar set of findings is given in the salary regressions of Table 3, which yield somewhat larger estimates of the elasticity of demand and show a different adjustment pattern. Regression (1), the mirror image of (1) in the previous table, indicates an elasticity of demand of about unity and a response to enrollments of 1.27 (1.21/.95). The addition of last period's enrollments, however, substantially reduces the estimated demand response to -.68 (1.0/1.47) and the enrollment impact to 1.10. Regression (3), which is analogous to Table 2, regression (2), yields virtually identical results with the employment and enrollment effects divided in the two periods. In (4), where lagged salaries are added, the effect of current faculty employment is eliminated and the elasticity of demand becomes -.53 (-1.0/1.89) with respect to salaries and .87 with respect to enrollments. The regression results are better with a one-period lag in faculty employment than with current employment (regression (6) compared to (5)); however, the two partial-adjustment specifications produce roughly the same elasticity estimates: -1.0 for the short-term impact of employment on salaries; -1.5 for the long-run effect, and a corresponding long-run elasticity of demand of -.67.

In the lagged-adjustment regressions in Table 3 the estimated response parameter, λ_2, is larger than in the corresponding employment regression of Table 2; this implies a more rapid response of salaries than of employment to market conditions. Differences in the estimated λ's, the greater role of past enrollments in explaining salaries, and the negligible impact of current employment on salaries in the regressions all support the notion of separate but interrelated price and quantity adjustment processes. The long-run elasticity of demand is estimated in the range of -.40 to -.70, with a magnitude not crucially dependent on the precise lagged-adjustment specification.

TABLE 4. Regression Estimates of the Determination of Faculty Salaries and Employment, 1920–1970[a]

Regression	Dependent Variable	Constant	ENR	ENR_{-1}	STK	ASAL	SAL_{-1}	FAC_{-1}	R^2	d.w.
(1)	FAC	-.63	.46 (5.8)	.15 (1.7)	.30 (6.0)	.005 (.1)			.998	0.52
(2)	SAL	3.19	.27 (1.3)	.07 (.3)	-.40 (3.1)	.71 (3.5)			.910	0.23
(3)	FAC	.07	.44 (8.8)	.09 (.9)	.15 (2.1)	.01 (.2)	-.17 (4.2)	.31 (2.0)	.999	2.23[b]
(4)	SAL	1.47	.32 (3.5)	.34 (2.9)	.08 (.7)	.70 (7.8)	.41 (5.8)	-1.07 (4.0)	.984	1.66[b]

[a] See footnote a, Table 2.
[b] A runs test of residuals also rejects the hypothesis of serial correlation. Regressions using a nonlinear search procedure to obtain an autocorrelation parameter with other coefficients also yielded similar results.

The way in which faculty employment and salaries are affected by shifts in demand and supply schedules is examined in Table 4 by least-squares estimation of the reduced form of the model of (18)-(20). Shifts in demand are measured by enrollments, changes in supply by the estimated stock of Ph.D. and Master's graduates qualified for faculty jobs and by the salary of high school teachers, an index of alternative opportunities.[29] While teaching in secondary schools is a significant option for many faculty, especially at the junior and community college levels, the variable was chosen primarily because it is the only professional income series covering the entire 1920–1970 period.[30] Two specifications are employed in the regressions, one without lagged dependent variables, regressions (1)-(2), and one with such variables, (3)-(4). The long-run impact of enrollments, the supply of qualified personnel, and alternative salaries are obtained in the latter case by solving the system after setting current and lagged variables equal. Because of the interaction between salaries and employment in both equations, the solution parameters differ in size and sometimes sign from the direct regression coefficients. With two supply and demand shift variables the structural parameters are overidentified. Rather than using simultaneous equation "averaging" to remove overidentification, estimates can be compared to determine the weaknesses or strengths of the model.

The regression results provide general support for applying the model to the faculty market and suggest considerable responsiveness of employment and salaries to exogenous developments. With one exception, all of the explanatory variables have economically sensible and quantitatively reasonable coefficients. The exception can be traced to faulty specification or measure-

[29]The stock is calculated by assuming 200,000 Ph.D.'s in 1960, on the basis of the percentage of persons with 4 or more years having a Ph.D. in NORC (1965). We also assume a 15-percent decadal depreciation rate on reported new Ph.D.'s.

[30]National Educational data reveal that in academic years 1963–1964 and 1964–1965 17 percent of all new academic hires and one-third of those in 2-year institutions were from secondary-school teaching. (NEA Research Report, 1965–R4.)

ment of variables in the supply equation, suggesting the need for additional work to obtain a short-run faculty supply relation with some degree of certainty.

Regressions (1)–(2), which omit lagged dependent variables, accord enrollments a positive impact on both salaries and employment, as expected of demand shift variables, and accord the stock of workers a positive effect on the number of faculty but a negative one on salaries, as is appropriate for a supply shift measure. While alternative salaries raise academic salaries, they have no apparent impact on employment. This indicates the weakness of teachers' salaries as a measure of alternative opportunities facing faculty and possibly also the omission of the cost of nonfaculty labor from the demand equation.[31]   Further evidence of misspecification, presumably of the lag structure of response, is indicated by the Durbin-Watson statistics.

Regressions (3) and (4) add lagged salaries and employment and yield generally better statistical results, though an anomaly remains, again apparently due to the problem of determining the supply equation. Solving (3) and (4) for the long-run elasticities of employment and salaries yields for employment .83 (with respect to enrollments); .33 (stock of workers) and −.50 (alternative salaries). For salaries the elasticities are −.33 (enrollments); −1.67 (stock of workers) and 1.96 (alternative salaries). The anomalous negative effect of enrollments on salaries, which reverses the direct positive coefficient of regression (4), results from the impact of the induced increase in employment in regression (3) on salaries. Since the ratio of the employment and salary parameters on enrollments is the elasticity of short-run supply in a simultaneous system of this form, the problem evidently arises from faulty specification or measurement of supply. Further estimates of a direct supply relation confirm this inference, showing small and statistically insignificant positive and negative coefficients on the faculty and alternative salaries.

[31] The problem is that with the wage of nonfaculty labor and alternative wages positively correlated, the positive effect of the former on employment could be balancing out the negative impact of the latter due to the omitted variables. Available data cannot readily distinguish between these two wages over the period under study.

125

On the other hand, when a supply equation is estimated for the 1948-1970 period with professional incomes as the alternative income variable, results are better.[32]   We conclude that the econometric calculations provide useful information on the demand response and the interrelated adjustment of salaries and employment, but are unable to pin down the short-run elasticity of supply.

C. Implications for the Future

Full-scale econometric forecasts of the state of the faculty labor market require information on the *long-run* supply of Ph.D. and related Master's graduates (taken as given in (18)-(20)). Our model can be used to evaluate future possibilities, in particular the extent to which salary adjustments can be expected to stabilize employment in a changing market and the supply responses needed to avert a severe market crisis.

Current projections of enrollments and numbers of Ph.D. graduates for the 1970-1980 decade suggest a market situation similar to that of 1969-1972. Enrollments are expected to grow by 50 percent and Ph.D. supply by 60 percent over the decade (Cartter, 1971), which would produce a moderate imbalance and downward pressure on salaries.[33]   Even with an inelastic demand for faculty, the market ought have no serious problem in adjusting to such a development. Moderate reductions in real faculty salaries that augment the total size of faculty, some increase in the Ph.D. share of the faculty, and some decreases in the proportion of Ph.D.'s teaching should rectify the situation. The market for faculty will be bad, but not *that* bad.

The demographic crunch, however, is expected to hit higher

[32] The estimates for 1920-1970 using nonlinear techniques to allow for serial correlation produce an estimated supply elasticity of .50 with respect to professors' salaries and −.11 with respect to the alternative, with standard errors of .34 and .34. By contrast the results for 1948-1970 only yield an elasticity of 1.36 for salaries and −1.55 for the alternative, with standard errors .35 and .55 respectively.

[33] I have used Cartter's forecasts of enrollments and Ph.D.'s as being the best of a large number of such studies. Even they overstate the growth of both enrollments and Ph.D.'s in the 1970's, but not the differential change in the demand and supply schedules.

education in the 1980's, when enrollments are expected to fall by 10 percent due to a decline in the number of college-age youth. If the supply of Ph.D.'s leveled off in the 1980's, however, this drop, while having deleterious effects on the economic status of faculty and the age structure of the profession, could also be alleviated by moderate demand-supply adjustments. The forecasted crisis depends critically on the assumption of continued rapid growth of Ph.D.'s at rates not very different from those in the late 1960's. Such supply behavior in the face of the market turnaround of 1969–1972 and an anticipated weak market in the 1970's seems highly implausible. Already graduate enrollments have dropped greatly in fields most affected by the turnaround, and it seems reasonable on the basis of supply studies (Freeman, 1971, 1972, and 1973) to expect additional supply responses to take up much of the adjustment burden. This market scenario does not, of course, mean that the process of adjusting to the end of the 1960's golden age for academics will be equitable or efficient.

IV. Conclusions

This study has examined the nonprofit demand for faculty in the higher educational system from the perspectives of the theory of derived demand, the institutional characteristics of academia, and a simple econometric model of demand. The paper has emphasized that demand for faculty is responsive to changes in the cost of employment, albeit with peculiarities due to nonprofit motivation and the distinct features of higher education.

Because of the nonprofit budget constraint, the short-run demand for labor will be more elastic with respect to wages and output in nonprofit than in for-profit enterprises, and prices will be more responsive to costs and less responsive to shifts in demand. In addition, nonprofit wages and employment will be more greatly influenced by shifts in supply and demand. The basic reason is that short-run supply follows the average rather than the marginal cost curve in the nonprofit case. Long-run factor demands can be expected to be identical in nonprofit and for-profit markets, given similar entry conditions. This requires

127

creation of additional nonprofit firms by subsidizers or purchases of products when costs rise above the minimum average cost.

The importance of the quality of faculty in higher education produces complex interactions between the number and quality of workers, which are likely to lead to greater quality than quantity adjustments, to changes in wages, rationing of places in high-level institutions, and a concentration of the most qualified in a limited number of universities. The "equitable" wage goal of universities, to reward comparable faculty similarly regardless of nonacademic opportunities, substantially narrows the interfield wage structure, producing less dispersion than in other sectors of the economy. Equitable wage policies exact a cost in terms of flexibility of response to market changes and are likely to be loosened in times of financial difficulties.

Tenure also reduces the responsiveness of the higher education system, particularly in periods of market decline when expansion of faculty cannot be used to reallocate resources across disciplines. Issues of academic freedom aside, tenure is critical in a system where senior employees control appointments. Internal production of faculty and the lag structure in producing Ph.D.'s create an accelerator-type adjustment process with long dampened cyclic fluctuations. As increasing proportions of cohorts enroll in college, the system becomes especially sensitive to demographic factors, notably the number of persons of college age.

The boom in higher education of the 1960's, which created a golden age for academics, terminated toward the end of the decade. With research and related expenditures no longer increasing, enrollments leveling off, and the number of Ph.D.'s seeking work increasing as a result of previous market conditions, the academic marketplace underwent a significant turnaround. Real salaries dropped from 1969 to 1972, employment conditions worsened, and new Ph.D.'s were forced to take less prestigious jobs. While adjustments in salaries and demand are likely to alleviate much of the market problem caused by greater shifts in supply than demand in the 1970's, the burden of adjusting to the 1980's market will necessarily fall on supply. A reasonable scenario will show far fewer Ph.D.'s than indicated in current forecasts.

128

Our econometric study shows that the demand for faculty is responsive to changes in enrollments and in salaries, with an elasticity of about unity with respect to the former, and -.4 to -.7 with respect to the latter. Salary and employment follow interrelated but distinct adjustment processes, and both are substantially affected by changes in the number of available workers.

COMMENTS

GEORGE E. JOHNSON

Freeman has explored a variety of questions associated with the analysis of nonprofit firms in general and academic institutions in particular. This is a huge subject, and it seems in retrospect very odd that labor economists have not focused on the general issues before. There are so many individual points made in Freeman's paper that I will be selective in my comments, discussing only three out of a potential of about twenty.

The first is the question of the reaction of the nonprofit firm to changes in prices in the short run. Freeman makes the interesting point that, whereas the for-profit firm will move along its marginal cost schedule when price rises, the nonprofit firm will move along its average cost schedule. (See his Figure 1 and related discussion.) The obvious implication is that the short-run effect of an increase in price will be greater in a nonprofit than a for-profit firm. While this conclusion follows from Freeman's assumptions, I believe there may not be as much difference between non- and for-profit firms in this respect as implied by his analysis. Consider a hypothetical example: the tuition and/or subsidy per student at Cisco Kid State College rises by a hundred dollars. With 20,000 students, this increases total revenue at CKSC by two million dollars. How will the college administration react to this situation? According to Freeman's analysis, they will hire more instructors and supporting staff and increase the size of the student body accordingly. In fact, the CKSC administration will take a longer view of the situation and realize that the scale of the college should be increased. New classrooms, laboratories, dormitories, offices, etc., must be built in order to maximize long-run output for a given stream of revenues. We would thus expect a good chunk of the two-million dollar windfall to be allocated to expansion of the physical plant of the college, not to increasing short-run output. This would permit a greater increase in output in the long run.

Freeman's suggestion that "managerial quality" would be lower

130

in non- than in for-profit firms does not, it seems to me, follow from his analysis. Although this discussion is more or less an afterthought in his paper, the question of whether nonprofit firms encourage maximum efficiency is certainly very important.

Freeman argues that exceptionally able businessmen will concentrate in for-profit firms where their talents are well paid. However, if it is also true that nonprofit firms attempt to maximize output subject to a zero-profit constraint, there is no reason why nonprofit firms should not select the level of quality of managerial staff that is consistent with cost minimization (and profit maximization). Returning to the university example, if the board of trustees at CKSC felt that the college's financial officers were misallocating resources, they would attempt to fire the relevant incompetents. In choosing replacements, the trustees will realize that they will have to pay market prices for administrators who are smart enough to allocate revenues optimally. Now it has been argued frequently that the top managers in the relatively monopolistic segment of private industry tend to set very high salaries and other emoluments for themselves at the expense of profits. To the extent that this is true, the most efficient managerial talent will be drawn into managing the production of soap, automobiles, and such, and managers of the highest quality will simply be too expensive for competitive firms and nonprofit enterprises. It would not be a good move for the trustees of CKSC to pay the former president of Universal Pollutants $500,000 per year so that he would, through the use of the best business methods, save the college $200,000 on its current scale of operations.

A major question in the analysis of labor markets in higher education concerns the influence of various institutional peculiarities on the nature of adjustment, and I think that Freeman has made some very interesting points in this regard. I especially concur with his discussion of the influences of equity notions in equalizing interdiscipline salary differentials. Some work I have been conducting with Frank Stafford has shown that the small size of interdiscipline differences is even more pronounced within school types, which means that the lower-paying schools concentrate on "cheaper" disciplines to a greater extent than the higher-paying schools. Interestingly, the uniformity of salary structures across disciplines is greater in government than in academic employment.

I find Freeman's dynamic model of the faculty labor market a trifle disappointing, especially given his previous discussion of the effects of the "internal labor market" and the tenure system. His model in (14)–(16) includes an implicit market-clearing equation, but it is not clear that the behavior of the institutions is consistent with immediate adjustment. Instead of his system, I would write out the following model:

(1) $$F^D = aG + bU - cS;$$

(2) $$F^S = PhD + [1 - \delta] F^S_{-1} \; ;$$

(3) $$PhD = G_{-1} = A + BS_{-1} + CX_{-1} \; ;$$

(4) $$X \equiv F^D - F^S \; ;$$

(5) $$\text{and } S - S_{-1} = \lambda X_{-1}.$$

where X is the rate of excess demand for faculty and λ is the slope of the salary adjustment function. Freeman's model is based on the assumption that $X = 0$ and that salaries adjust accordingly rather than in response to excess demand pressures as embodied in (5).

What I find to be one of the most disturbing features of the academic labor market at the present time is the possibility that salaries may not fall very rapidly in the face of excess supply pressures. In terms of the model embodied in (1) through (5), this is represented by a small value of λ. Suppose that λ were zero, which means that salaries simply go their merry way independent of supply/demand pressures. Then the salary level, set in terms relative to some comparison group like other professional labor, is fixed at S_*, and the "equilibrium" rate of excess demand for faculty is given by:

$$\overline{X} = \frac{1}{C[1 - a\delta] + \delta} \left[\delta bU - [1 - a\delta]A - [[1 - \delta a]B + \delta c]S_* \right].$$

This implies that the rate of excess demand for academics will be higher the greater is the number of undergraduates, the less desirable the academic profession is judged on nonpecuniary grounds, and the lower is the salary level for academics.

There is abundant casual evidence that wages in academia adjust upward: Simply look at what happened in 1958–1968. There are many signs, however, that institutional forces may not allow the equilibration of supply and demand in the academic labor market during the 1970's. One of the most important of these forces is unionization, a factor that hardly existed in academia five years ago. The push for unionization probably represents a desire on the part of senior faculty to institutionalize the high relative salary levels that were induced by the excess demand conditions of the early and mid-1960's. If unionization is successful in turning these quasi-rents into outright monopoly rents, the academic profession will continue to be a difficult craft to enter. Further, the scarcity of younger practitioners will tend to slow down the rate at which new knowledge is created, which will, along with the graduate-student acceleration effect discussed by Freeman, tend to shift the demand curve for faculty to the left. This leads to a rather gloomy forecast of the medium-run outlook for the academic labor market. However, we can hope that this forecast, like most economic forecasts of the more conventional sort, is wrong.

JOHN F. BURTON, JR., AND CHARLES E. KRIDER

The Incidence of Strikes in Public Employment

The rapid growth of unions in the public sector probably has been the most significant development of the last decade in American industrial relations. The most obvious manifestation of the development has been the increasing reliance by public employees on strikes as a method of improving their working conditions. Despite nearly universal illegality, the number and notoriety of public-sector strikes has swelled.

This paper examines the incidence of strikes in the local government, noneducation sector. The first section presents some historical comparisons between strikes in the entire economy and those in the government sector. The second and third sections review earlier studies of strike activity and develop general hypotheses about the causes of strikes. The next sections translate the general hypotheses into testable propositions and present our empirical results for local government strikes in the 50 states during 1968–1971. A final section summarizes our findings and discusses the policy implications.

Note: We appreciate the advice provided by Robert J. Flanagan, Lee K. Benham, Myron Roomkin, and other members of the Labor Workshop of the University of Chicago, and by Daniel Hamermesh, John Pencavel and others who attended the Conference on Labor in Nonprofit Industry and Government held at Princeton University in May 1973. Eric Klempner performed much of the computational work and provided advice for the paper. This paper was prepared as part of the *Studies of Unionism in Government*, which are being conducted by the Brookings Institution with financial support from the Ford Foundation. The views are the authors' and are not presented as those of the officers, trustees, or staff members of the Brookings Institution or of the Ford Foundation.

135

TABLE 1. Work Stoppages in the Entire Economy, Annual Averages 1946-1971

	Work Stoppages		Workers Involved		Man-Days Idle		Duration[a]	FTE Employees
Years	Number (1)	per million FTE Employees (2)	Number (thousands) (3)	per thousand FTE Employees (4)	Number (thousands) (5)	per thousand FTE Employees (6)	Mean in days (7)	(thousands) (8)
1946-50	4109	85.6	2834	59.2	54800	1146.4	18.3	47985
1951-55	4547	83.7	2468	45.4	32220	592.8	12.8	54278
1956-60	3647	65.0	1710	30.5	32320	575.9	18.4	56155
1961-65	3592	60.2	1362	22.8	19440	324.8	14.5	59646
1966	4405	66.6	1960	29.6	25400	384.2	13.0	66114
1967	4595	67.7	2870	42.3	42100	619.9	14.7	67913
1968	5045	72.2	2649	37.9	49018	701.9	18.5	69832
1969	5700	79.4	2481	34.6	42869	597.0	17.3	71803
1970	5716	79.8	3305	46.2	66414	927.7	20.1	71587
1971	5138	72.2	3280	46.1	47589	668.9	14.5	71148

Sources: Data on work stoppages, workers involved, and man-days idle are from Bureau of Labor Statistics, Bulletin 1777, *Analysis of Work Stoppages 1971*. Data on full-time equivalent (FTE) employees are from U.S., Department of Commerce, Office of Business Economics, *The National Income and Product Accounts of the United States, 1929-65, Statistical Tables*, Table 6.4, and from Table 6.4 of the July issues of the *Survey of Current Business* for 1968-73.

[a] Duration is the number of man-days idle (col. 5) divided by the number of workers involved (col. 3).

I. The Postwar Strike Record

Several dimensions of strike activity can be traced in the postwar period. Published statistics pertaining to the economy, reproduced in Table 1, are the number of work stoppages beginning in the year (column 1), the number of workers involved in strikes beginning in the year (column 3), and the number of man-days idle during the year (column 5). In order to facilitate comparisons through time and between the entire economy and the government sector, these measures of strike activity have been related to the number of full-time equivalent (FTE) employees (column 8). The results are the number of strikes per one million FTE employees (column 2), the number of striking employees per one thousand FTE employees (column 4), and the number of man-days idle per one thousand FTE employees (column 6). The mean duration of strikes (column 7) has been calculated by determining the number of man-days idle during the year per striking worker.[1]

Table 2 presents the same data for the state and local sector for 1946–1971. The coverage of all state and local employees is used, even though the primary concern of this paper is local government, noneducation employees, because historical data for the more narrow category are unavailable. Table 3 presents data for 1968–1971 for the local government, noneducation sector.

The per-employee data in Table 1 indicate that the entire economy has experienced a diminution of strike activity during the past 25 years, although since 1967 there has been a decided reversal in the trend. The data in Table 2 on strikes by state and local government employees present an even more dramatic story for recent years. All measures of strike activity have surged to records; but even with this recent surge, the state and local sector is much less conflict-prone than the rest of the economy.

[1] Our figures on mean duration shown in Tables 1 and 2 differ from those published by the Bureau of Labor Statistics because their figures are simple averages (each stoppage is given equal weight regardless of size), while our figures are weighted averages (each stoppage is given a weight proportional to the number of workers involved). Their figures also pertain to strikes ending in the year, while our figures approximate the duration of strikes in effect during the year.

137

TABLE 2. Work Stoppages in the State and Local Sector, Annual Averages 1946–1971

Years	Work Stoppages		Workers Involved		Man-Days Idle		Duration	FTE Employees
	Number (1)	per million FTE Employees (2)	Number (thousands) (3)	per thousand FTE Employees (4)	Number (thousands) (5)	per thousand FTE Employees (6)	Mean in days (7)	(thousands) (8)
1946–50	27	8.3	3.8	1.2	22.0	6.7	6.0	3393
1951–55	28	7.1	4.5	1.1	26.6	6.6	5.8	4115
1956–60	23	4.5	7.4	1.4	18.6	3.5	4.0	5096
1961–65	33	5.2	14.6	2.3	58.6	9.0	4.5	6244
1966	142	19.7	105.0	14.5	455.0	63.0	4.3	7221
1967	181	24.1	132.0	17.6	1250.0	166.7	9.5	7498
1968	251	32.0	200.2	25.5	2535.6	323.0	12.7	7850
1969	409	50.2	159.4	19.6	744.6	91.4	4.7	8150
1970	409	48.1	177.7	20.9	1375.1	161.8	7.7	8501
1971	327	37.0	151.6	17.2	893.3	101.1	5.9	8832

Sources: Data on work stoppages, workers involved, and man-days idle are from Bureau of Labor Statistics. 1946–1957 data are from "Work Stoppages, Government Employees, 1942–61," Report No. 247; 1958–1968 data are from "Work Stoppages in Government, 1958–68," Report No. 348; 1969–1970 data are from "Government Work Stoppages, 1960, 1969, and 1970," Summary Report; 1971 data are from source cited in Table 1. Source of data on full-time equivalent employees is cited in Table 1.

TABLE 3. Work Stoppages in the Local Government, Noneducation Sector, Annual Averages 1968–1971[a]

Years	Work Stoppages		Workers Involved		Man-Days Idle		Duration	FTE Employees
	Number (1)	per million FTE Employees (2)	Number (thousands) (3)	per thousand FTE Employees (4)	Number (thousands) (5)	per thousand FTE Employees (6)	Mean in days (7)	(thousands) (8)
1968	132	51.6	37.2	14.5	322.2	125.8	8.7	2561
1969	152	57.7	26.1	9.9	177.9	67.6	6.8	2633
1970	197	68.9	41.8	14.6	287.8	100.6	6.9	2860
1971	142	48.0	54.6	18.5	239.2	80.8	4.4	2958

Sources: Number of work stoppages, workers involved, and man-days idle were calculated from unpublished data provided by the Bureau of Labor Statistics. Data on full-time equivalent (FTE) employees in the local government, noneducation sector are from U.S. Bureau of the Census, Public Employment in 1968, Table 8 and from corresponding publications for 1969–1971.

[a] All figures relate to strikes beginning in years shown.

Data for 1968–1971 for the local noneducation sector (Table 3) indicate that, after adjustment for the size of the labor force, this sector has more strikes, but with fewer workers involved and fewer man-days idle than the balance of the state and local sector. The probable reason is that teachers' strikes, which account for the bulk of the government employee strikes not included in our analysis, apparently involve more employees and last longer than strikes in the noneducation sector.

II. Previous Studies of Strikes

This section provides a selective review of earlier studies of strike activity. The survey is limited to empirical examinations, with the exception of Hicks (1932), who provided a theory of strikes that has been an important input to much of the subsequent empirical research. Hicks felt that in general it will be possible to get more favorable terms by negotiating than by striking, and, therefore, "The majority of actual strikes are doubtless the result of faulty negotiation" (p. 146).

The fault that leads to strikes is lack of information; indeed, "Adequate knowledge will always make a settlement possible" (Hicks, 1932, p. 147). An explicit delineation of two causes of lack of information appears useful, although the distinction is only implicit in Hicks. One cause, which we term "uncertainty," results from an inaccurate assessment by one party of the other party's bargaining position or ability to sustain a strike. The other cause, termed "expectations," occurs because the parties may react differently to a given set of facts. Thus, even if each party fully understands the other's position, a strike may occur because the parties differ in their expectations about what is a reasonable settlement under the circumstances. Both "uncertainty" and "expectations" as causes of strikes are due to inadequate knowledge, but we believe it is worth distinguishing between misinformation due to a misperception of the other party's intentions and misinformation due to the parties' different assessments of the environment within which bargaining is taking place.

In an elaboration of his view that inadequate information causes strikes, Hicks (1932, p. 147) suggests the possibility of "a difference of opinion between the Union leaders and their rank and file." Indeed, conciliation probably increases this evil: union leaders and employers gain knowledge through conciliation, thus reducing the chances of strikes, but the conciliation efforts may have little influence on the ordinary member. This is an important reason why union officials are forced against their will into a very high proportion of strikes. Hicks, in essence, argues that lack of knowledge is the primary cause of strikes, and that three parties—the employer, the union leader, and the ordinary member—are central to the strike decision.[2]

Our understanding of the strike process was enhanced by Rees (1952) in his study of the relationship between strikes and the business cycle. Rees found a high correspondence between strike cycles and the business cycle for monthly data for 1915–1938, and very little correspondence for the war and postwar years, 1939–1950. The lack of association in the latter period is not surprising, but even in the earlier period the correspondence was only clear between business activity and the number of strikes beginning in each month. The number of workers involved in strikes beginning in each month (for which monthly data are available since 1927) was an erratic series that had to be smoothed by a five-month moving average to reveal its cyclical movements, and even this series was only used as a rough check on the series on the number of strikes. Annual data on the average duration of strikes are available since 1927, but Rees found no relation between duration and the business cycle. Rees presented no statistical analysis of data on the number of man-days idle. For the series on the number of strikes beginning in each month, Rees found that the turning points led the business cycle turning points at the peaks and lagged at the troughs.

Rees (p. 382) argued that most strikes "are caused by social and psychological forces or by economic forces which are noncyclical in nature." These causes are not specifically identified, but Rees's explanation of the general correspondence between the number of strikes and business activity and the lead and lag relationships

[2] Hicks (1932, p. 146) also asserts that some strikes are necessary to keep the union in fighting trim. This cause of strikes, though of relative unimportance in Hicks's theory, is incorporated in our analysis in Section III.

141

at peaks and troughs does extend Hicks's theory because Rees added bargaining power as a determinant of strikes. When business conditions are favorable, the union's bargaining power is increased because of factors such as the employer's reluctance to lose his share of an expanding market and the strikers' awareness of employment possibilities elsewhere if the employer discharges them. For reasons not made clear by Rees, employers do not react to their deteriorating bargaining power in good times by granting concessions without a strike, but rather the unions apparently are required to exercise their enhanced power.

While the general correlation between strikes and business activity is explained by fluctuations in bargaining power, the lead-lag relationships between the cycles are explained by Rees on another basis. In the period when strikes and business activity are nearing their peaks, there is a divergence of expectations between employers and unions. The unions pay close attention to employment, which generally does not lead at the peak. Employers, however, focus their attention on activities which do lead at the peak, such as orders, and they will resist demands for which the unions are still willing to fight. "The strike peak probably represents a maximum in the divergence of expectations between employers and unions" (Rees, 1952, p. 381). The lag of the strike series at the trough represents a "wait and see" attitude by union leaders who want assurance the revival is genuine before risking their members' jobs.

Rees's results were updated by Weintraub (1966). He found that the correspondence between strike cycles and the business cycles, which had existed between 1915–1938 but had disappeared in the war and postwar years 1939–1950, reappeared for the period 1949–1961. The lead and lag relationships among the strike cycles and business cycles were similar to the relationships found by Rees for the earlier years.

Weintraub did not analyze data on the number of employees on strike, the average duration of strikes, or man-days lost. Even the analysis of the cyclical behavior of the number of strikes beginning in each month seemed strained. For example, Weintraub (p. 234) indicated that, for 1949–1961, "there was a cycle of strikes for every reference cycle listed by the NBER." Yet his chart shows that between the successive business cycle troughs in October 1949 and August 1954 there were three troughs in the strike series.

The most recent examination of the relationship between strike activity and business cycles is by Scully (1971), whose approach differed from the Rees and Weintraub studies in several ways. His measures of strike activity included the number of strikes beginning in each month, the number of strikes in effect during the month, the number of workers involved in strikes beginning in the month, the number of workers involved in strikes in effect during the month, and man-days idle during the month. Also, instead of using the NBER reference cycle, Scully used monthly data on layoffs and on the Federal Reserve Board index of industrial production. Finally, Scully used spectral and cross-spectral analysis to test for the existence of a relationship between strike activity and the business cycle. The essence of spectral analysis is the identification of the relative importance of cycles of different length that exist in time-series data. For example, many economic time series have important annual cycles. Cross-spectral analysis tests for leads and lags between the cycles in two time series.

Scully found that the most important cycles in the strike series are shorter than the important cycles in business activity, even after the annual cycle in strike activity is ignored. Furthermore, with the exception of cycles shorter than twenty-seven months, there is a lack of coherence or association between strikes and business activity. Since the term "business cycles" refers to expansions and contractions of the economy that typically exceed twenty-seven months, the conclusion that strike cycles and business cycles are statistically associated must be rejected. This also means that analysis of the leads and lags between strike cycles and business cycles is irrelevant.

Scully (p. 374) felt his empirical evidence "confirms Hicks' observation that strikes are irrational events emerging from faulty negotiations and, hence, are likely to have a very strong random component above the strong annual element in the strike series." This restatement seems more nihilistic than Hicks intended, although fully consistent with Scully's interpretation of the time-series data. His other venture into theorizing about strikes is

143

more elaborate and insightful. Noting that Rees had postulated more strikes during a period of business expansion because of the union's improved bargaining strength, Scully argued that the concurrent weakening of the employer's bargaining position might make him more willing to settle without a strike. Moreover, in economic downturns unions may be less anxious to strike because of their lower bargaining power, but employers may induce strikes because of their strong position. In short, Scully believes that a priori arguments about the impact of cyclical variations in relative bargaining power on the frequency of strikes are inconclusive.

Another approach to the explanation of variations through time in the amount of strike activity was provided by Ashenfelter and Johnson (1969). They argued that conventional bargaining theory relied on two explanations of why strikes occur. First, one party may misjudge the other's intentions and a strike results because of inadequate knowledge. (In our terms, this is a strike due to uncertainty.) Second, a breakdown in negotiations may occur because the two parties are irrational. They could not see how either of these explanations could be related to any of the observable variables in the system, and concluded that conventional bargaining theory was not very helpful in deriving implications about the frequency or duration of strikes.

Ashenfelter and Johnson (p. 37) therefore offered an alternative bargaining model. This model recognized three parties in the negotiation process: management, union leadership, and union rank and file. Strikes can result when the membership's expected wage increase is greater than the amount management will accept, and the union's leaders incur a strike to lower the membership's expectations. After the strike lasts long enough, "the leadership feels that the minimum acceptable wage increase has fallen to a level at which it can safely sign with management, and the strike ends."

In essence, strikes occur because the union membership and management have different "expectations" about what constitutes a reasonable settlement, and the strike is the equilibrating mechanism for the divergent expectations. The parties have different expectations because they look at different aspects of the

144

economic environment in determining what is a reasonable wage increase. Firms consider profits: a strike will lower profits immediately, but the lower wage settlement that results from the strike will eventually increase profits. Ashenfelter and Johnson postulate that the greater the previous profit level relative to the previous wage bill, the less likely are strikes to occur because of employer resistance to union wage demands. The union membership, however, is more likely to demand a higher wage increase when previous profits are high, and so the net impact of higher profits on the level of strikes is uncertain a priori. The membership's expectations for wage increases are also likely to be higher the lower the level of unemployment and the slower real wages have been increasing.

The Ashenfelter-Johnson model is tested on quarterly data for 1952-I to 1967-II on the number of strikes beginning in each quarter. The results provide strong statistical support for the model: strikes are inversely related both to the level of unemployment and to the previous rate of increase in real wages. Only the level of profits is not related to the number of strikes in a statistically significant manner; this is consistent with the model's prediction of the offsetting impact of higher profits on the expectations of the employer and union members.

The Ashenfelter-Johnson article is a major contribution to the strike literature, and among the successful uses of the model are examinations of strike activity in Canada (Smith, 1973) and in Britain (Pencavel, 1970). Nonetheless, there are limitations to the model.[3] For example, despite their assertion that the model pro-

---

[3] In addition to the limitations discussed in the text, we believe their bargaining model may be unnecessarily complex. The model distinguishes three parties to the negotiations and stresses the role of the strike in reducing divergent expectations between the union leadership and the union rank and file. However, even if the leadership always perfectly reflects the views of the rank and file, so that the union has a unitary viewpoint, it does not appear that any of the testable hypotheses of the model are affected. In the two-party model, the strike becomes a mechanism to bring the union view about what is a reasonable settlement into line with the management view, with profits, unemployment, and real wages having the same expected relationship with strike activity as in the Ashenfelter-Johnson three-party model.

145

vides "predictions concerning the probability of a strike's occurrence and the expected duration of such a strike" (Ashenfelter and Johnson, 1969, p. 39), no empirical analysis of the latter aspect of strike activity is presented. Nor is any attempt made to predict the number of workers involved in strikes or man-days idle.

A recent examination of strike activity by Roomkin (1972) suggests further limitations of the Ashenfelter-Johnson model. Roomkin extended the time period through 1970-IV (from the original 1952-I to 1967-II periods). The regression coefficients for the individual variables generally were still significant, but the values of the coefficients in the Roomkin regression were statistically different from those in the original regression. Roomkin found that the extended regression did not support the Ashenfelter-Johnson model, produced markedly varying results when applied to selected industrial sectors (such as construction, mining, and durable manufacturing), and that there appeared to be a significant potential for aggregation error in a single economy-wide strike equation.[4]

Most empirical studies of strikes have attempted to explain variations through time in economy-wide aggregates of strike activity.[5] Among the limited number of studies of disaggregated strike data is the Kerr and Siegel (1954) international comparison of the interindustry propensity to strike. Kerr and Siegel examined data from eleven countries on the number of man-days lost relative to employment in all industries for which data were available. They then ranked industries in five categories based on their typical strike propensities. The range was from a high propensity in the mining, maritime, and longshore industries to a low propensity in the railroad, agriculture, and trade industries. Data on the government sector were sparse, but "on the basis of general knowledge alone," government employees were confidently placed in the low-propensity-to-strike category.

[4] In contrast, Pencavel (1970, p. 254) found no evidence of aggregation error in his application of the Ashenfelter-Johnson model to the British economy.

[5] Other studies concerned with economy-wide aggregates of strike activity are Ross (1961) and Dubin (1965).

146

Two hypotheses were offered as the most important explanations of strike-proneness. First, the location of the worker in society determines his propensity to strike, and this location is heavily influenced by the industrial environment. The prototype of a strike-prone industry is logging, in which the workers form isolated masses physically separated from society. The employees are largely homogeneous, performing the same work with little opportunity to move up in the occupational structure or to move out of the industry. "The strike for this isolated mass is a kind of colonial revolt against far-removed authority, an outlet for accumulated tensions, and a substitute for occupational and social mobility." (Kerr and Siegel, 1954, p. 193). The opposite of the isolated mass is the integrated individual or the integrated group. "Integrated" is used in the sociological sense to mean absorbed in society at large.

The second hypothesis is that the inherent nature of the job determines the kinds of workers employed and their attitudes, and these workers, in turn, cause conflict or peace. "If the job is physically difficult and unpleasant, unskilled or semiskilled, and casual or seasonal, and fosters an independent spirit (as in the logger in the woods), it will draw tough, inconstant, combative, and virile workers, and they will be inclined to strike" (Kerr and Siegel, 1954, p. 195). In contrast, if the job is physically easy and performed in pleasant surroundings, skilled and responsible, steady, and subject to set rules and close supervision, it will attract women or the most submissive type of man who will abhor strikes. Kerr and Siegel note exceptions to the second hypothesis, such as teamsters who do not strike enough and textile workers who strike too often. Nonetheless, they feel this hypothesis and the first are more useful in explaining differences in strike propensities among industries than factors such as the structure of the product market, profitability of the industry, the state of technological change, or the sensitivity of the industry to the business cycle. Unfortunately, no empirical analysis of these factors is presented, nor are the two hypotheses offered by Kerr and Siegel subjected to any test of their predictive power.

There is a study of strikes by government employees that draws

147

on the Kerr-Siegel framework for its analysis.[6]   Krislov (1961) examined work stoppages of government employees between 1942 and 1959. His general conclusions were that the average number of strikes per year in the latter part of the period (1955–1959) was substantially lower than in the earlier part of the period.   Also, government strikes involved relatively few employees and were of relatively short duration, compared to the rest of the economy. Among Krislov's specific findings was that strikes were concentrated among sanitation employees, utility employees including transportation workers, and education employees–usually teachers. Indeed, strikes by street cleaners and garbage collectors accounted for about half of all local government strikes. This finding was viewed as a confirmation of the Kerr and Siegel conclusion that workers who form a homogeneous and undifferentiated group–who were an "isolated mass"–were likely to have a high propensity to strike.

Another interesting aspect of this study concerns the impact of public policy on the number of strikes. Eight states enacted no-strike laws for public employees between 1942 and 1959, and Krislov compared the number of strikes before and after enactment of these laws. In one state (New York) the number of strikes increased, in four the number declined, and in three the number did not change appreciably. As a control group, Krislov examined the experience in five states that enacted no such legislation and compared the number of strikes in the 1942–1947 period with the number in the 1948–1957 period. (1947 was the median year in which states enacted no-strike laws.) He found that, in the states without laws, the number of strikes did not change appreciably in three, while it declined in two. Krislov concluded that enactment of a no-strike law will reduce the number of strikes, but that, "the objective can be obtained without passage of such legislation" (p. 92). We would be hard pressed to disagree with Krislov's analysis.

This survey of strike studies suggest that our empirical knowl-

---

[6] Most articles on strikes by government employees are descriptive rather than analytical. A recent example is Young and Brewer (1970), which includes references to several other descriptive articles.

edge of the public and private sectors is both narrow and fragile. Narrow because most examinations have concentrated on the number of strikes. Other measures of strike activity, such as the number of striking employees and the number of man-days lost, have received less attention, and the duration of strikes has been virtually ignored. Our knowledge can also be characterized as narrow because most studies have concentrated on national time-series data; studies of disaggregated or cross-sectional behavior are uncommon. The evidence is fragile because the results are sensitive to the specific time period or level of aggregation from which data are used.

III. Some General Hypotheses about Strikes

We do not believe the studies surveyed in the previous section can be integrated into a unitary explanation or theory of strikes, but a few general hypotheses about strikes can be identified. The general hypotheses are based on the concepts of uncertainty, expectations, bargaining power, and psychological or sociological factors.[7]

Consistent with our discussion in Section II, we view uncertainty as a form of misinformation in which one party makes an inaccurate assessment of the other party's position on substantive

[7] Section III provides several explanations of the propensity to strike, without attempting to differentiate among the various aspects of strike activity such as average duration or man-days idle per thousand FTE employees. A more complete model would consider the relationships among these aspects; e.g., for a given population of workers, there may be a tradeoff between the number of striking workers and the average duration of the strikes. If the number of strikers and average duration are, in effect, substitutes, then man-days idle per thousand FTE employees may be the best overall measure of the propensity to strike. However, man-days idle is the product of the number of striking employees and the average strike duration, and duration may be a particularly erratic aspect of strike activity. This view of duration is consistent with the Walton and McKersie (1965) analysis of settlement dynamics during a strike. If this view is correct, then duration and man-days idle will be particularly hard to predict, and a model explaining the propensity to strike is likely to do a better job predicting the number of strikes or the number of striking employees.

issues or ability to substain a strike.[8] If all other variables are held constant, uncertainty is positively associated with the likelihood of a strike. Given perfect knowledge, the propensity to strike should be low, and perhaps even zero. Hicks asserts that adequate knowledge will always make a settlement possible; however, we feel some strikes may occur with perfect information. Hicks (1932, p. 146), for example, provides an exception to his own rule by stating "A Union which never strikes may lose the ability to organize a formidable strike." The exact shape of the function is impossible to postulate; that a positive relation exists is our basic hypothesis about the relationship between uncertainty and strike activity.

Strikes may occur because of inconsistent expectations of the parties. The term "expectations" refers to a settlement expected by a party, and will usually be based upon an interpretation of current and predicted economic events. If the opponent's offer is below a party's expectations, a strike may occur even if the intentions and positions of both sides are fully known (i.e., even if there is no uncertainty). The cause of such a strike would be a divergence of expectations. For this divergence to occur, there must be an incorrect assessment of economic events by at least one of the participants. A union, for example, may expect a settlement higher than market conditions warrant because of an emphasis on inappropriate economic indicators. On the assumption that the expectations of the participants will at least in part be formed independently, any change in the environment that increases the expectations of union leaders or members about a reasonable settlement, or decreases management's expectations, would be positively associated with strikes.

Bargaining power is another concept which should help explain the incidence of strikes. Krider (1971) has examined the relationship between strike activity and the definition of bargaining

[8]We use the term "uncertainty" in a more narrow sense than the recent literature on probabilistic economics, which is surveyed in McCall (1971). "Uncertainty" describes a bargaining situation where each party has a given position on substantive issues and has a given ability to sustain a strike, but where at least one party makes an erroneous assessment of the other party's substantive position or ability to strike.

power used by Chamberlain and Kuhn (1965). Here we will use a more simplified notion of bargaining power.[9] A union's relative bargaining power is measured by its ability to obtain wages greater than the employer would have voluntarily paid on the basis of market conditions. A strong union would be able to obtain wages considerably in excess of the market wage, while a very weak union would not even be able to force the employer to pay what the market would dictate.

Rees (1952) suggests that bargaining power will influence the propensity to strike. Unions are more likely to strike when market conditions are favorable because their bargaining power is high. Similarly, union bargaining power is low in bad times and hence fewer strikes occur. The implication of Rees's viewpoint is illustrated by line RR in Figure 1, which shows the relationship between changes through time in relative bargaining power for a particular union and its propensity to strike.

Our analysis is not concerned with the varying propensity of a given union to strike through time as its bargaining power ebbs and flows, but with the relative propensity of different unions to strike as a function of their relative bargaining power. The reasons offered by Rees why a union will be more likely to strike when its bargaining power is great can be adapted to an explanation of variations among unions in their propensity to strike. The implication is that, at a given point in time, unions with greater bargaining power are more likely to strike than weaker unions. However, we believe a more likely relationship is that illustrated by line BK in Figure 1. A weak union has little reason to strike since the market dictates a higher wage rate than it could secure through a strike. Under such circumstances, the employer presumably voluntarily grants the market wage if only to reduce the quit rate among his employees. A strike would not occur since the union could gain nothing by matching its bargaining

---

[9] Chamberlain and Kuhn (1965) argue bargaining power cannot be defined as an inherent attribute of the parties, but rather varies with the size of the contract demand. Krider (1971) shows that by determining the size of the wage increase that will equalize union and employer bargaining power in each bargaining relationship, interunion comparisons can be made in terms of the size of the equalizing wage increase for each union.

FIGURE 1.

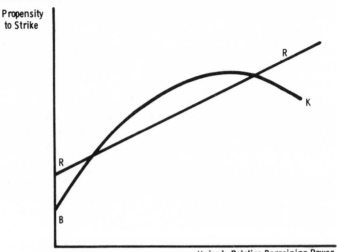

power against that of the employer. Unions with greater bargaining power have an incentive to strike in order to obtain wage increases above the market rate. This explains the positive slope of BK as we move from weak to moderately strong unions. This conclusion is consistent with Rees.

However, in contrast to Rees, we believe that dominant unions are also less likely to strike than unions with moderate strength. The powerful union seeks and accepts less than the maximum wage it could obtain from full use of its bargaining power. The employer is likely to settle rather than to take a strike in such circumstances, since a confrontation with the union would find the employer overpowered.

Why should a strong union be reluctant to force its advantage to the limit, thus precipitating a strike? We believe that unions will not place much value on wages in excess of the wage increases being received by other unions viewed by the leaders and members as appropriate comparisons. This view on the limited exercise of power by very strong unions is consistent with the work of Ross (1948). Walton and McKersie (1965, p. 26) have reached a similar conclusion about the value of extra high wage increases:

> The value of higher settlements to the union official actually becomes negative. This is based on the assumption that settlements can be so high as to make his life difficult in certain ways. Higher figures may raise the expectations of the membership to have similar settlements in the future or to influence the expectations of other groups he also represents.

An alternative explanation of why strong unions do not precipitate strikes by exploiting their power fully is that such use of power in the short run may seriously affect the employer's competitive position or may engender public ire and thus jeopardize the union's long-run capacity to obtain large wage increases.[10]

The argument that strong unions are less strike prone because they do not use all their bargaining power is consistent with some of the empirical evidence on the relation between the degree of union organization of an industry and the extent of union influence on the relative wage. As summarized by Rees (1973a, pp. 151–153), the union approaches its maximum effect on relative wages well before it organizes the entire industry.

Assuming that line BK in Figure 1 summarizes the relationship between the propensity to strike and a union's relative bargaining power, a potential problem looms for empirical examinations, since an increase in bargaining power can be associated with more or fewer strikes. In the local government sector, however, we believe the problem is not severe. Specifically, we believe that, during the period of our empirical examination, most local government unions were weak or only moderately strong, so the factors we can identify that would be associated with increases in bargaining power would all pertain to the portion of the function with a positive slope.

A final broad category of explanations of the propensity to strike includes those psychological or sociological factors that

---

[10] Leaders of strong unions also may not precipitate strikes by translating all of the bargaining power into higher wages because their objective may be a quiet life. For a discussion of the nonpecuniary uses of monopoly power, see Alchian and Kessel (1962).

affect the predisposition of particular employees to strike. Unfortunately, it is difficult to find general concepts in this area. One can say that not all employees or work groups have the same predisposition toward the use of strike as a legitimate tactic in collective bargaining, and that not all work groups have the same capacity to organize strikes; but translating statements at this level of generality into testable propositions is difficult. For example, Kerr and Siegel offer the hypothesis that those employees who form isolated masses apart from the general society and share common job-related grievances are more likely to strike than other employees. We are unable to identify empirical counterparts to this hypothesis that have general applicability. A specific hypothesis relevant for the public-sector area, drawing upon the Kerr-Siegel approach, was utilized by Krislov in his study of government employee work stoppages. Krislov viewed sanitation employees as the prototype of workers with a high propensity to strike, and we will test that specific hypothesis.

Another fairly specific hypothesis involving psychological or sociological factors is that the size of the work group will affect the likelihood of strikes. Presumably, small work groups have more direct contact with management and thus less need to resolve disputes through strikes. Moreover, there is considerable evidence that group size tends to be negatively related to work performance and perhaps satisfaction (see Korman, 1971, pp. 107–112), and this would also suggest a tendency for large work groups to engage in a disproportionate number of strikes. Cleland (1955, p. 62), in one of the few empirical studies of the effect of plant size on industrial relations, found that "small plant size allows the intimate contact necessary to know one's workers and to provide them with a large variety of personal services, both of which contribute to good industrial relations." The personal touch in small plants was a major factor in the lower incidence of strikes in these plants. We do not have a measure of the size of work groups in the local government sector. However, we do have information on the proportion of local government employment in large cities in each state, and, on the assumption that larger cities have larger work groups, we use these data to test the hypothesis that large cities are more likely to have strikes.

154

IV. Some Specific Hypotheses about Strikes
in the Local Government Sector

The general hypotheses about strikes developed in the previous section must now be adapted to the local government, noneducation sector, the subject of our empirical examination. Figure 2 presents our view of the appropriate framework for the analysis of local government strikes. Three broad categories of factors affect the incidence of local government strikes in a state: the state environment, including the economic and political climate; the extent of public-sector unionization; and the statutory policy for labor relations in the local government sector. Three aspects of public policy are identified: statutes establishing third-party procedures for impasse resolution; statutes setting the basic policy toward collective bargaining; and statutes that establish a policy toward strikes.

These broad categories of factors interact in the determination of strikes as shown by the arrows in Figure 2. Our main concern is the direct impact of each factor on strikes, but some of the indirect effects (such as the impact of environment on unionization and thereby on strikes) will be discussed. On the assumption that we have properly specified the model, the regression coefficients shown in the next section should only reflect the direct impact of variables on strikes.

The categories identified in Figure 2 are too general to lead to

FIGURE 2.

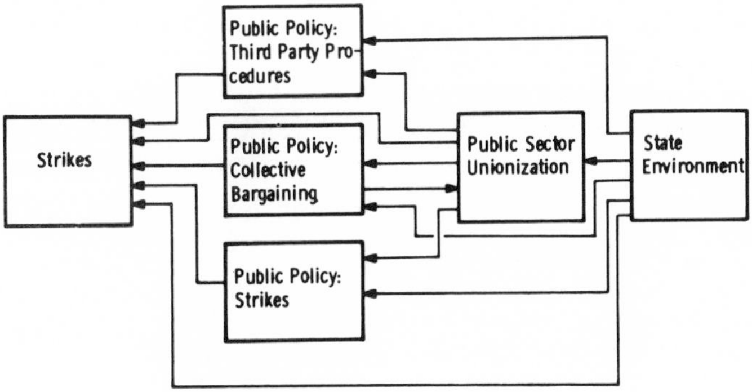

testable hypotheses; the balance of this section identifies specific variables within these general categories and indicates the expected relationship between these variables and the incidence of strikes. (The variables and their sources are listed in the Appendix, Table A1.)

The dependent variables are the number of work stoppages per million full-time equivalent employees (STKPER), the number of workers involved in strikes per thousand full-time equivalent employees (EESPER), the mean duration in days of the strikes (STKDUR), and the number of man-days idle per thousand full-time equivalent employees (DYSPER). Because of the lack of success in previous studies in explaining duration and man-days idle, our primary interest is the number of work stoppages and the number of workers involved, and the discussion of the independent variables that follows is largely directed toward an explanation of these two aspects of strike activity.

The statutory provisions governing collective bargaining by local government employees were cataloged.[11] Some states have statutes that provide third-party procedures for impasse resolution. We have created a dummy variable (ANYFFM) with a value of 1 for each state with any fact-finding or mediation procedure available for local government employees. We expect the coefficient to be negative, both because we expect third-party procedures to reduce the amount of uncertainty that each party has about the other party's position and because we expect the third-party procedures to lead to a convergence of the expectations of the parties about what is a reasonable settlement. We thus differ with Hicks's view about the impact of conciliation on expectations.

In some states there is a statutory policy for strikes by local government employees. We use a dummy variable (STKPPP) with a value of 1 for those statutes that prohibit, or prohibit and penalize, strikes by local government employees; the coefficient

[11] Tables summarizing state statutory policy for collective bargaining by local government employees will be included in a forthcoming volume by John F. Burton, Jr., and Arnold R. Weber to be published by the Brookings Institution in its series of *Studies of Unionism in Government*.

for this variable is expected to be negative. Although strikes by public employees are invariably illegal in the absence of such statutes, nonetheless we believe the statutes make strikes even more costly to public employees, thus reducing their bargaining power and propensity to strike.

A third aspect of statutory policy is the basic collective bargaining law for local government employees. In two states (North Carolina and Texas) bargaining is illegal (ILLEGL), and public employers are prohibited from signing contracts with unions. There are three variants of statutes that encourage collective bargaining. Permissive laws (PMLW1+) authorize public employers to negotiate with public employees, but bargaining is not required, nor can agreements be binding until ratified by the legislative body. Meet and confer laws (MCLW1+) require employers to meet and confer with their employees, but agreements are not binding on the employer either until a legislature ratifies the agreement or under any circumstances. Good faith laws (GFLW1+) require public employers to bargain in good faith and authorizes binding contracts. A dummy variable has been created for each of these types of laws. We expect the coefficient on ILLEGL to be negative primarily because such a law will reduce the bargaining power of unions. There should also be an indirect impact of this type of law on the extent of public sector unionization.

The expected sign of the coefficients for permissive laws (PMLW1+), meet and confer laws (MCLW1+), and good faith laws (GFLW1+) singly, or in combination (LWXX1+), is ambiguous. These laws should increase union bargaining power and increase the expectations of union leaders and rank and file members, which would tend to increase strike activity. In the short run, enactment of these laws should also increase uncertainty, thereby inducing strikes, although after the laws have been in effect for several years it is possible that the amount of uncertainty is less than it would have been had the parties been operating without statutory guidance. Since most of the laws in the public sector are relatively new, we would not expect the uncertainty-reducing result of these statutes to be demonstrable in

157

our empirical work.[12]   However, one attribute of these laws should reduce strike activity immediately, namely the establishment of a recognition procedure that eliminates the need for recognition strikes, a common source of public-sector strikes in states without collective bargaining laws. In a sense the relative bargaining power of a union becomes infinite on the recognition issue when recognition is guaranteed by statute to a majority-status union. Whether the strike-reducing aspect of collective bargaining laws that results from elimination of the recognition issue exactly, more, or less than offsets the increase in strikes on other issues that we expect to flow from enactment of bargaining laws is unclear on a priori grounds.

States with a high proportion of their public-sector labor force unionized (PUBUNZ) are expected to have more strikes than states with less extensive unionization. Unionized employees should have greater bargaining power and higher wage expectations than nonunionized employees, and both factors would increase the chances of strikes. Increased public-sector unionization may also have an indirect impact on the number of strikes. Strongly unionized states are more likely to have public policies that encourage collective bargaining and are less repressive toward strikes. Public-sector unions may also make more likely the enactment of statutes that provide impasse resolution procedures, which is a factor that would tend to reduce strikes with strong public-sector unions. However, this indirect consequence of public-sector unions on the likelihood of strikes is likely to be overcome by the factors that would increase the number of strikes in the presence of greater unionization.

Figure 2 also contains the state environment as one of the categories that influences public sector strikes. We include in this category those economic, political, and sociological factors that appear to have an impact on the public collective bargaining system, but that themselves are largely unaffected by public-sector bargaining.

---

[12] A final reason why the presence of one of the three statutory forms of encouraging bargaining should increase strikes is that the laws encourage public unionization and thus indirectly the number of strikes.

The extent of private-sector unionization (PVTUNZ) in the state is expected to be positively associated with the number of public-sector strikes.[13] Public unions will have greater bargaining power in a state with extensive private unionization, because the support of private unions will make it less costly for public unions to strike and will make it easier for public employers to respond favorably to their employees' demands. Extensive private unionization can also be expected to increase the expectations of public-union members about a reasonable wage increase. A variable that is the obverse of the extent of private unionization is the presence of a right-to-work law in the state (RTTOWK). This law is indicative of a general public attitude unfavorable to unionization, which should reduce the bargaining power and the expectations of public-union members.

Several economic variables should influence the extent of strikes. The state's unemployment rate (UN) should be negatively related to the number of strikes in the state. Consistent with the Rees (1952) and the Ashenfelter and Johnson (1969) studies, we assume that economic factors in the labor market are likely to have their primary impact on expectations of union leaders and union members, while other economic factors are more likely to influence the expectations of management. Thus the unemployment rate in a state should be inversely related to the number of strikes because higher unemployment should reduce the expectations of the members about a reasonable wage settlement. Higher unemployment should also reduce the public union's bargaining power. We have also measured the ratio of public- to private-sector earnings in each state (ERNRAT) and the change in that earnings ratio in the immediate past (DERNRT), and we expect both variables to be negatively related to strike activity. As this wage ratio increases, the expectations of union members about further wage increases should decline. The bargaining power of the unions should also decline, since, among other things, it will be harder to gain support from

[13] More precisely, PVTUNZ represents total union membership in a state (including public union members) as a percentage of the state's total nonagricultural labor force.

159

private unions as public wages began to pull ahead of those else-where in the state.

Ashenfelter and Johnson (1969) suggested that the level of profits provided a proxy for the employer's expectations about a reasonable wage increase. Higher profits increased the expecta-tions of employers about a reasonable wage increase, thereby reducing the likelihood of strikes. Unfortunately, higher profits also increased the expectations of employees about reasonable wage increases, thus increasing the likelihood of strikes and mak-ing the net impact of higher profits on strikes ambiguous. In the public sector there are, of course, no data on profits. The economic variable that seems to be of most concern to public employers in governing their expectations about reasonable wage increases is a level of taxes, and we have calculated taxes as a percentage of personal income in each state (TAXPCT). A reason why the coefficient should be positive is that a higher tax rate should lower the expectations of employers about a reasonable wage increase, thereby inducing strikes. However, higher taxes should reduce the bargaining power of unions, thus tending to reduce the number of strikes. On net, however, we expect the coefficient to be positive.

Two variables draw on psychological or sociological explana-tions of strike behavior. The percentage of local government employees in sanitation (SANPCT) is expected to be positively related to the number of strikes. Sanitation workers appear to have more bargaining power than most public-sector employees, and this increased bargaining power should increase their pro-pensity to strike. Also, more strikes are expected based on the Kerr-Siegel (1954) and Krislov (1961) views about the strike propensity of such workers.[14] A similar variable is the percentage of public employment in each state located in cities of 50,000 or more (50KPCT). The literature suggests that large units are more strike prone, and, on the assumption that bigger cities have

[14] An additional reason why public sanitation workers might be relatively strike-prone compared to other public-sector employees is that a relatively high proportion of sanitation workers are in the private sector and thus can freely strike, and this behavior pattern may be emulated by their public-sector counterparts.

bigger work groups, more strikes in large cities are expected. Also, big cities are probably more vulnerable to strikes, and we would thus expect the greater bargaining power of unions in big cities to lead to more strikes.

V. Empirical Results

The test of a theory is its predictive power, and, with that criterion, our theory is something less than fully vindicated. Regressions using the full set of dependent variables listed in Table A1 and subsets of the independent variables were run for each of the four measures of strike activity. The results for the average duration (STKDUR) regressions are so poor they have been relegated to the Appendix (Table A3). The balance of this section discusses only the results using number of strikes (STKPER), number of striking employees (EESPER), and number of man-days idle (DYSPER) as dependent variables. The results for the latter variable (DYSPER) are weaker than for the other two, which is not surprising given the poor results for the average duration (STKDUR) regressions, since man-days idle is a product of average duration and the number of striking employees. Preliminary analysis of the data showed evidence of heteroscedasticity, so this section relies on observations weighted by each state's number of full-time equivalent employees in the local government, noneducation sector.[15]

[15] One of the assumptions of the linear regression model is that the disturbances are uncorrelated random variables with constant variance. In the case where heteroscedasticity exists because the disturbance variance is a function of the size of the sample underlying each data observation, the deficiency can be overcome by weighting each observation by its sample size. Goldfeld and Quandt (1965) have proposed a test for heteroscedasticity, and an alternative test is available based on theoretical work by Henri Theil. The Theil test has certain advantages, as briefly described in Burton (1969) and detailed in Theil (1971, Chapter 5). However, the computer program necessary to perform the Theil test for heteroscedasticity is unavailable at the University of Chicago, and so the Goldfeld and Quandt test was used. Because the test would reduce the number of degrees of freedom considerably if all of the independent variables shown in Table 4 were used, the test was performed using the small model with four independent

161

Tables 4–6 present results for regressions using the full set of independent variables. There are regressions for the individual years 1968, 1969, 1970, and 1971, and for pooled data for 1968–1971. The overall explanatory power of the regressions is limited. Some regressions are quite respectable, but many are not, and we are impressed by the instability of the model from year to year. Coefficients for the individual variables are generally insignificant and often have signs inconsistent with our expectations. Even those variables that have significant coefficients in some years are insignificant in most; further, sign changes in significant coefficients for the same variable are found.

The record of success for the independent variables varies. Among the environmental variables, private unionization (PVTUNZ) was expected to have a positive coefficient and the right-to-work law (RTTOWK) a negative coefficient, and these signs appear in a substantial majority of the regressions. PVTUNZ is significant at the 10 percent level four times in Tables 4–6, always with the right sign. However, RTTOWK is significant only three times, and once (in a regression with DYSPER as the dependent variable) with the incorrect sign. Another variable with equal lack of success is the unemployment rate (UN), which was expected to have a negative coefficient and does for two of the three significant coefficients.

Other environmental variables generally are also unsuccessful. The earnings ratio (ERNRAT) and the change in earnings ratio (DERNRT) were expected to have negative coefficients. The former is never significant; DERNRT is negative and significant seven times, the best result for any of the economic variables. The tax percentage (TAXPCT) is significant in five regressions, but always has the wrong sign.

---

variables that is represented in Tables 7–9. The test provided evidence of heteroscedasticity for all regressions involving number of strikes (STKPER) or number of striking employees (EESPER) as the dependent variable, thus justifying the use of weighted regressions for these dependent variables. There is also evidence of heteroscedasticity in two of the four years for the regressions involving the number of man-days idle (DYSPER). In order to simplify the discussion, our analysis relies on weighted regressions for all years and for all dependent variables.

TABLE 4. Determinants of Interstate Variations in Strikes per Million FTE Employees[a]

	1968	1969	1970	1971	1968-71 pooled
Constant	461.8	248.4	45.34	133.0	132.6
	(4.8)	(2.5)	(0.3)	(1.6)	(2.6)
Private Unionization	0.61	2.97	3.27	3.53	2.80
	(0.4)	(1.6)	(1.4)	(2.2)	(3.2)
Public Unionization	1.47	0.08	−1.25	0.34	−0.14
	(2.7)	(0.1)	(1.4)	(0.5)	(0.4)
Earnings Ratio	−97.38	−141.8	2.99	43.45	−27.29
	(1.5)	(1.3)	(0.0)	(0.5)	(0.7)
Change in Earnings Ratio	−6.59	−2.29	4.14	1.03	−1.90
	(2.8)	(0.9)	(1.1)	(0.6)	(2.2)
Unemployment Rate	−11.72	−13.84	8.42	−5.64	4.33
	(1.0)	(0.9)	(0.6)	(0.7)	(1.3)
Tax Percentage	−35.11	−11.43	−4.17	−19.10	−13.28
	(4.5)	(1.2)	(0.4)	(2.4)	(3.3)
Percent Employment in Cities over 50,000	−0.01	−0.62	−21.62	−0.69	−0.32
	(1.2)	(0.5)	(0.3)	(1.4)	(1.1)
Percent Employment in Sanitation	13.61	14.63	8.46	10.16	8.41
	(2.2)	(2.3)	(1.1)	(1.7)	(2.8)
Right to Work Law	−31.63	−36.95	−64.68	−45.15	−33.91
	(1.3)	(1.2)	(1.7)	(1.6)	(2.3)
Permissive Law	−15.61	−108.1	−31.50	14.27	−28.83
	(0.3)	(1.7)	(0.5)	(0.3)	(1.2)
Meet and Confer Law	60.83	−31.75	−93.38	−23.10	−21.26
	(1.9)	(0.6)	(1.7)	(0.5)	(1.1)
Good Faith Law	90.55	−89.73	−60.43	−40.72	−36.60
	(1.8)	(1.5)	(1.0)	(0.9)	(1.8)
Bargaining Illegal	42.62	−15.96	−21.14	−30.99	−4.89
	(1.3)	(0.3)	(0.4)	(0.9)	(0.3)
Third Party Procedure Law	0.62	100.40	44.45	15.27	33.51
	(0.0)	(1.8)	(0.9)	(0.4)	(2.0)
Strikes Prohibited or Penalized	−44.71	3.08	10.28	18.39	−1.21
	(1.9)	(1.2)	(0.3)	(0.9)	(0.1)
R^2	.59	.52	.38	.59	.34

[a]Absolute values of t-statistics here and in Tables 5–9.

TABLE 5. Determinants of Interstate Variation in Striking Employees per Thousand FTE Employees

	1968	1969	1970	1971	1968–71 pooled
Constant	73.20	21.01	−40.81	−63.52	−16.36
	(2.1)	(0.5)	(0.9)	(2.2)	(0.9)
Private Unionization	0.67	0.15	−0.21	1.21	0.53
	(1.3)	(0.2)	(0.3)	(3.1)	(1.6)
Public Unionization	0.19	0.15	0.18	0.40	0.23
	(1.0)	(0.6)	(0.6)	(2.6)	(1.9)
Earnings Ratio	−27.04	−17.47	40.22	9.89	11.94
	(1.2)	(0.5)	(1.3)	(0.5)	(0.8)
Change in Earnings Ratio	−1.18	−1.81	−0.79	−0.70	−1.00
	(1.4)	(2.0)	(0.7)	(1.7)	(3.1)
Unemployment Rate	−.44	−2.20	5.87	−7.34	2.50
	(0.1)	(0.4)	(1.4)	(3.9)	(2.0)
Tax Percent	−7.43	−0.27	−1.18	2.74	−2.39
	(2.6)	(0.1)	(0.4)	(1.4)	(1.6)
Percentage Employment in Cities over 50,000	0.33	0.04	−0.26	−0.15	−.04
	(1.0)	(0.1)	(1.4)	(1.2)	(0.4)
Percent Employment in Sanitation	2.52	4.26	3.18	7.20	3.27
	(1.2)	(1.9)	(1.4)	(5.0)	(3.0)
Right to Work Law	3.63	−14.01	−11.14	−2.01	−3.10
	(0.4)	(1.3)	(0.9)	(0.3)	(0.6)
Permissive Law	−0.15	−11.71	−11.01	29.84	−1.16
	(0.0)	(0.5)	(0.6)	(2.8)	(0.1)
Meet and Confer Law	9.44	−6.41	−2.31	29.35	−2.86
	(0.8)	(0.3)	(0.1)	(2.7)	(0.4)
Good Faith Law	15.43	−17.76	−21.20	42.52	−4.69
	(0.8)	(0.8)	(1.1)	(3.9)	(0.6)
Bargaining Illegal	1.39	−3.20	−3.39	14.24	4.80
	(0.1)	(0.2)	(0.2)	(1.7)	(0.7)
Third Party Procedure Law	11.50	10.72	4.53	−22.83	4.15
	(0.9)	(0.5)	(0.3)	(2.4)	(0.7)
Strikes Prohibited or Penalized	−24.32	−1.35	2.77	−1.36	−5.45
	(2.9)	(0.1)	(0.3)	(0.3)	(1.3)
R^2	.43	.28	.31	.86	.20

TABLE 6. Determinants of Interstate Variations in Man-Days Idle per Thousand FTE Employees

	1968	1969	1970	1971	1968–71 pooled
Constant	729.9	199.7	−148.6	−303.7	−31.25
	(1.3)	(0.5)	(0.4)	(2.0)	(0.2)
Private Unionization	1.62	1.39	−0.20	7.61	4.64
	(0.2)	(0.2)	(0.0)	(3.6)	(1.5)
Public Unionization	5.42	−2.30	1.38	1.19	1.69
	(1.7)	(0.9)	(0.6)	(1.4)	(1.5)
Earnings Ratio	−621.6	−260.3	4.00	−9.41	−62.83
	(1.7)	(0.7)	(0.0)	(0.1)	(0.5)
Change in Earnings Ratio	−10.32	4.38	−13.19	−4.91	−5.77
	(0.7)	(0.5)	(1.4)	(2.2)	(1.9)
Unemployment Rate	68.96	10.02	49.48	−28.99	10.72
	(1.0)	(0.2)	(1.5)	(2.9)	(0.9)
Tax Percentage	−111.9	−0.17	−1.98	12.74	−16.01
	(2.4)	(0.0)	(0.1)	(1.2)	(1.1)
Percent Employment in Cities over 50,000	18.36	−1.32	−1.53	−0.59	−0.31
	(3.2)	(0.3)	(1.0)	(0.9)	(0.3)
Percent Employment in Sanitation	−17.02	40.95	16.52	35.19	28.22
	(0.5)	(1.9)	(0.9)	(4.6)	(2.7)
Right to Work Law	468.6	−82.71	−33.23	23.88	61.95
	(3.2)	(0.8)	(0.3)	(0.6)	(1.2)
Permissive Law	50.38	−46.59	−189.4	93.84	−36.51
	(0.2)	(0.2)	(0.1)	(1.6)	(0.4)
Meet and Confer Law	135.4	117.8	−38.51	170.0	30.95
	(0.7)	(0.7)	(0.3)	(3.0)	(0.5)
Good Faith Law	−300.1	6.82	−188.0	210.1	−9.80
	(1.0)	(0.1)	(1.2)	(3.6)	(0.1)
Bargaining Illegal	−302.0	−145.4	−103.6	79.44	−54.40
	(1.5)	(0.9)	(0.8)	(1.7)	(0.8)
Third Party Procedure Law	403.2	37.71	39.05	−97.00	23.05
	(1.9)	(0.2)	(0.3)	(1.9)	(0.4)
Strikes Prohibited or Penalized	−354.4	43.77	87.69	−35.28	−33.56
	(2.6)	(0.5)	(1.2)	(1.3)	(0.8)
R^2	.47	.24	.30	.80	.10

JOHN F. BURTON, JR., & CHARLES E. KRIDER

The final environmental variables are the percentage of employment in sanitation (SANPCT) and the percentage of employment in cities of 50,000 and over (50KPCT), for both of which positive signs were expected. The sign on 50KPCT almost always violates our expectation, although the only significant coefficient is positive.[16] SANPCT wins the environmental variable sweepstakes by having the right sign in 14 of 15 regressions, usually with a significant coefficient.

Public unionization (PUBUNZ) has surprisingly weak results. The coefficient is almost always positive, but is only thrice significant. Perhaps the fault lies in the accuracy of the measurement of public unionization, but we are not inclined to subscribe fully to this position since the variable works well in another context.[17]

The influence of public policy on strike activity by public employees is apparently limited. The coefficients on the variables for good faith laws (GFLW1+), meet and confer laws (MCLW1+), and permissive laws (PMLW1+) are significant only nine times out of 45 opportunities in Tables 4-6, with seven of the significant coefficients positive. If laws encouraging collective bargaining perhaps have a mild tendency to encourage strikes, laws making bargaining illegal (ILLEGL) show no potency: indeed, the only significant coefficient is positive. Further, the coefficient on the

[16] The mean value for 50KPCT increases substantially between 1969 and 1970, as shown in Table A2, reflecting the once-a-decade reclassification of cities on the basis of size. This discontinuity must be considered when evaluating the regression results for 50KPCT, particularly the regressions with pooled 1968-1971 data.

[17] As part of our general examination of public collective bargaining, we are developing a model to explain the extent of public-sector unionization in each state. An example of our results, using unweighted data for 1969, is

$$PUBUNZ = 6.92 + 13.67 \, LWXX3+ \; -21.57 \, ILLEGL + \; 0.54 \, 50KPCT$$
$$(1.0) \quad (2.6) \qquad\qquad (2.0) \qquad\qquad (4.0)$$
$$+0.79 \, PVTUNZ, \qquad R^2 = .60$$
$$(2.9)$$

All variables are defined in Table A1 except LWXX3+, which indicates the presence of a permissive, meet-and-confer, or good-faith law in the state for three or more years.

166

variable measuring statutory prohibition or penalty for strikes (STKPPP) is significant only three times, always negative. The final public policy variable is ANYFFM, which measures a statutory provision of fact-finding or mediation. For ANYFFM, three of the five significant coefficients are positive, again suggesting the limited impact of public policy on the strike propensity.

We ran regressions that also included a set of dummy variables indicating the Census region in which each state is located. There is no a priori reason to expect one region to have more strikes than another after all the other independent variables are taken into account, but it is possible that there is an area effect operating, whereby public-sector unrest spreads from one state to other nearby states. Results with the regressions using regional dummies differ in certain particulars from the results in Tables 4–6, but the general inability to explain strikes persists. There is no consistent tendency for any region to have an unusual amount of strike activity after the effect of the other independent variables is considered. Still another variant we attempted was to redefine the dependent variables to exclude strikes that involved recognition as one of the issues. We hypothesized that recognition strikes are typically more volatile because of the immaturity of the bargaining relationship, and that strikes over issues other than recognition should therefore be more predictable. However, the regressions excluding recognition strikes were not superior statistically to the regressions in Tables 4–6.[18]

The results in Tables 4–6 and the variants described in the preceding paragraph use the full set of independent variables. We also ran regressions with a limited number of independent variables, since there is a potential multicollinearity problem because of the high correlation among some of the independent vari-

[18] Another variant on the regressions in Tables 4–6 we attempted was to use combined-years data. For example, we used 50 observations for which all variables had the average value for 1968 and 1969. Similarly, we used two-year averages for 1970 and 1971, and four-year averages for 1968–1971. In some instances, the combined years data provided results that were superior to the individual years data, but the opposite was true for other results. Overall there was no improvement in our empirical work from the use of combined data, and the results are therefore not shown.

ables.[19] The culmination of our efforts to limit the variables is the model represented in Tables 7–9. This small model was developed by running a series of regressions confined to the 1969 data until we found a model with reasonable explanatory power; this model was then applied to other years in our sample.

With one exception, the regressions explaining the number of strikes (STKPER) or the number of striking employees (STKPER) have an R^2 with an implied F-ratio that is significant.[20] The results for man-days idle (DYSPER) are less impressive, although both the 1971 and 1968–1971 pooled regressions are significant. As measured by the coefficient of determination, only a limited proportion of the interstate variation in strike activity can be explained by this small model. Nonetheless, it appears that certain environmental variables can consistently explain a portion of the interstate variation in strike activity. Particularly impressive as an explanatory variable is private unionization (PVTUNZ), which has a significant and positive coefficient for 11 of the 15 regressions in Tables 7–9. The change in earnings ratio (DERNRT) and the percent employment in sanitation (SANPCT) explain little of the variation in man-days idle (Table 9), but each variable is significant in half of the regressions in Tables 7 and 8. Least impressive of the independent variables in the small model is tax percentage (TAXPCT); 8 of the 15 coefficients in Tables 7–9 are significant, but 6 of the significant coefficients have a negative sign, inconsistent with our hypothesis.

The small model in Tables 7–9 contains only variables that measure aspects of the state's environment because we could not find a public policy variable that was consistently significant. We did find that the presence of any law encouraging collective bargaining (LWXX1+) has a positive and significant coefficient (when used in combination with the four independent variables

---

[19] High correlations are especially prevalent among the independent variables measuring public policy. In 1971, for example, the simple correlation coefficient between LWXX1+ (law encouraging bargaining) and ANYFFM (third party procedure law) is 0.75.

[20] Unweighted regressions using the special model with four independent variables were run on subsets of the data to test for heteroscedasticity; a discussion of heteroscedasticity is included in n. 15.

TABLE 7. Determinants of Interstate Variations in Strikes per Million
FTE Employees

	1968	1969	1970	1971	1968–71 pooled
Constant	171.6	126.3	101.8	114.2	122.3
	(3.1)	(1.9)	(1.4)	(1.9)	(4.0)
Private Unionization	2.25	2.98	3.64	4.37	3.05
	(2.6)	(2.9)	(2.9)	(5.3)	(6.4)
Change in Earnings Ratio	−4.18	−3.04	0.32	0.38	−1.74
	(1.8)	(1.3)	(0.1)	(0.3)	(2.2)
Tax Percentage	−18.93	−15.94	−13.91	−18.11	−14.91
	(4.3)	(3.0)	(2.2)	(4.2)	(6.4)
Percent Employed in	6.59	6.94	4.80	3.45	3.82
Sanitation	(1.4)	(1.5)	(0.9)	(0.8)	(1.8)
R^2	.33	.32	.19	.46	.26

TABLE 8. Determinants of Interstate Variations in Striking Employees per Thousand
FTE Employees

	1968	1969	1970	1971	1968–71 pooled
Constant	7.93	−11.73	8.32	−130.5	−26.13
	(0.4)	(0.5)	(0.3)	(6.6)	(2.4)
Private Unionization	0.77	0.65	0.22	1.82	0.77
	(2.7)	(1.9)	(0.6)	(6.7)	(4.4)
Change in Earnings Ratio	−0.87	−1.75	0.45	−0.78	−0.72
	(1.1)	(2.3)	(0.5)	(1.8)	(2.5)
Tax Percentage	2.46	−0.26	−0.01	5.99	0.90
	(1.7)	(0.2)	(0.0)	(4.3)	(1.1)
Percent Employed in	3.15	3.48	−0.06	8.45	2.85
Sanitation	(2.0)	(2.3)	(0.0)	(6.2)	(3.6)
R^2	.17	.19	.02	.69	.14

TABLE 9. Determinants of Interstate Variations in Man-Days Idle per Thousand
FTE Employees

	1968	1969	1970	1971	1968–71 pooled
Constant	3.31	90.68	117.1	−530.6	−75.08
	(0.0)	(0.4)	(0.6)	(5.7)	(0.7)
Private Unionization	2.25	1.63	4.13	8.17	4.20
	(0.4)	(0.5)	(1.3)	(6.4)	(2.6)
Change in Earnings Ratio	−8.88	−2.70	−6.76	−3.21	−4.35
	(0.6)	(0.4)	(1.0)	(1.6)	(0.6)
Tax Percentage	−6.84	−13.63	−11.28	21.82	−2.67
	(0.2)	(0.8)	(0.7)	(3.3)	(0.3)
Percent Employment in	39.01	19.87	−0.02	37.70	22.47
Sanitation	(1.3)	(1.3)	(0.0)	(5.9)	(3.1)
R^2	.05	.09	.08	.65	.07

JOHN F. BURTON, JR., & CHARLES E. KRIDER

included in Tables 7–9) for 1971 regressions explaining the number of striking employees (STKPER) and the number of man-days idle (DYSPER). These regressions suggest that a public policy that encourages collective bargaining also promotes strike activity. This finding is not supported by our overall results, however, since in similar regressions for 1968, 1969, 1970, and 1968–1971 pooled data, the coefficient for LWXX1+ is never significant.[21]

VI. Conclusions

We examined previous studies of strike activity. We identified some general hypotheses about strikes based on this survey and derived testable hypotheses about this model for the local government sector. Unfortunately, our analysis of the data for all local government, noneducation strikes that took place between 1968 and 1971 reveals limited explanatory power for our hypotheses. With a few exceptions, most of the variations among states in strike activity in a particular year cannot be explained by our variables, and those variables that appear important in one year often are unimportant or have an opposite effect in other years.

There are a variety of possible reasons for our limited success.

[21] The statistical results included in Tables 4–9 are based on ordinary least-squares (OLS) regressions. If the directions of causation in Figure 2 are correct, however, several of the independent variables used in the analysis are endogenous. This means there is a possibility of simultaneous-equations bias in the regression coefficients. A discussion of simultaneous equations models is contained in Theil (1971, Chapters 9–10).

Arguably, in addition to the four independent variables included in Tables 7–9, a properly specified model should include the variable LWXX1+, the presence of a law encouraging collective bargaining. On the assumptions that LWXX1+ is endogenous and that the system is not recursive, one of the appropriate statistical techniques is two-stage least-squares (2SLS), as described by Theil (1971, pp. 451–460). We ran 2SLS regressions comparable to the OLS regressions in Tables 7–9 except that LWXX1+ was added as an endogenous independent variable. A total of 30 2SLS regressions were run, since there are three dependent variables, five time periods, and two combinations of instrumental variables. In no case did the t-statistic for the regression coefficient for LWXX1+ reach the conventional .10 significance level.

170

The strike data may be inaccurate because of limitations in the procedure used by the Bureau of Labor Standards to compile the information.[22]   There may, of course, be variables we have not considered or statistical techniques we have not used that would reveal systematic behavior in strike activity.   The simplest explanation, though, is that most public-sector strike activity is unpredictable.

Our hypotheses do explain some of the differences among states in public-sector strike activity.   The variables with the best explanatory power across years and states are those pertaining to the state's environment. For example, the proportion of the local government employment in sanitation consistently is positively associated with the number of strikes and strikers in the state.

The environmental factors are largely beyond the control of public policy, while those elements that can be controlled by public policy seem to have little impact on strikes. For example, the statutory prohibition on strikes has little apparent impact on the incidence of strikes, nor does the enactment of a law either prohibiting or encouraging collective bargaining by public employees appear to affect materially the number of local government strikes.   Another aspect of public policy that does not appear to influence strike activity is the availability of fact-finding or mediation.

One way of looking at our results concerning the impact of public policy on strikes is to view such statutory efforts as futile, but there is another way of viewing the evidence that we prefer to stress. Those states that encourage collective bargaining because they believe this is a meritorious way to determine working conditions for public employees do not incur a rash of strikes as a consequence.   In this sense, our findings may encourage the enactment of statutes supporting bargaining rights for public employees.

While we are sympathetic to the enactment of such statutes, we

[22]The Bureau of Labor Statistics primarily relies on newspaper reports to learn of public-sector strikes, and an unknown number of strikes are unreported. The 1972 Census of Governments included a question about strikes, and when the data are available, a partial evaluation of the accuracy of the BLS data will be possible.

do not mean to suggest that the evidence in this paper in favor of their enactment is very strong.[23]   Indeed, the most compelling conclusion of our work for us is that the industrial relations research community and policy makers have almost no evidence on which to base assertions about the impact of public policy on strike activity.

[23] We believe that most local government employees should have the right to bargain and to strike (see Burton and Krider, 1970). However, in this paper we are concerned solely with the determinants of strike activity and make no normative judgments about the desirable quantity of strike activity.

APPENDIX

TABLE A1. Sources of Data Used in the Statistical Analysis and Exact
Description of the Variables

A. *Dependent Variables*

Abbreviation	*Description and Sources of Data*
STKPER	The number of strikes per million full-time equivalent (FTE) employees.
EESPER	The number of employees on strike per thousand FTE employees.
DYSPER	The number of man-days idle per thousand FTE employees.
STKDUR	The mean duration of strikes. The number of man-days idle divided by the number of employees on strike.
	Sources: Strike data from Bureau of Labor Statistics files which were examined by Charles Krider; *data on number of full-time equivalent employees* in local government, non-education sector from U.S., Dept. of Commerce, Bureau of the Census, *Public Employment in 1968* (1969, 1970, 1971), Table 8.

B. *Independent Variables Other Than Public Policy Variables*

Abbreviation	*Description and Sources of Data*
PVTUNZ	*Private unionization.* Total membership in labor unions as a percent of the nonagricultural labor force.
	Source: U.S., Dept. of Labor, Bureau of Labor Statistics, *Directory of National Unions and Employee Associations 1971* (Bull. 1750). The 1969 value was interpolated and the 1971 value was projected on the basis of 1968 and 1970 data.
PUBUNZ	*Public Unionization.* The percent of noneducation, local government employees who were represented by a labor union in a recognized bargaining unit in 1968.
	Source: Unpublished data from Jack Stieber, Director, School of Labor and Industrial Relations, Michigan State University. For a description of the data, see Stieber, Jack, "Employee Representation in Municipal Government," in *The Municipal Year Book 1969*, pp. 31–57. Washington: The International City Management Association, 1969.
ERNRAT	*Earnings ratio.* Ratio of public sector-employee earnings to private-sector employee earnings. The public-sector

173

employee earnings are average monthly earnings of full-time, local government, noneducation employees. The private-sector employee earnings are the average weekly earnings of manufacturing production workers times $4\frac{1}{3}$ (which converts the data to monthly figures).

DERNRT   *Change in earnings ratio.* The percent change in the earnings ratio from three to one year ago.

Sources: Public sector earnings in U.S., Dept. of Commerce, Bureau of the Census, *Public Employment in 1968* (1969, 1970, 1971), Table 7; *Private sector earnings*, U.S., Dept. of Labor, Bureau of Labor Statistics, *Employment and Earnings in States and Areas 1939–71* (Bull. 1370–9).

UN   *Unemployment rate.* The unemployment rate for the state's civilian labor force.

Source: U.S., Dept. of Labor, *Manpower Report of the President*, 1972, Table D-4.

TAXPCT   *Tax percentage.* Per capita state and local government taxes as a percent of per capita personal income.

Sources: Tax data from U.S., Dept. of Commerce, Bureau of the Census, *Governmental Finances in 1967–68* (1968–69, 1969–70, 1970–71), Table 26; *personal income data* from U.S., Dept. of Commerce, Bureau of the Census, *Survey of Current Business*, August 1968 (1969, 1970, 1971).

50KPCT   *Percent employment in cities over 50,000.* The percent of FTE noneducation, local government employment in cities with a population 50,000 or over.

SANPCT   *Percent employment in sanitation.* The percent of FTE noneducation, local government employment in sanitation.

Sources: Total number of full-time equivalent employees source is given above; *number of full-time equivalent employees in cities over 50,000*, U.S., Dept. of Commerce, Bureau of the Census, *City Employment in 1968* (1969, 1970, 1971), Table 3; *number of full-time equivalent employees in sanitation* from U.S., Dept. of Commerce, Bureau of the Census, *Public Employment in 1968* (1969, 1970, 1971), Table 8.

RTTOWK   *Right to work law.* A dummy variable for a right to work law. (1 = law; 0 = no law.)

Source: U.S., Dept. of Labor, Bureau of Labor Statistics, *Directory of National Unions and Employee Associations 1971* (Bull. 1750), Table 18.

174

C. *Public Policy Variables*

Abbreviation	Description and Source of Data
PMLW1+	*Permissive law.* A dummy variable for a permissive collective bargaining law. (1 = law; 0 = no law.)
MCLW1+	*Meet and confer law.* A dummy variable for a meet and confer collective bargaining law. (1 = law; 0 = no law.)
GFLW1+	*Good faith law.* A dummy variable for a good faith collective bargaining law. (1 = law; 0 = no law.)
LWXX1+	*Bargaining encouraged.* A dummy variable for a state with a good faith, permissive, or meet and confer collective bargaining law. (1 = law; 0 = no law.) (This variable is used in place of GFLW1+, PMLW1+, and MCLW1+ in certain regressions.)
ILLEGL	*Bargaining illegal.* A dummy variable for a law which prohibits collective bargaining. (1 = law; 0 = no law.)
ANYFFM	*Third party procedure law.* A dummy variable for a law with procedures for resolving bargaining impasses through mediation or fact finding or both. (1 = law; 0 = no law.)
STKPPP	*Strikes prohibited or penalized.* A dummy variable for a law which prohibits strikes or which prohibits and penalizes strikes. (1 = law; 0 = no law.)
	Source: Based on tables that will be included in *Collective Bargaining in the Public Sector,* by John F. Burton, Jr. and Arnold R. Weber, a volume which will be published by the Brookings Institution in its series of *Studies of Unionism in Government.*

175

TABLE A2. Means and Standard Deviations of Dependent and Independent Variables, by Year

	1968	1969	1970	1971	1968-71
Strikes per 1,000,000 FTE	48.7	55.4	92.7	54.3	62.8
Employees	(72.0)	(68.6)	(129.2)	(96.7)	(95.7)
Employees on Strike per	10.7	12.5	17.8	12.2	13.3
1,000 FTE Employees	(21.2)	(30.8)	(36.5)	(30.4)	(30.1)
Private Unionization	24.1	23.9	23.8	23.6	23.9
	(8.7)	(8.7)	(8.8)	(9.0)	(8.7)
Public Unionization	42.7	42.7	42.7	42.7	42.7
	(21.8)	(21.8)	(21.8)	(21.8)	(21.8)
Change in Earnings Ratio	4.8	3.9	0.9	4.8	3.6
	(4.8)	(5.1)	(4.3)	(5.2)	(5.1)
Earnings Ratio	.934	.943	.979	.981	.959
	(.148)	(.144)	(.165)	(.164)	(.156)
Unemployment Rate	3.81	3.68	4.84	5.64	4.49
	(1.15)	(1.09)	(1.33)	(1.51)	(1.50)
Tax Percentage	9.9	10.2	10.8	10.9	10.4
	(1.3)	(1.3)	(1.3)	(1.4)	(1.4)
Percent Employment in	27.6	27.5	37.3	37.1	32.4
Cities over 50,000	(16.8)	(16.6)	(30.7)	(30.7)	(25.0)
Percent Employment in	4.58	4.64	4.42	4.27	4.48
Sanitation	(2.23)	(2.44)	(2.32)	(2.15)	(2.27)
Right to Work Law	.380	.380	.380	.380	.380
	(.490)	(.490)	(.490)	(.490)	(.490)
Good Faith Law	.140	.180	.200	.260	.195
	(.351)	(.388)	(.404)	(.443)	(.397)
Permissive Law	.080	.100	.100	.100	.095
	(.274)	(.303)	(.303)	(.303)	(.294)
Meet and Confer Law	.060	.060	.080	.060	.065
	(.240)	(.240)	(.274)	(.240)	(.247)
Bargaining Illegal	.040	.040	.040	.040	.040
	(.198)	(.198)	(.198)	(.198)	(.198)
Third Party Procedure Law	.240	.320	.320	.380	.315
	(.431)	(.471)	(.471)	(.490)	(.466)
Strikes Prohibited or	.280	.320	.340	.320	.315
Penalized	(.454)	(.471)	(.479)	(.471)	(.466)
Permissive, Good Faith or	.280	.340	.380	.420	.355
Meet and Confer Law	(.454)	(.479)	(.490)	(.499)	(.480)
Man-days idle per 1,000	85.5	84.9	99.9	47.5	79.5
FTE Employees	(263.4)	(235.9)	(160.6)	(108.2)	(201.0)
Average Duration of Strikes	8.03	10.27	7.43	5.83	7.96
	(12.39)	(15.05)	(10.25)	(7.99)	(11.74)

TABLE A3. Determinants of Interstate Variations in Duration of Strikes[a]
(Duration measured in Days)

	1968–71 pooled
Constant	20.02
	(0.7)
Private Unionization	0.16
	(0.4)
Public Unionization	0.10
	(0.7)
Earnings Ratio	−19.08
	(0.9)
Change in Earnings Ratio	−0.83
	(0.9)
Unemployment Rate	2.39
	(0.9)
Tax Percentage	−2.42
	(1.2)
Percent Employment in Cities over 50,000	0.28
	(1.7)
Percent Employment in Sanitation	0.90
	(0.7)
Right to Work Law	11.90
	(1.8)
Permissive Law	−2.26
	(0.2)
Meet and Confer Law	3.25
	(0.3)
Good Faith Law	−10.45
	(0.8)
Bargaining Illegal	−9.18
	(1.1)
Third Party Procedure Law	7.88
	(0.7)
Strikes Prohibited or Penalized	−5.70
	(1.0)
R^2	.40

[a]Absolute value of t-statistics in parentheses. There is a single observation for each state with at least one strike in this period.

COMMENTS

JACK STIEBER

In few areas of public policy have the "experts" had so little influence as in the statutory treatment of strikes in public employment. Most labor specialists oppose a blanket prohibition of strikes by government employees; yet almost all states with laws regulating collective bargaining in public employment have such a prohibition. Acceptance of compulsory arbitration as a way of resolving disputes in public employment is growing, even though it is not favored, except perhaps for police and firefighter disputes, by most labor specialists including experienced arbitrators. The Burton-Krider paper helps explain this gap between the so-called experts and the makers of public policy by showing how little we know about the factors influencing the incidence of public-employee strikes.

Before considering the substance of the Burton-Krider paper, it should be noted that a number of random factors have compounded the inherently difficult task the authors set for themselves: to determine systematic relationships between certain variables and local government strikes.

1) With few exceptions, laws governing public-employee collective bargaining were relatively new during the period under study, 1968–1971. Interpretations of key provisions were in doubt, and both labor and management were often ignorant of their obligations and responsibilities under the laws. This could affect the relationship between public policy and strikes. 2) In almost all instances the parties were engaged in negotiating their first or at most their second contract, a period often fraught with uncertainty and hostility. During this period, it is not unusual for strikes to occur for relatively irrational reasons. 3) Organization of public employees was proceeding at a very rapid pace with a high degree of interunion competition. Unions felt the need to prove themselves, and a strike is one way of doing this. 4) The

178

existence of nonunion public-employee associations, with no commitment to collective bargaining, confused and complicated the problem of measuring such variables as the extent of organization and bargaining power.

In short, the authors were trying to measure the influence of various factors on public-employee strikes during a period that may be compared with the first few years after enactment of the Wagner Act in 1935. I cannot recall any such research during this earlier period, and even the more recent efforts to explain private-sector strikes have not been very successful, as detailed by the authors in their comprehensive summary of earlier studies.

Turning to some of the independent variables used by the authors in their regressions, I believe that the measures of union bargaining power, public unionization, and private unionization suffer on the one hand from statistical defects, and on the other from a dubious relationship between public- and private-sector unions. Because of the absence of figures on membership in bona fide unions in local government, the authors have used data on local government employees represented by unions and employee associations developed in a survey conducted for me in 1968 by the International City Managers Association. These figures include employees represented by associations, some of which do not even believe in collective bargaining, let alone strikes. It is therefore not surprising that the authors found a "surprisingly weak" relationship between public-employee unionization and strikes.

A problem with using private-sector unionization as a measure of bargaining power of public-sector unions is that unions in private industry, particularly the construction unions that control central labor councils in many cities, have often failed to support efforts by public-employee unions to organize government workers. This attitude sometimes reflected the view that collective bargaining was not adaptable to public employment. But in some instances, private-sector unions regarded public-employee unions as threatening satisfactory political deals they had worked out on behalf of their members.

In place of a "profit" variable which has been used in studies of private-sector strikes, the authors used the ratio of taxes to

179

personal income, expecting a positive coefficient because "A higher tax rate should lower the expectations of employers about a reasonable wage increase, thereby inducing strikes." This influence was rated stronger than the countervailing pressure of higher taxes to reduce the bargaining power of unions, thus tending to reduce the number of strikes. The authors apparently neglected to consider the greater ability of cities with a higher tax rate to pay higher wages, thus contributing to the negative influence on strikes. Since with one exception the resulting significant coefficients were negative, it appears that the negative influence on strikes of this variable was greater than anticipated. In any event, this is a poor proxy for profits in private industry, and not too much significance should be ascribed to the results.

I was as surprised as the authors at the poor results from the variable measuring the proportion of public employment in cities of 50,000 and over. This was expected to be positively correlated with strikes, but instead the coefficient was almost always negative. Available statistics show a strong propensity for strikes to occur more frequently in large cities. Perhaps the cut-off point on city size was too low; a measure of employment in cities with over 100,000 population might yield better results.

I do not share the authors' disappointment on results from public policy variables. The consistent negative correlation between strikes and laws providing for fact-finding and mediation suggests that more money should be appropriated by states for agencies administering mediation and fact-finding procedures. Conversely, the poor results from variables measuring different kinds of laws (good-faith, meet-and-confer and permissive-bargaining) suggest that interpretation and administration of statutes may be as important as content. This latter observation applies particularly to laws prohibiting strikes, which are rarely enforced. For example, the Michigan law prohibits public-employee strikes, but the Michigan Supreme Court has held that courts should exercise their traditional equity powers, including an evaluation of whether good-faith bargaining has occurred and irreparable damage would result, in determining whether to enjoin such strikes. Certainly this decision has had the effect of reducing any negative influence on strikes that the statutory strike prohibition might have had.

There are three additional variables that might have yielded more significant coefficients than some of those used by the authors: the extent of interunion competition to represent public employees; the proportion of blacks and other minorities in the local population; and the relationship between teacher strikes and stoppages involving noneducational employees. Public-employee organization has been characterized by a great deal of competition among unions and between unions and nonunion associations. Such rivalry often leads to promises that raise employee expectations regarding the results of unionization and subsequently to efforts by organizations to deliver on these promises. I would postulate that strikes occur more frequently in the aftermath of rivalry to represent employees than in situations where only one organization is involved and is recognized either voluntarily or as a result of a representation election.

It is common knowledge that many public-employee strikes include a racial component. Common factors are a history of blacks being concentrated in dirty, menial, and low-paying jobs, often working under white supervisors; certain jobs being regarded as "for blacks only" who are barred from consideration for other jobs; discrimination against minority group employees in certain departments, etc. This suggests a positive relationship between the proportion of nonwhites in government employment and the number of strikes in a locality.

By excluding teacher strikes from their study, the authors have omitted an important variable that may affect strikes among other public employees. In many states, teachers have engaged in more strikes than have all other public employees combined. It is probable that in many cities other employees have voted to strike after observing the militancy of teachers and the results of strikes by teacher unions. If this is so, there should be a positive correlation between the number of teacher strikes and stoppages among other public employees.

A major distinction between the Burton-Krider study and studies of private-sector strikes is the tremendous importance in public employment of so-called "job actions," which are not included in strike statistics, but are often employed as a substitute for the strike. Such job actions include slowdowns, mass sick calls, "blue flu" epidemics, demonstrations and picketing, mass resignations, moratoriums on issuing summonses and other ingenious ways for government employees to let employers know their dissatisfaction without actually striking. As long as job actions continue to be utilized as strike substitutes by government employees, researchers trying to determine systematic relationships between certain variables and strikes will be laboring under an almost insurmountable handicap.

DONALD E. FREY

Wage Determination in Public Schools and the Effects of Unionization

School administrators and other public officials have in recent years been confronted by increasingly militant, organized teachers. Some estimate of the impact of collective bargaining on teachers' wages is mandatory for any serious educational planning. To determine whether collective bargaining has raised teachers' wages requires an explicit theory of the determination of wages and employment in school districts. In Section I a formal model of wage determination in public education is presented; in Section II the sources of data required for an empirical test of the model are reviewed, and in Section III statistical results that tend to confirm the model are presented along with a number of interesting implications. In most of what follows, equations and mathematical notation serve mainly to summarize what is primarily a verbal exposition.

I. A Model of the Salary Decisions of Local School Boards

A theory of the behavior of school boards, as of any economic agent, may seek generality, perhaps at the price of an inability to show specific results; conversely it may seek specificity, perhaps at the price of making restrictive assumptions. The following model is relatively specific. In some cases the form of an equation may be specified; in other cases a variable may be excluded from a function when a case could be made for its inclusion. We do attempt to justify specific choices of this sort. Furthermore, when different assumptions would lead to different

Note: The author expresses his thanks to the discussant, Hirschel Kasper, and also to Albert Rees and Daniel Hamermesh for many insights they offered at an early stage in this research. Remaining errors are solely mine.

183

results, some indication is given in the text. The model is general, however, in the sense that it starts with first principles and proceeds to results, which hopefully are more than obvious or trivial implications of the initial assumptions.

A. Elements of the Model

Data regularly published by teachers' associations, state departments of education, and other organizations indicate that professional educators are vitally concerned with such things as teacher-student ratios, the teaching experience of the average faculty member, and the proportion of a faculty holding various kinds of certification. Although teachers' associations may view the teacher-student ratio as an index of working conditions, they and the school boards write about the ratio as though it were one component of an index of the educational quality of a school system. Similarly, the great concern for experience and certification is consistent with the hypothesis that these are viewed as determinants of educational quality.[1]

We assume that school boards consider educational quality to depend upon the teacher-student ratio and the caliber of the faculty. For simplicity we consider only two characteristics that define the "caliber" of the faculty: *experience* indicates the years of teaching of the average teacher, and *ability* indicates any attributes other than experience that the school board believes are important. Ability is assumed to be an economic good.[2] The quality index, which represents the subjective views of the school board, is:

---

[1] Much recent research has failed to find positive evidence that educational inputs such as teacher-student ratios are very effective in determining student performance. Our educational quality index does not necessarily take issue with these findings; it requires only that school boards *believe* that teacher-student ratios, ability and experience are important, and that the boards act upon such a belief.

[2] If every school board had an entirely different definition of the attributes that constitute teaching ability, then, so long as all school systems were very small relative to the teacher market, ability would not be an economic good. School boards would bid up the price of ability only if there were some agreement about the desired attributes.

TABLE 1. Abbreviations and Definitions of Variables

Endogenous Variables

B	Base pay. The salary for an academic year of a teacher with no previous experience who holds the bachelor's degree or equivalent.
I	Increment in salary per year of experience. The average salary increment per year of experience up to some maximum level of experience.
A	Ability of the average faculty member. A set of capabilities believed by the school board to contribute to educational quality.
EX	Experience of the average faculty member. Attribute believed to contribute to educational quality.
T	Number of teachers in the district.
Q	Educational quality.

Exogenous Variables

H	A variable taking one positive value for an elementary system and another positive value for a system including high schools.
AW	Alternative wage, the wage available to teachers in alternative employment.
AM	Amenities, the presence of pleasant working conditions.
TXB	Tax base, the equalized property value per pupil in the district.
INC	Median family income of a community.
S	The number of pupils in average daily attendance in the district.

$$(1) \qquad Q = H[T/S]^{\alpha} q(A, EX),$$

where all the variables are defined in Table 1; α is a parameter that is less than unity and q indicates some unspecified function. Educational quality, Q, is assumed to depend upon the teacher-student ratio, T/S, the average ability of the faculty, A, the average experience of the faculty, EX, and whether the school system is an elementary system or comprehensive system, H. The equation does not indicate whether ability and experience interact with each other in producing educational quality. However, the relationship between the teacher-student ratio and the other two inputs is multiplicative, since it is meaningless to speak of ability or experience contributing to educational quality if there are no teachers available. Ability and experience are embodied in teachers, and equation (1) makes this fact apparent. The variable H simply recognizes that a teacher-student ratio considered "good" in an elementary system might not be good in a

185

high school. Equation (1) purposely ignores nonpersonnel factors such as the age or condition of school buildings.

Equation (1) contains average ability rather than the ability of various categories of teachers; this is because the school board has at its disposal a device capable of influencing only average ability. The single salary schedule essentially prevents school administrators from offering very high salaries to certain particularly capable teachers, despite a few dodges that may be used to circumvent a strict application of the schedule.[3] Rather than tailoring its salary offers to the individual candidates for employment, the board must set a schedule of wages applicable to all teachers and make a choice from among the candidates who make themselves available at those rates. With such a general tool at its disposal, the board is likely to set appropriately general goals like the attainment of some average level of ability and experience.

If a school district wishes to improve its capacity to recruit and hold highly able teachers, it must increase its salary schedule relative to that of alternative occupations. Recruiting power is probably improved most readily by increasing base pay. Base pay is important because most teachers actively seeking employment are new graduates, and in any event base pay has an impact on other pay grades as well. Perry and Wildman (1970, p. 151) support this estimate of the central importance of base pay in recruiting when they state, "The primary link between the school system and the labor market tends to be at the base of the service dimension and of the salary schedule." This is also the view of Benson (1968, p. 304).

Equation (2) incorporates this view and indicates the level of base pay required for the school district to recruit and hold a faculty of some level of ability:

[3]Sometimes teachers are able to earn extra income by supervising student activities. Very promising teacher candidates might be offered relatively well-paid jobs of this sort in addition to their normal duties as a way to circumvent the strict application of the single salary schedule. Such opportunities for circumvention are relatively rare; furthermore, the wide use of such dodges by school boards would result in serious morale problems among faculty members not so favored.

(2) $$B = B(A; AW, AM).$$

Note that equation (2) does not indicate that base pay must increase as the number of teachers increases. The assumption implicit in this is that the elasticity of supply of teachers of given ability *to a school district* is infinite; salaries must be increased only to employ teachers of greater ability. (No claim is being made that the aggregate market supply of teachers of each ability category is of infinite elasticity.) This assumption should approximate reality if school districts are very small relative to the total employment of teachers. The consequences of relaxing this assumption will be explored in Section III.

Equation (2) states that the wage available to teachers in alternative work, AW, determines the base pay needed to obtain teachers of some given level of ability. If the alternative wage increases, the base pay must increase, *ceteris paribus.* Should the base pay fail to increase in response to an increase in the alternative wage, the district would experience a deterioration in the ability of its faculty. In the long run, the elasticity of teachers' wages with respect to the alternative wage should be one. Any wage differential not justified by hours of work, required training, or amenities would be eliminated.[4] The specification also

---

[4] Depending on the occupation, teachers may be relatively good or relatively poor substitutes for workers in other employment. Changes in wages in alternative occupations for which teachers are relatively good substitute workers should be reflected in teachers' wages relatively quickly; the reverse is true for occupations where teachers make poor substitute workers. Teachers are probably relatively good substitutes for workers in several occupations. This view implies a particular perspective on so-called teacher "surpluses" and "shortages." There are probably a number of occupations to which and from which teachers are rather mobile. This means that a general "shortage" of teachers could occur if thousands of school districts acting independently depressed wages substantially below those prevailing in alternative occupations. This seems highly unlikely. Analysis of the "shortage literature" of the mid-sixties reveals that there never was a general shortage of teachers. Schools had unfilled openings only in special disciplines such as mathematics. Teachers of mathematics, obviously, were able to earn a far higher alternative wage during the sixties than most teachers. Since the single salary schedule prevented a premium being paid in certain fields, a shortage developed *in those fields.*

emphasizes the amenity value, *AM*, of working in certain school districts. We are not concerned with the nonpecuniary benefits associated with *any* teaching job (e.g., ample vacations, hours coinciding with those of one's children, etc.). The variable *AM* distinguishes differences in amenities among districts; unpleasant work may command high wages.[5] Just as a certain level of base pay allows the district to influence the average ability of its faculty, so the district is able to reduce turnover and increase the average level of experience by rewarding experience more highly. We thus have:

$$(3) \qquad I = I(EX; AW, AM).$$

We assume that a community, or a majority of its voters, assigns some dollar value to the educational quality produced by its school system. An egalitarian community may do so in the following manner. For the average child, educational quality of level Q^* is believed to have some value K^*; that is, a function K indicates the dollar value per child for every possible level of

---

The concept of a general shortage, however, is inconceivable. Currently, there is much talk of a teacher "surplus." In the sense that a greater number of newly certificated candidates are being graduated than there are open jobs, there may be a "surplus." However, alternative occupations are available to these candidates, and there are few unemployed teachers as such. Furthermore, there is no certainty that teaching is the first choice of occupations, even among those undergraduates who chose to obtain a certificate. It is unlikely that the current certificate surplus will depress teachers' wages relative to wages in occupations which are relatively close alternatives to teaching.

[5]That some teachers consider a certain school district to be "unpleasant" does not necessarily mean that such a district must pay higher wages than more amenity-laden districts in order to hire teachers of equal ability. If school districts are small relative to the teacher market, and if teachers' tastes are relatively diverse with respect to what constitutes an amenity or disamenity, then even districts that a majority of teachers consider to be unpleasant can fill their needs at the going rate by hiring from the minority of teachers that does not find the working conditions distasteful. Teachers' tastes probably *are* diverse in this respect. If an urban school district is small relative to the market, it may not have to pay a very large "disamenity premium" even if a majority of teachers view the district with distaste.

educational quality. Presumably the value of a *marginal* improvement in educational quality is always positive but decreasing over the relevant range. The total value of educational quality ($TVEQ$) is defined as the value to a typical student multiplied by the total number of students:

$$(4) \qquad TVEQ = S \cdot K(Q; INC, TXB),$$

where INC indicates community income, and TXB indicates the tax base of the community. The function K may be interpreted as showing the maximum amount per child that the community would bid to obtain some level of educational quality.

The tax base, TXB, and level of income in the community, INC, also help determine what the community will bid to obtain educational quality. If education were simply an investment in productive skills, tax base and income would have no impact on the willingness of the community to buy extra educational quality; neither one would cause the demand curve of the community for educational quality to shift. Any rational community, rich or poor, would simply value an increment of educational quality at the present value of the anticipated future earnings of the students attributable to that increment. The present value of educational quality, not the ability to pay for it, would determine the demand curve for educational quality.

Education, however, is not merely a producer's durable investment, it is also a consumption good. If education is at least partially a consumption good, the consumer theory tells us that income and tax base should have an impact on the demand curve for educational quality. Equation (4) reflects the view that education is at least partially a consumer's good. Thus, as community income and tax base grow, the demand for educational quality (i.e., $TVEQ$) increases.

Various ad hoc theories of wage determination in public education have assumed that community wealth, as measured by income or tax base, has a *direct* impact on teachers' salaries (and ability) (Owen, 1972). The present model, however, reflects the view that greater wealth of a community increases the demand for educational quality, a concept one step removed from teacher ability. Increased demand for educational quality may, of course, increase the derived demand for teacher ability and thereby raise salaries; on the other hand, it need not. It is more satisfactory to *conclude* that community wealth influences the demand for teacher ability than to assume it.

The total salary cost (*TSC*) to the district is defined as the average salary multiplied by the number of teachers:

(5) $$TSC = T\,[B + EX \cdot I].$$

Clearly, the total salary cost will rise if the school board attempts to increase educational quality in the district by hiring more able teachers.

Among the plausible objectives of a school board are: (1) maximizing educational quality, as long as total cost of the quality does not exceed the total value of educational quality as perceived by the community; (2) minimizing costs, as long as some acceptable minimum level of quality is maintained; and (3) maximizing the "surplus" of the value of educational quality above its costs of production.

Objective (1) is unlikely. Diminishing marginal value of educational quality means that the last few units of quality produced in maximizing quality would be viewed by the community as costing more than they were worth. Why would a community that is cognizant of both the value and cost of educational quality, as we have assumed, adopt a goal that results in the production of incremental units of educational quality that cost more than they are worth? Hidden agendas may, of course, exist, prompting some school boards to adopt this goal. For example, the board may gain prestige by producing more educational quality than the citizens want, or school boards may be pressured by their professional administrators whose hidden agenda is to maximize quality. This goal results in maximized employment of teachers, which enlarges the supervising responsibilities of administrators and possibly administrators' salaries. If, however, the community is aware of the value and cost of educational quality, such hidden agendas would soon be discovered and defeated.

Objective (2) is similarly unlikely for reasons already suggested. So long as a community perceives that the value of marginal increases in educational quality exceeds the cost, it will resist stopping at some minimum level of educational quality.

The school board will adopt objective (3) for the very reasons that it rejects the others. The maximization of the difference between the value of educational quality and its costs is analogous to maximizing the sum of consumer's surplus and producer's surplus. Objective (3) suggests maximizing:

$$(6) \qquad G = S \cdot K - T[B + EX \cdot I],$$

with respect to ability, experience, and the number of teachers, factors that are under the control of the school board. The first-order conditions require that the partial derivatives of G with respect to A, EX, and T be zero. We require that the value of the marginal quality product of each factor be equal to the marginal cost of each factor:

$$(7) \qquad Z[\partial q/\partial A] = T[\partial B/\partial A];$$

$$(8) \qquad Z[\partial q/\partial EX] = T\{[\partial I/\partial EX]\,EX + I\};$$

$$(9) \qquad \alpha Z T^{-1} q = B + EX \cdot I,$$

where $Z = HS^{1-\alpha}\,T^{\alpha}[\partial K/\partial Q]$. These conditions for a maximum are three equations in three unknowns. We may use equations (2) and (3) and the solution values for A, EX, and T to solve for the equilibrium values of base pay, B, and the experience increments, I.

Equation (7) may be modified to reflect the fact that an increase in teachers' salaries does not instantaneously improve average faculty ability to the level that may be desired by the school board. When a school board desires to improve the average ability of teachers in the district, the single salary schedule requires that the base pay of *all* teachers in the district be raised. The higher base pay then permits the school board to employ new recruits from among more capable candidates. Thus in the first year after the salary schedule has been improved, only the newest employees of the school district reflect the impact of higher wages in the sense that they are more capable teachers. Only after some years of recruiting does the actual average level

191

of faculty ability reach the desired level. For a period of years a school board that is trying to improve faculty ability must "over-pay" older faculty members of lower ability. Changing from one equilibrium level of faculty ability to a higher level imposes an extra fixed cost on the school district. This problem would not exist if a school board desired to *decrease* the level of ability of the faculty by reducing salaries.

A school board may take this fixed cost into account and view it as an investment on which it must earn a return. Such a return may be obtained by allowing the value of the marginal quality product, *VMQP*, of faculty ability to exceed the marginal cost of ability, *MC*, in the new equilibrium:

$$(7') \qquad Z\,[\partial q/\partial A] = \gamma T(\partial B/\partial A).$$

The term γ indicates the proportion by which the *VMQP* of ability must exceed the *MC* of ability. Needless to say, γ is a constant only for purposes of static analysis. In a dynamic model it would be a function of the initial level of faculty ability, the final level of faculty ability, the speed of adjustment, and so on.

The modification represented by equation $(7')$ does not change the major results that follow. However, there are some implications to be derived from taking explicit account of the fixed costs involved in changing the attributes of a school's faculty. First, the larger is the fixed cost (and thus the larger is γ), the smaller must be the final equilibrium level of faculty ability chosen by a school board. Similarly, the larger is γ, the lower must be the final equilibrium level of educational quality. The term γ will be very close to 1 and therefore unimportant for analysis, if new school districts immediately hire the kind of faculty that is optimal, and if any subsequent changes in the optimal level of faculty ability are small. The term γ will also be close to 1 if any changes in the desired level of faculty ability occur only rarely, so that any fixed costs may be returned over a large number of years.

B. Interpretation of the Model and Results

In each of the first-order equations (7)–(9) the first term is simply the amount that the community is willing to pay for the educational quality produced by a marginal increase in ability, experience, or number of teachers. Each term on the right-hand side of the equations is the marginal cost of an input. We note that the marginal cost of teachers in the long run is simply the average salary.

That the value of the marginal product of a factor should equal the marginal cost of the factor is a standard result of the theory of the firm. However, the marginal cost of ability (or experience) is not a fixed, parametric price; the marginal cost of ability varies as the size of the faculty varies. To help understand this, consider two school districts, one with a faculty of 100 teachers, the other with a faculty of 200. Suppose both districts can in the long run raise the average ability of their faculties by one unit by raising salaries $100 per teacher. Although the *per-teacher* cost of an added unit of average ability is the same for both districts, the marginal cost for the smaller district will be $10,000 (= $100 X 100 teachers), and for the larger district will be $20,000 (= $100 X 200 teachers). The marginal cost of ability (and experience) is proportional to the number of teachers in the faculty. This should be helpful in understanding the following discussion.

One useful variation of the standard marginal conditions is that the ratio of the marginal costs of two inputs be equal to the ratio of their marginal products. Consider these ratios for the pair of inputs, ability and teachers. Dividing equation (7) by (9) gives:

$$(10) \qquad \frac{T\,[\partial q/\partial A]}{\alpha q} = \frac{T\,[\partial B/\partial A]}{B + EX \cdot I}.$$

We note that T appears in the numerator on both sides of the equation and nowhere else. This means that *once in equilibrium* the school board will continue on its equilibrium "expansion path" simply by increasing or decreasing the number of teachers. (Note that a γ in the numerator of the right-hand side would change nothing.) A similar result would be obtained by dividing (8) by (9).

A diagrammatic exposition of this result is given in Figure 1. The locus of all combinations of inputs creating equal levels of quality is called in the diagram an "isoqual." The slope of an

193

FIGURE 1. Diagrammatic Interpretation of Equation (10)

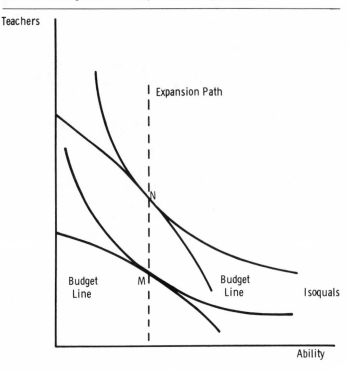

isoqual at any given point represents the ratio of the marginal quality product of ability to the marginal quality product of another teacher. The total cost function allows us to find the locus of all combinations of ability and faculty size that may be obtained at a given total salary cost. Since the tradeoff between number of teachers and ability of faculty need not be at a constant rate of exchange, we have drawn budget lines that are somewhat bowed. The slope at any point on these budget lines, or "ability-teacher frontiers," represents the ratio of the marginal cost of ability to the marginal cost of a teacher.

Figure 1 indicates that, if there were a possible equilibrium at point M, then there would be another at point N that lies on a vertical line through M. The equilibrium chosen by a community will depend on the value it places upon educational quality. (Note that $\gamma > 1$ would shift the vertical expansion path MN to the left.) This discussion allows us to present the following formal results with a minimum of discussion: (1) starting from equilibrium, an increase in the community's tax base or income results only in an increased teacher-student ratio and no change of ability or experience of the faculty. Thus an increase in community income or its tax base has no impact on wages paid.[6] The practical implication of this is important. Poor school districts apparently should pay about the same level of salaries as rich school districts, all else equal. Wealth per se does not result in suburban districts' outbidding inner cities for more capable or more experienced teachers. Rather, the model predicts that wealth is spent on better teacher-student ratios. (2) Whether a school district administers elementary schools only, or both elementary and high schools, the salary schedule should be the same. This result holds for the same reason that result (1) holds. The presence of a high school in this model is handled mathematically analogously to a difference in tax base or community income. (3) The salaries of teachers vary as the alternative wage varies. The labor market where a district is located has the only important impact on teachers' salaries. The main exception is that amenities or disamenities of local districts may influence salaries. Results (1) and (2) have eliminated any other possible influences on salaries of teachers in nonunionized school districts.

C. The Theory and Collective Bargaining

Although it is not a model of collective bargaining per se, the theory just presented contributes to the understanding of collective bargaining in education. Collective bargaining may be viewed as a process whereby wage variables that were once unilaterally determined by a school board are jointly determined by the school board and teachers' association. Presumably the board sets as its target the level of wages (B and I) that would prevail if it could unilaterally set wages. (This does not deny that the board may offer less than its real target wage at some point dur-

---

[6] A formal proof may be found in Frey (1972).

ing negotiations as a bargaining ploy.) The target wages of the
school board are the optimal wage rates determined by the
model of the previous section. The actual wage to emerge from
negotiations may be viewed as the target wage times a multiplier
that reflects the success of the union. In the case of base pay:

(11) $$B_n = B_t \cdot e^{\rho U},$$

where B_n is the negotiated wage, B_t is the target wage determined
in our model, ρ is a coefficient reflecting the strength of the
union, and U represents the presence or absence of bargaining in
the school district ($U = 0$, no bargaining; $U = 1$, bargaining). The
absence of bargaining in the district means that the "negotiated"
wage is equal to the optimal target wage of the school board.

If a union were to succeed in obtaining negotiated wages above
the target levels, the ability and experience of the faculty would
also be set at higher levels, via equations (2) and (3), than the
school board would have unilaterally chosen. If faculty size is
not negotiable, a school board adhering to the objective suggested
earlier would employ (9) to determine the optimum number of
teachers, given the results of the wage bargaining. The implication of (9) is that a successful increase in wages, B and I, results
in fewer teachers being employed than without bargaining over
wages.

Of some interest is the magnitude of the elasticity of employment with respect to teachers' wages. Although an inelastic
demand for labor is not a sufficient condition for a union's
success, it is certainly a necessary condition. Equation (9) reveals
that the degree of which faculty ability and experience improve
in response to higher negotiated wages influences the magnitude
of the employment response to the wage change. In our model a
faculty becomes more capable as a result of increased wage rates.
This increase in the productivity of teachers results in the loss of
fewer jobs for a given wage increase than if wage changes did not
have an eventual impact on teacher quality (and productivity).

It is still difficult to tell whether the demand for teachers is
elastic or inelastic on the basis of this discussion. Assume that the
demand actually is inelastic; this is a precondition for large union

effects on wages. An inelastic demand curve for teachers is still worthless to the union if the union lacks power. "Power" means either the ability to control entry into the teaching profession or the ability to win wage increases by imposing costs on school boards by means of strikes.

Aside from closed shops, which do not exist in public education, the power to control entry to a profession is usually through licensing. In teaching, the certification process could be used to limit entry to the profession. In actuality, certification is controlled by state governments and state governments have not allowed certification to restrict supply. Indeed, it is difficult to see why a government that controls certification would use it to restrict entry to a profession where the government itself is the only employer. The very fact that teachers' associations have long criticized the number of substandard certificates issued by state governments indicates that teachers' unions achieved no control over the certification process.

This leaves the strike as a possible source of power for teachers' unions. It is not clear that the strike or threat of strike gives teachers' unions a credible source of leverage in the bargaining situation. A union in the private sector employs the strike because it imposes costs upon profit-maximizing firms. The strike cuts off revenues while at least some of the firm's costs continue to accrue. The situation in public education is notable for its dissimilarity. A school board is not a profit-maximizing institution; furthermore, its source of revenue is not threatened by a strike. Unless the employees of the tax office are members of friendly unions, the revenue the school board needs to operate will be unaffected by a strike. Although state aid may be lost during a strike, the parallel with a profit-maximizing firm is tenuous and unconvincing.

The strike in public employment is obviously not a tactic designed to exert market pressure on an institution; rather, it is a political device. The question ultimately becomes one of the political impact of strikes: does a strike generate more support for teachers' demands than it causes antagonism against teachers? There are no a priori reasons for suggesting what the political

TABLE 2. The Impact of Collective Bargaining in the Public Sector: A Summary

Name of Researcher	Wage Variable	Estimated Impact of Bargaining	Alternative Wage Control Variable (Or Equivalent) Present
Kasper (1970)	Teachers average statewide wage	Less than 4 percent	Not Consistently
Thornton (1971)	a) Teachers' base pay, 83 cities b) Teachers' maximum pay	Less than 4 percent More than 25 percent[a]	Yes
Landon-Baird (1972)	Teachers' base pay, 44 cities	Less than 5 percent	No
Hall-Carroll (1973)	Elementary teachers' average salary, in one labor market	Less than 2 percent	Yes
Schmenner (1973)	Teachers' base pay, 11 very large cities	a) 12-14 percent (total union impact) b) 6.8-9.3 percent (bargaining impact alone)	Yes
Ashenfelter (1971)	a) Firefighters' annual salary b) Firefighters hourly wage	No statistically significant impact, most years 8.7-16 percent, in cities of 25–50,000 population; generally none in larger cities	Yes

[a]Thornton presented evidence casting doubt on this estimate.

effects of a teachers' strike will be. The issue finally becomes an empirical one; Table 2 presents the evidence to date regarding the impact of unions on wages in the public sector.

II. Testing the Model: Sources of Data

The wage equations that occupy the rest of the discussion are based upon the theory of Section I. These equations are estimated using data generated by 298 school districts in New Jersey over a period of six years. Confining all observations to one state avoids relying upon published data from diverse sources that may use noncomparable definitions of the variables in question. Limiting the empirical study to one state also guarantees a uniform legal framework under which the school districts operated. All districts with more than 750 pupils in average daily attendance, except regional high school districts, are included in the sample. The six years covered by the study span several years when virtually no substantive collective bargaining occurred and one year when active bargaining occurred in about 70 percent of all districts in the sample.

Although some of the endogenous variables in Section I, such as ability and educational quality, are difficult to quantify, our main concern is with the wages of teachers. The salary schedules of teachers are published regularly. We ignore the undefinable variables and treat each wage variable as a function of all the exogenous variables in the model, in essence providing reduced-form estimates.

A key variable in the theory is base pay, B, the annual salary received by a new teacher holding the bachelor-level degree. The level of base pay in all the school districts in the sample is published by the New Jersey Education Association in an annual series entitled *New Jersey Teacher Salary Guides*. This same source provided data concerning the maximum pay level for teachers holding the bachelor-level degree.

The alternative wage provides, at least in the long run, an option to employment in teaching. Increases in the alternative wage ultimately force a school district to adjust its wage or allow the ability of its faculty to deteriorate. The more perfectly

199

substitutable are teachers and workers in the alternative occupation, the less time it takes for long-run adjustments to be made. Teachers in one district are almost perfect substitutes for teachers in a neighboring district; this might suggest to the unwary that the alternative wage for teachers in district C is the wage in district D. This prescription is seriously flawed. If the alternative wage in district C were the wage in D, then the alternative wage for teachers in D would be the wage in C. This means that a feedback loop exists and the wage in D is not really exogenous to the model. For purposes of statistical estimation, it is impossible to determine the salary level in one district in terms of the salary in neighboring districts; simultaneous equations bias would seriously hinder such an attempt. We require a truly exogenous wage.

The Bureau of Labor Statistics publishes in *Area Wage Surveys* the straight-time earnings for several occupations; the number of occupations actually surveyed varies with the labor market. Since the wages of industrial nurses were surveyed for all the labor markets of the state of New Jersey, and since nurses and teachers share some important common characteristics, this wage was chosen as the exogenous alternative wage. The nursing profession provides a good benchmark occupation because both teaching and nursing require relatively highly educated workers who are predominantly female.

Although I am skeptical as to the magnitude of any effect on wage differences across school districts that amenities or disamenities may have, the possibility of some amenity effect clearly exists. We therefore seek a variable to serve as a proxy for the pleasantness or unpleasantness of working in a particular district. Our theory suggests that district size (number of pupils) per se should not influence the wages of teachers; however, district size may be a good proxy for the magnitude of the disamenities associated with a particular district. We propose that the unpleasantness of a job increases with the size of the district. As enrollments increase the likelihood of racial, ethnic, or religious factions or animosities developing in the system increases. All else equal, we would expect social tensions or hostilities to be more apparent in larger districts. Open hostilities are much more difficult where a large proportion of teachers, parents, and even pupils know one another. The tensions that develop in the largest school systems are undoubtedly disamenities. Additionally, the largest systems are responsible for a disproportionately large number of children from poverty-stricken or broken families. Some teachers may consider the extra effort required to work successfully with these children a disamenity. The variable actually chosen to represent the size of the district was the average daily attendance of the district. This is published by the New Jersey Department of Education in the *Annual Report of the Commissioner.*

Community income influences the community's demand for educational quality. Standard theory of the consumer leads us to expect that higher incomes lead families to be willing to pay more for educational quality or to buy more quality at a constant price. It is not our purpose to discuss how citizen's incomes are turned into voting behavior and hence into behavior by school boards. The connection between variables such as community income and the behavior of school boards is discussed by Barzel (1973) among others. Whatever the mechanism, we expect higher incomes to increase the demand for educational quality. The variable actually employed is the median family income of the community as derived from the 1960 Census.[7]

If the voters of a community and the taxpayers were exactly the same set of people, there would be little point in considering tax base in addition to median family income. A substantial portion of property tax receipts, however, is paid by nonresident landowners, corporations, and so on; their contributions decrease the real burden of education borne by the resident voters of the community. As the property tax base per pupil rises, all else

---

[7]Community income for any given year was derived from the 1960 *Census of Population*, PC(1)-C. The median family income in each community in 1959, as given in the 1960 Census, was multiplied by the ratio of median family income in the northeast in the year of interest to the median family income in the northeast in 1959.

201

equal, we expect the demand for educational quality to increase.[8] The equalized property value per pupil is published in the *Annual Report of the Commissioner* cited previously.

State aid to local school districts makes the districts effectively richer and should influence the demand for educational quality in the same manner as does tax base or community income. In preliminary cross-section regressions by year, state aid per pupil was never a significant variable. During the period of this study, the largest portion of state aid was in the form of flat per-pupil grants to districts. Thus in any given year per-pupil aid varied little from district to district. However, per-pupil aid to districts varied from one year to the next during the period studied. As may be expected, a variable representing per-pupil state aid proved to have a significant impact in a regression equation pooling data from several years. Finally, federal aid to school districts, including aid mandated by the Elementary and Secondary Education Act, did not appear to have a significant impact in preliminary regressions.

Collective bargaining was represented by a dummy variable, U. In 1968 New Jersey enacted a public employment law that required school boards to bargain with teachers' organizations that wished to bargain. Although there had been virtually no substantive collective bargaining prior to 1968, local teachers' associations did exist in most districts throughout the state. Many of these local associations viewed the public employment act as a mandate to begin bargaining. During 1968–1969 a large number of districts entered negotiations to set salaries for the academic year 1969–1970; completed contracts were filed with the Public Employment Relations Commission. The dummy variable, U, was constructed representing all districts with contracts on file for 1969–1970. The year 1969–1970 is virtually the only year in the sample permitting a cross-section analysis of the impact of bargaining; after 1969–1970 there was nearly universal bargaining.

---

[8] Inclusion of the property tax base in the wage equations eliminates the need to include a tax *rate* as a variable. The tax rate, all else equal, is determined by the tax base per pupil.

A variable representing the presence of a high school in the district was included in a set of preliminary regression equations. The coefficient was positive and never significant. This is consistent with result (2) of Section I.

III. Empirical Results

A. The Base Pay of Teachers

Cross-section regressions of base pay as a function of all the exogenous variables in our model were estimated for each of the six years, 1964–1965 through 1969–1970, with 298 observations in each year. The equations for the six years were estimated by ordinary least-squares and by three-stage least-squares for seemingly unrelated equations; the coefficients were not substantially changed by the method of estimation.[9] Table 3 shows coefficients and the absolute values of the t-statistics; since the functional form of the equations is log-linear, the coefficients should be interpreted as elasticities.

The coefficients of the tax base and community income variables are extremely small, so small that no serious modification of the specification of the model of Section I seems warranted. Two characteristics of that model led to the result that teachers' wages would be unresponsive to demand variables such as community income or tax base: (1) the particular multiplicative form of the quality index, equation (1); and (2) the assumption that the supply of teachers of given ability to a district is infinitely elastic, equation (2). Slight modification of either of these equations could generate the results of Table 3. For example, if the elasticity of supply of teachers of given ability were slightly less than infinite, the model would predict a very slight sensitivity of wages to wealth, as shown in Table 3. Less than infinite elasticity allows the price of teachers of given ability to rise relative to the price of ability per se if wealthy districts employ larger faculties than poorer districts. This shift of relative prices would favor

---

[9] Each of the cross-section equations is a reduced-form equation, and therefore seemingly unrelated to the others. However, it is possible to estimate the equations for all six years simultaneously (see Zellner, 1962).

TABLE 3. Cross-Section Wage Equations: Dependent Variable is Logarithm of Base Pay

Year	Type of Estimate	Constant	S	TXB	INC	AW	U	U·AW	R^2
1964-65	Ord. Lst. Squares	.29 (.97)[a]	.009 (5.6)	.014 (3.9)	.033 (3.7)	.67 (9.4)			.656
	3-Stg. Lst. Squares	.85 (3.1)	.010 (6.1)	.015 (4.3)	.041 (4.6)	.54 (8.3)			
1965-66	Ord. Lst. Squares	.83 (3.7)	.008 (4.4)	.014 (3.4)	.034 (3.3)	.56 (10.0)			.637
	3-Stg. Lst. Squares	1.17 (5.5)	.009 (4.8)	.014 (3.7)	.042 (2.1)	.47 (9.3)			
1966-67	Ord. Lst. Squares	1.91 (9.3)	.012 (5.8)	.028 (6.6)	.017 (1.5)	.35 (7.2)			.598
	3-Stg. Lst. Squares	2.10 (11.2)	.013 (6.4)	.027 (6.6)	.024 (2.1)	.29 (6.6)			
1967-68	Ord. Lst. Squares	1.09 (3.6)	.009 (4.1)	.019 (4.4)	.014 (1.2)	.55 (8.1)			.537
	3-Stg. Lst. Squares	1.27 (4.4)	.009 (4.1)	.018 (4.3)	.017 (1.6)	.51 (7.8)			
1968-69	Ord. Lst. Squares	-.52 (1.2)	.013 (5.5)	.017 (3.8)	.049 (4.2)	.82 (8.6)			.557
	3-Stg. Lst. Squares	-1.36 (.3)	.012 (5.6)	.017 (3.8)	.053 (4.6)	.74 (8.0)			
1969-70	Ord. Lst. Squares	-.72 (1.2)	.011 (5.7)	.028 (7.2)	.041 (3.9)	.87 (7.2)			.553
	Ord. Lst. Squares	.80 (1.1)	.011 (5.8)	.027 (6.9)	.041 (4.6)	.57 (3.7)	-2.86 (3.0)	.57 (3.0)	.588
	3-Stg. Lst. Squares	2.6 (3.4)	.011 (6.7)	.027 (7.1)	.052 (5.3)	.18 (1.0)	-3.60 (3.6)	.72 (3.6)	

[a]Absolute values of t-statistics in parentheses.

204

ability per se, resulting in larger salaries for more capable teachers. Needless to say, such a slight modification of specification does not alter the basic structure of the model. Indeed, the smallness of the coefficients of tax base and community income, as reported in Table 3, is striking.

The skeptic may argue that community income and tax base have very low elasticities only because equalizing state aid to school districts was at work behind the scenes. If there were a large program of equalizing state aid, differences in the tax base or income of communities would be more apparent than real. For the years 1964–1965 and 1965–1966 there was no state aid of a nature that would equalize the resources of districts. Nevertheless, the estimated elasticities for those two years are not significantly different from many of the elasticities for later years when a very small amount of equalizing aid was available.

Table 4 presents estimates of the extent to which differences in tax base and community income created differentials in the base pay of teachers for each of the six years of the study. A poor district (tax base per pupil of $18,000) would in 1964–1965 offer only about $79 less in base pay than a rich district (tax base per pupil of $60,000), all else equal. This is a rather small differential in wages given the large disparity of tax base between the two communities. Column (3) of Table 4 reveals a drift over time toward slightly larger differentials, from $79 in 1964 to about $188 in 1969. Part of this drift is due to larger elasticities in the later years, part to the increased magnitude of the mean base pay over time. Of the growth of the differential from $79 to $188, about $50 is due to growth in base pay over time.

Variations in community income are even less effective in causing differentials in teachers' salaries than are variations in tax base, because community income varies less than tax base across communities. Tax base may be altered significantly by the presence of industrial parks, summer resort property, farms, and a host of other types of real estate. Indeed, in New Jersey the communities with the largest equalized value per pupil are not "rich" suburbs, but seashore communities with large amounts of resort property relative to the small permanent populations. Nor is it true that communities that have large family incomes also

TABLE 4. Impact of Variations in Tax Base and Income on Base Pay, in Percent and Dollars, 1964–1970

Year	Difference (%) of Tax Base between Poor and Rich Districts[a] (1)	Differential (%) of Base Pay due to Differences of Tax Base[b] (2)	Differential ($) of Base Pay due to Differences of Tax Base[c] (3)	Difference (%) of Income between Poor and Rich Districts[d] (4)	Differential (%) of Base Pay due to Differences of Income[d] (5)	Differential ($) of Base Pay due to Differences of Income[d] (6)
1964–65	108	1.6	79	34	1.4	69
1965–66	110	1.5	76	34	1.4	71
1966–67	110	3.0	159	34	.81	43
1967–68	111	2.0	114	34	.58	33
1968–69	110	1.9	114	34	1.8	110
1969–70	105	2.8	188	34	1.7	114

[a]A rich district is defined as having a tax base one standard deviation above the average tax base. A poor district has a tax base valued at one standard deviation below the mean. (1) reports the geometric mean of the difference between the two as a percent of the high tax base and as a percent of the low, or poor, tax base.
[b]Computed by multiplying (1) by the appropriate 3-stage estimate of elasticity in Table 3.
[c]Computed by multiplying the decimal form of (2) by the average base pay in the state for each year: $4950; $5100; $5300; $5675; $6100; $6725, for 1964–1965, 1965–1966, etc.
[d]Computed analogously to first three columns.

tend to have very large tax bases. The simple correlation coefficient of community income and tax base was less than .4. It would be wrong to suggest that the effects of income and tax base differences strongly reinforce each other in causing teachers' salaries to vary across districts.

Turning again to Table 3, we see that the coefficients on the alternative wage variable are much larger than on any other explanatory variable. The elasticity of base pay with respect to the alternative wage was not one in any of these estimates, although we would expect the elasticity to be one in the long run. However, the cross-section estimates need not be viewed as unbiased long-run estimates.[10] (The estimated elasticity was one when

---

[10] Suppose the observed value for the alternative wage is composed of the true alternative wage in the labor market and an error term. For simplicity, assume that teachers' base pay, B, is exactly related to the true component of the alternative wage, AW:

$$B = a + b \cdot AW,$$

where, to be consistent with our regressions, the variables should be viewed here as logarithms. Assume also that:

$$B_o = B + v,$$

and

$$AW_o = AW + u,$$

where the o subscript signifies the observed variables, and v and u are error terms that are independent of each other. Then by substitution:

$$B_o = a + bAW_o + (-bu + v).$$

It is apparent that not only is B_o related to the error term, but so is AW_o, leading to biased estimates of b. Furthermore:

$$\text{Probability limit } b = \frac{b}{1 + \dfrac{\text{Var}(u)}{\text{Var}(AW)}}.$$

This indicates that the estimate is also inconsistent. In our particular case, pooling data from several years will serve to increase $\text{Var}(AW)$ enormously relative to $\text{Var}(u)$, causing the estimate of b to approach the true value of b. Therefore, in any regression using pooled data, the coefficient of alternative wage should be much closer in value to one than in the cross-section regressions.

207

data for the six years were pooled in results discussed below.) Table 5 shows the differentials in base pay induced by variations in alternative wages. Although the variation of the alternative wage from one labor market to another in any given year was rather small, it accounted for more variation in base pay than did the vast variation in tax base. This strongly confirms the prediction that the labor market in which a school district is located is far more important than the wealth of the district in establishing teachers' salaries.

On a national scale the importance of labor-market considerations rather than the wealth of a school district would be even more apparent. In our study we were confined to several labor markets in a relatively small state; variation in the alternative wage was rather minor. On the other hand, percent variations in tax base in New Jersey are about as large as are likely to be found anywhere. Suppose on a national scale that the percentage variation of alternative wages were as much as 25 percent, while the variation in tax base were as much as 200 percent. Assuming that

TABLE 5. The Impact of Variations in the Alternative Wage Rate on Teachers' Base Pay, in Percent and Dollars, 1964-70.

Year	Percent Variation Between Low and High AW^a (1)		Percent Differential of Base Pay Due to Variation of AW^b (2)		Dollar Differential of Base Pay Due to Variation of AW^c (3)	
	(a)	(b)	(a)	(b)	(a)	(b)
1964-65	4.6	5.2	2.5	2.8	124	138
1965-66	6.8	8.9	3.2	4.2	163	214
1966-67	8.1	12.2	2.4	3.6	127	190
1967-68	5.8	7.8	2.9	3.9	165	221
1968-69	4.3	5.8	3.2	4.3	195	262
1969-70	2.9	4.1	2.5	3.6	168	241

[a]Series A is the percent difference between the alternative wage one standard deviation above/below the average alternative wage as a percent of mean alternative wage. Series B is the percent difference between the lowest and highest alternative wages in all labor markets of the state.

[b]Computed by multiplying (1) by the appropriate elasticity in Table 3. Three-stage estimates were employed except for 1969-70.

[c]Computed by multiplying the decimal form of (2) by average base pay for each year. (See note to Table 4 for average base pay.)

PUBLIC SCHOOLS

our coefficients were valid for the nation, we could compute Table 6. These computations are hardly valid as representations of the actual behavior of teachers' wages on the national level, but they do illustrate the considerable importance of labor-market variables compared to other possible determinants of teachers' wages.

The last determinant of wages, other than collective bargaining, is the working environment of a school district. The variable serving as a proxy for the pleasantness or unpleasantness of teaching in a school district is the size of enrollment in the district. Table 3 reveals that district size possesses a small but significant coefficient, while Table 7 shows its impact on teachers' wages. Several representative cities have been chosen, ranging from the largest in the state to relatively modest cities. Whether or not the figures in Table 7 represent *large* payments for the disamenities of large-city teaching is left to the reader. Assuming a ten-month contract, the largest monthly disamenity premium would appear to be about $21.

Assuming that a disamenity premium of $21 per month or less is judged to be small, two interpretations are possible. The first has been suggested already: if teachers' personal tastes about what constitutes bad working conditions differ, then large districts (presumably with bad working conditions) may be hiring from a minority of teachers that simply does not require a large disamenity premium. In this view, bad working conditions would not necessarily result in either large disamenity premia *or* a decline in faculty ability. The other interpretation of the ap-

TABLE 6. Hypothetical Impact of Alternative Wage and Tax Base on Teachers' Base Pay Nationally, 1969–1970

	Assumed Percent Variation Nationally	Percent Differential of Base Pay Due to Each Independent Variable	Dollar Differential of Base Pay Due to Each Independent Variable[a]
Tax Base	200	6	$400
Alternative			
Wage	25	22	$1480

[a]The computation in this column assumes an average base pay of $6700.

209

TABLE 7. The Impact of District Enrollment on Base Pay, 1969–1970

City	Enrollment In City (1)	Average Enrollment in Surrounding County (2)	Percent Difference[a] (3)	Percent Differential in Base Pay Due To Enrollment[b] (4)	Dollar Differential in Base Pay Due To Enrollment (5)
Newark	76,000	6,000	330	3.3	215
Jersey City	37,000	5,600	220	2.2	146
Camden	20,000	3,000	220	2.2	146
Trenton	17,000	5,666	115	1.15	75

[a]Geometric mean of difference in size as percent of city's enrollment and as percent of average county enrollment.
[b]Column (3) times appropriate elasticity in Table 3.

parently small disamenity premia is that large urban school districts allow faculty ability levels to deteriorate rather than compensate fully for bad working conditions with large wage premia. It is not possible to distinguish between the two interpretations within the limits of this study.

B. The Impact of Collective Bargaining

In 1969–1970 a number of school districts operated with negotiated salary schedules for the first time. A dummy variable, U, representing bargained contracts was entered into the cross-section wage equation, but it failed to have a significant coefficient. Three explanations are possible: 1) bargaining in 70 percent of the districts may have influenced the 30 percent that did not formally file contracts; 2) bargaining may have had no impact; 3) bargaining may have had an impact that could not be detected by a simple dummy variable. The first explanation, employing the concept of "spillover" effects, is tested below with pooled data.

Collective bargaining may interact with other determinants in influencing the salaries of teachers. For example, "poor" school districts may face strong political pressure to resist teachers' demands; indeed, such pressures might actually be generated by the advent of well-publicized negotiations. On the other hand, unions bargaining with "rich" districts might be under severe pressure to achieve large gains. Thus, poor districts may bargain smaller increases than when wages were quietly set unilaterally without generating political controversy. On the other hand, rich districts may bargain larger wage increases than were set without bargaining. Bargaining may also make school boards and teachers more sensitive to prevailing labor markets conditions in setting wage scales. Justifying demands and counterproposals might force bargaining parties to examine more closely alternative wages and market conditions than when wages were set unilaterally. (School boards setting salaries unilaterally may employ rules of thumb that are somewhat insensitive to market conditions.) If this hypothesis is true, we would expect base pay in bargaining districts to reflect prevailing alternative wages more closely than base pay in nonbargaining districts.

In order to study these possibilities, interaction variables were created by multiplying all exogenous variables in the wage equation by the bargaining dummy variable. Each new interaction variable was paired with the bargaining dummy and entered in the wage equation for 1969–1970. This resulted in the discovery that bargaining districts were significantly more sensitive to the alternative wage variables than were nonbargaining districts. This may be seen in Table 3.

One important characteristic of this formulation is that the impact of unionism on wages varies depending on the particular labor market in which the bargaining district was located. Table 8 reveals the degree of impact of collective bargaining in the various labor markets of the state. When the *mean* value of the alternative wage is employed in computing the impact of collective bargaining, the net effect of bargaining is almost exactly zero. The weighted average in Table 8 indicates a small positive impact of bargaining because proportionally more bargaining districts are located in high- than low-wage labor markets. Bargaining districts are thus concentrated where bargaining tends to do teachers some good.

The weighted average of the impact of bargaining in Table 8 uses the proportion of all bargaining *districts* in each labor mar-

TABLE 8.   The Impact of Collective Bargaining on Base Pay by Labor Market, 1969

Labor Markets Ranked by Size of AW[a]	Impact (%) of Bargaining[b] (1)	Proportion of All Districts with Union Contracts (2)	(1) $\times$ (2) (3)	Incidence of Bargaining in Market (4)
High	+1.4	.456	.638	.78
Second	+ .2	.228	.045	.70
Third	− .2	.038	−.007	.50
Fourth	− .6	.179	−.107	.75
Fifth	−1.7	.097	−.165	.50
		Weighted Average =	.404 percent	

[a]For purposes of this study the state was divided into 7 labor markets, 2 of which were consolidated with the others in calculating this table due to similarity of wage rates.

[b]Derived from $[-3.60 + .72 \ln (AW_i)] \cdot 100$, where i indicates a particular labor market.

212

ket, not the proportion of all *teachers* covered by contracts in each labor market. Since school districts in high-wage labor markets employ more teachers than districts in low-wage markets, a teacher-weighted average would reveal a somewhat larger impact of collective bargaining. Table 9 is based upon relatively crude computations from raw data, and so should be taken as indicative of general magnitudes, not as a precise tabulation.

The impact of bargaining is certainly not large. An increase of .4 percent (Table 8) relative to nonbargaining districts represents only about $30 annually in 1969–1970. The dollar amount of an impact of .55 percent (Table 9) is only about $40. The largest impact of bargaining in any of the labor markets is about 1.4 percent, about $100 per year. These rather small estimates of the impact of collective bargaining are consistent with the results of other studies (see Table 2). So far we have considered only cross-section results, which may underestimate the effect of bargaining if threat effects of unions are important.

That collective bargaining might result in salary scales becoming more attuned to prevailing labor market conditions is plausible. Why, however, should bargaining in some labor markets have lowered salaries below those in nonbargaining districts? Why should unionization ever lower relative wages? It is possible that school boards in low-wage markets were able to defeat the demands of the new unions. If the school boards had such power, why did they fail to use it in those districts, located in the

TABLE 9. Impact of Bargaining on Base Pay, Using Teacher-Weighted Average

Labor Markets Ranked By Wage	Proportion of All Teachers With Union Contract[a] (1)	Impact (%) of Bargaining (2)	(1) × (2) percent (3)
High	.53	1.4	.74
Second	.18	.2	.036
Third	.07	− .2	−.014
Fourth	.14	− .6	−.084
Fifth	.07	−1.7	−.119
		Teacher-Weighted Average = .559	

[a]Does not sum to one due to rounding.

213

same labor market, that did *not* bargain? Surely power used against organized teachers can readily be turned against unorganized teachers. The only possible rationalization of this is that nonbargaining school boards did not employ their latent power, while something in the process of bargaining encouraged school boards in bargaining districts to employ their power. Possibly nonbargaining districts continued to set wages in an habitual manner, making use of rules of thumb and failing to exercise latent power to depress wages. Bargaining may have shaken the other districts out of habitual patterns and caused them to exert their latent power to depress wages (or at least resist wage increases).

Even this explanation leaves some issues to be resolved. Why should school boards in low-wage markets have the power to resist union demands, while those in high-wage markets apparently lack such power? Were the teachers' organizations in the low-wage markets somehow weaker than unions in the high-wage markets? This latter idea seems likely: low-wage labor markets are typically located in the rural areas of the state, and vice versa. The state teachers' association is likely to concentrate its professional resources in the urban districts rather than the rural ones. If pro-union sentiment in the public at large were to play a large role in supporting teachers' demands, such public support is more likely in urban than rural areas. Finally, if the incidence of collective bargaining in a labor market is any index of the strength of unionization, the unions in the high-wage labor markets would have to be considered stronger than those in the low-wage markets (see Column 4, Table 8).

If negotiated wage scales appear more sensitive to labor-market conditions than nonnegotiated scales, is such sensitivity due to bargaining, or did districts that already were more sensitive to labor market conditions merely have a higher propensity to bargain than other districts? Thornton (1971) found that bargaining in 1969–1970 apparently raised relative wages in the districts he studied. However, he found that the same bargaining variables introduced into wage equations for 1958, when no bargaining occurred, had positive and significant coefficients. Those districts that bargained in 1969 apparently had a tendency at least as early as 1958 to pay relatively high wages anyway.

In order to test Thornton's suggestion, the bargaining and interaction variables were introduced into the wage equations for the five years prior to 1969–1970, the first year of official negotiations. In four of the five years the coefficients were insignificant, although they were significant in 1966–1967. The magnitudes of these coefficients were never as much as one-half the magnitudes of the coefficients in 1969–1970, the bargaining year. This would suggest that some small tendency existed for bargaining to occur in districts that already were relatively sensitive to labor market conditions, but that negotiations surely accentuated this sensitivity.

Despite the demonstrated increased sensitivity of bargaining districts to labor-market conditions, we have failed to discover more than a trivial impact of bargaining on wages in the typical school district. This appearance of a weak performance by the teachers' associations might be explained by spillover effects. Suppose the threat of teacher militancy induced nonbargaining districts to increase their salary schedules for 1969–1970 as much as bargaining districts increased theirs. In an effort to convince teachers, who for the most part were already organized in local chapters of the New Jersey Education Association, that active bargaining gains little, nonbargaining boards might have been unusually generous in determining the 1969–1970 salary schedules. A cross-section regression equation, which in essence compares the wage in the average nonbargaining district with the wage in the average bargaining district, would detect no difference in wage due to bargaining. After all, the wage in the nonbargaining districts was, in fact, responsive to the bargaining that was occurring in other districts. It would be incorrect to conclude that bargaining had no effect on wages; rather, because bargaining influenced wages in *all* districts, it was simply impossible to measure the full impact of negotiations.

One way to overcome this difficulty is to compare bargained wages with nonbargained wages that could not possibly have been influenced by spillover and threat effects. Fortunately this is a simple matter, since we have data for the years 1964–1969, when there was virtually no bargaining at all in the state, and obviously no spillover or threat effects. By pooling data for 1964–1970, it is possible to obtain another estimate of the impact of bargaining, for which the problem of spillover effects would be minimized. The following equation was estimated by ordinary least squares for the years 1964–1970:

$$\ln B = -1.18 + .008 \ln S + .014 \ln TXB + .022 \ln INC$$
$$+ .966 \ln AW + .013 U + .059 \ln (\text{State Aid}).$$

The number of observations is 1,788 and the R^2 was .943. All coefficients are statistically significant at the 1 percent level.[11] The estimated elasticity of base pay with respect to the alternative wage is not significantly different from 1. Pooled data thus yield an estimate that confirms the predicted long-run elasticity of 1. The estimated impact of bargaining on wages in the average district is 1.3 percent with this equation. Even an allowance for the threat effect, therefore, fails to produce a large estimate of the impact of teachers' unions on base pay.

C. Further Results: The Maximum Pay of Teachers

Does collective bargaining have the same impact on other aspects of the single salary schedule as upon base pay? The following equation was estimated by ordinary least squares for the year 1969–1970:

$$\ln (\text{Maximum Pay}) = -1.06 + .016 \ln S + .066 \ln TXB$$
$$+ .057 \ln INC + .977 \ln AW - 3.60 U + .728 U \ln AW.$$

The number of observations is 298; the R^2 is .606, and all the coefficients in the equation are statistically significant.

---

[11] The logarithm of per-pupil state aid is included in this pooled regression equation, although it was not in the cross-section regressions. State aid was not a significant explanatory variable in the cross-section work for given years because per-pupil aid for all districts was almost equal for any given year. However, between years the legislature of the state frequently increased per-pupil state aid. Aid thus appears as a variable in this equation and possesses a significant coefficient.

Maximum pay is defined as the largest annual salary that a teacher holding the bachelor's degree can earn after accumulating experience up to some maximum level. Without repeating the discussion of the preceding sections, we note that the demand variables such as tax base and community income have rather small coefficients, and that the main determinant of teachers' maximum pay appears to be the alternative wage.

The impact of collective bargaining is essentially the same for maximum pay as it was for base pay, although a three-stage least-squares estimate, comparable to the one in Table 3, would undoubtedly give somewhat different coefficients. The impact of bargaining on maximum pay would be $60–$70, using a teacher-weighted estimate of the impact. The impact of bargaining on maximum pay levels in the high-wage labor market would only be $155–$160; this is still a relatively small impact upon wages.

IV. Conclusions

The evidence tends to support the theory presented in Section I. When one considers the very large differences in the wealth of communities, the salary differentials created by such variation of wealth are exceedingly small. Although this finding runs counter to much ad hoc theorizing, which holds there to be a large direct link between community wealth and teachers' wages, our empirical result does not stand alone. Hall and Carroll (1973), who also correctly controlled for labor market conditions by restricting their sample to schools within one labor market, reported a similar result, although they did not appreciate their finding and may even have been puzzled by it.

One implication of this is that wealthy school systems may not greatly outbid poorer school districts for more capable teachers. Reacting to the evidence that wealth does not influence teachers' wages directly, some readers may suggest a more subtle wealth effect: richer districts may not need to pay higher wages because they attract more capable teachers simply by being more pleasant places in which to work. In such a view, the theory in Section I, which predicted a negligible wealth effect on wages, is rejected,

217

and it is suggested that, but for the amenities of rich school districts, the impact of wealth on wages would be observed.

Within the context of the empirical work, it is difficult conclusively to dismiss this view. However, we may examine the relative merits of the theory of Section I and this view, which claims that a wealth effect on teachers' wages would be observed but for offsetting amenities. The theory of Section I predicted a negligible wealth effect on salaries. Can proponents of the competing view explain why the two offsetting effects seem almost precisely to cancel each other? This is a rather large coincidence, particularly when our theory predicts the negligible impact of wealth on wages. If amenities associated with wealth are so strong as to offset any direct impact of wealth on wages, why not *more* than offset it so that wealthy districts would pay *smaller* wages than poor districts? These are not quibbles, and they suggest serious problems with this alternative interpretation of the empirical work.

Another implication of our work is that increased state aid to education, which may be interpreted as an effective increase in the wealth of a community, will not be translated automatically into a windfall for teachers. Moynihan (1972, p. 74) has suggested that increased state or federal aid will simply enrich teachers, rather than benefiting pupils; we disagree.[12]

A second major conclusion is that district size has a very small impact on teachers' wages. Assuming that district size does generate disamenities, two interpretations of our finding are possible. Teachers' personal tastes may be diverse, and large school districts may be able to hire from among candidates who do not perceive a disamenity. One may also argue that large school districts simply allow the ability of their faculties to decline without attempting to compensate fully for the disamenity. Within the confines of this study it has been impossible to disentangle the two possibilities.

---

[12] It is possible that the *aggregate* short-run supply of teachers is less than infinitely elastic, and that an increase in aggregate demand due to a large increase in state aid to school districts could cause a short-run increase in teachers' wages. Our results suggest, however, that increased state aid will not *directly* induce districts to raise wages.

218

The major determinant of teachers' wages is the alternative wage. Since the wages of teachers are sensitive to alternative wages over time as well as across distance, we may conclude that teachers' wages will continue to rise at a rapid rate as long as general wage inflation is rapid. Little relief from this major cause of rising educational expenses would seem apparent.

Collective bargaining seems to have a very small impact on teachers' wages. One hesitates to generalize this result: if the impact of bargaining in public employment depends heavily on political considerations, then results from one state at one point in time may differ greatly from results in school systems located in very different political climates. Horton (1973) has outlined the unique political circumstances in New York City that have allowed a wage explosion in unionized public employment in that city. It is understandable, notwithstanding our results, that Schmenner (1973) found large wage impacts of bargaining in the eleven very large cities he studied.

COMMENTS

HIRSCHEL KASPER

The stimulating paper by Professor Frey represents another step forward in the process of understanding the impact of collective bargaining in the public sector. His study makes a number of interesting and useful contributions. The major one, it seems to me, is his attempt to tie together the wage impact of unionization with the quantity and quality of public services, in this case education. Research on the wage effects of public-sector unions is interesting, and Frey adds to the dozen or so studies in that area, but such studies assume greater importance when they go beyond the factor market to the broad spectrum of goods and services that we buy collectively with our taxes and fees. (I should make it clear, however, that I do not regard a two-sector general equilibrium model à la Johnson and Mieszkowski (1970) as the *optimum optimorum*.)

Frey's paper is an improvement over much of the earlier work, since the nature of his population, school districts within a single state, avoids many of the possible problems that faced earlier writers in defining the relevant labor market, the unit of observation. All the teachers and school districts in his study operate under the same rules with respect to matters such as rules of entry into the occupation. Mobility across the units of observation is thus easier institutionally than mobility out of the population.

Noteworthy, also, is the extreme congruence of his estimates of the impact of bargaining on teachers' wages with the earlier work done by others (Lipsky and Drotning, 1973; Hall and Carroll, 1973; Landon and Baird, 1972; Thornton, 1971; and Kasper, 1970 and 1971b). As a matter of fact, the estimates are all so close to each other that, while all of us may be right, it may also be that we have misspecified our equations in a systematic manner. It is encouraging to know that we have reached very similar conclusions, but I know of no economic law that states that the impact of collective bargaining has to be less than 5 percent regardless of whether the population is defined as teachers or school districts in all the states, large SMSA's, big cities, or all the school districts within a single state, taken at any and every moment of time (in the late 1960's!).

The wage impact of unions is probably not the most interesting result of this paper, at least to its author. Frey seems more taken by his estimates that income and wealth variables have only a negligible effect on salaries, and that to a large extent teachers' salaries are determined by the supply side via alternative employment opportunities. So let me turn to a brief consideration of those results and the underlying theory.

Frey asserts that not only is the supply of teachers perfectly elastic at the going wage but that the supply of each and every level of quality of teachers is also perfectly elastic for each school district. If this were in fact the case, demand would have no impact on wages. But the assertion would obtain very little support from school administrators and (black and white) taxpayers, not to mention the bored and tired school children, who would be appalled to learn that there is no economic limit to the number of good teachers who are available. The form and implications of his model would be quite different if the marginal costs of both ability and teachers varied with the number of teachers employed in the district.

As I read the paper I found myself unable to keep separate two kinds of quality: (1) the quality of the educational process, the degree to which students are stimulated, become aware and learn; and (2) the quality of teachers, as measured by their experience and other variables. It is one thing to assert that teacher ability is an economic good that can be purchased in the market, but it is a very different thing to assume that school superintendents are able to employ teachers who yield a quality of education of students with a reasonably small variance. Since the study examines the base salary, it is necessary to recognize that it is really discussing the *expected* quality of new, inexperienced teachers.

To the extent that superintendents can affect quality by select-

221

ing higher ability teachers, they directly affect the district-wide quality of teachers on the margin, although the average quality may change only negligibly. If one were to offer higher salaries than competitors in order to attract more educated, better trained, more verbal teachers and thus improve the quality of education in the district, experienced teachers with similar characteristics would demand higher salaries also on grounds of equity. The marginal costs of educational quality are apt to rise steeply.

Increased base salaries are not the only avenue open to districts that want to raise the quality of their teachers. The district can seek to change the internal relations within a given salary structure, including the criteria necessary to move along the salary schedule, in order to encourage its continuing teachers to seek additional education, training, and degrees. It should also be remembered that not all new teachers are inexperienced recent college graduates; a large proportion of the new teachers in most districts do have some teaching experience and do not begin at the base salary.

The absence in the empirical work of the usual flock of measures of educational quality, especially the student-teacher ratio, is surprising. No single measure of quality is entirely satisfactory, but average class size is probably the least bad. The cost to the teachers of smaller class size is apt to be foregone higher salaries, if school districts operate as if they had a wages fund, as I think they often do.

Frey concentrates on school boards as the buyers of educational quality and teachers, but it is possible to imagine a model wherein the school boards themselves are an argument in the demand for education by the community. I cannot say much about the determinants of the behavior of school boards, but I am sufficiently unsure of the facts on this matter that I am not willing to concede that there are only three possible objective functions of school boards. School boards may not be independent decision-making units, but I still wish I knew why people seek election to them.

In many states, although I assume not in New Jersey, school districts are a subset of a larger governmental unit; funds can then be directly transferred to education from, say, welfare, policing, or transportation. (Taxpayers, too, exercise some choice over the domain of public services.). In other words, decisions about school finances may in general result from more complex objective functions than Frey suggests for New Jersey. In this connection it would have been interesting to see the impact of "political" variables on salary. Teachers at the state and district levels exercise political power on both the underlying legislation that guides bargaining and on the identities of the elected officials.

I think that Frey's empirical results are interesting, accurate, and useful. If I can draw an arbitrary distinction between his results and his conclusions, I would say that it is the latter which give me some pause. His conclusions have been drawn, I think, with an eye on policy, and it is not always easy to stay within the confines of your empirical research if you want to talk policy.

I find it hard to say much that is constructive about either the specific variables in the equations or about the estimates. It is always possible to quibble, so I shall. For example, I do not believe that size of school district is a useful proxy for disamenities. If school tensions are exacerbated when "a large proportion of teachers, parents and even pupils know one another," then it seems more likely that small school districts and small schools will have more tension than the large anonymous bureaucratic districts and schools. Moreover, disamenities are more often associated with specific schools within a single district than, as implied by Frey's model, with the district as a whole. An alternative interpretation of the finding that there is a positive relation between base salary and district size is that the supply of teachers to a district is less than perfectly elastic and that there are increasing marginal costs in the employment of teachers.

I think that I would be more willing to concede that "wealth is spent on better teacher-student ratios" rather than on higher salaries if Frey had reported some regressions of wealth on average class size. It seems reasonable to assume that the supply of teacher ability is such that, the higher the salary, the more ability the district can buy. If, however, districts pay more attention to the ability of experienced teachers than to new ones,

223

wealth might not have any effect on base salaries but rather on the various steps of the salary schedule and on the *average* salary of teachers. In that case Frey's results may be seen as an elaboration on the work of others rather than a contrary conclusion.

I wonder whether Frey's construction of his "income" variable imparts any bias to his estimates. Is there any kind of "regression toward the mean" problem here? If differences in the recent rates of growth of community income had any effect on the differences in teacher salaries, it might have been obscured by forcing all communities into a single growth-rate mold.

The empirical problem of selecting a control group is always a difficult matter. Nursing may be a good alternative to teaching, but perhaps not for the reason Frey indicates, the predominance of females. Men constitute about 35 percent of all classroom teachers in New Jersey and 57 percent of the secondary school teachers in that state. I doubt whether so many men are yet in nursing, and I wish that Frey had tried some other control groups in addition to nursing—but not policemen (Kasper, 1970). Eckaus (1973) found that rates of return to education were very sensitive to the choice of a control group, and Frey's results may be also.

Even if judgment is withheld on the elasticity of supply of teachers, to the extent that unions raise nurses' wages above the market, an excess supply of teachers may be generated. It may be asked, why won't the employing agency select the most able teachers? Unless there is an inverse correlation between opportunity cost and ability, the pool of applicants, even if chosen randomly, should marginally raise the mean of teachers' ability. If the correlation between opportunity cost and teacher ability is positive, it would most likely be that above-market wages would lead to better teachers.

As I look at Frey's results in Table 3, I wonder whether he has not been too hard on himself. Has he unfortunately thrown out all his small coefficients on the assumption that they were only so much bath water? Assume, as he says, that both income and the tax base are of little importance to salary levels, and that there is a positive relation between salaries and the number of pupils. By assumption, the supply of teachers is perfectly elastic. The reader may feel that, aside from a constant term, which is sometimes highly significant and other times not at all, we are left with essentially a simple regression of the salaries of teachers on the salaries of nurses.

Certainly the policy implications derived from the use of the nurses' wage must be made with caution, since it is ambiguous whether this alternative wage is a pure supply variable. Could nurses' salaries be acting as measures for community income, wealth, or tastes for public and/or social services? I note that the significance of the coefficients for median family income fluctuates sharply (compare 1966-1967 and 1967-1968 with the other years), a seemingly unlikely occurrence unless some other highly correlated variable is implicitly compensating. It is also possible that the nurses' wages might be reflecting regional price differentials. One would then want to draw inferences with respect to the real incomes of teachers, not the elasticity of supply.

I still believe that the dependent variable should accurately reflect whatever salary measure school boards set in their sights (Kasper, 1972). If they look at base pay and calculate the costs upward from that during negotiations, base pay should be the variable. If boards are interested in costs in general and permit unions to make some shifts within the salary distribution, then average wage increases are a better measure of the bargaining effort. I sympathize with empiricists who use available data and do not intend to cast either the first or the *n*th stone, but we ought to gather some institutional knowledge so we can examine whatever variable the parties tell us might be worth examining. Different salary measures may warrant different models.

As events would have it, I have become involved as a mediator in some negotiations involving teachers and so have had a small opportunity to match both theory and statistics with one experience. If I had to expend my one degree of freedom on an equation, I would select a model that explicitly recognized a tradeoff between salaries and class size, because they are not independent. In addition, I have new doubts about the ability of a measure such as the tax base to capture the wealth and willingness of a district to spend funds for education. Variables such as tax effort, millage rate, or even the proportion of dollars voted in bond issues and tax levies relative to the total amount of dollars that have been on recent ballots may come closer to measuring the demands for education and teachers. Finally, I would reiterate my earlier doubts about using base pay rather than some average salary as the dependent variable. I noted that teacher negotiating committees are generally drawn from the more experienced teachers who thereby have a direct financial stake in salary adjustments other than those for entering, inexperienced teachers. Moreover, if a teacher "surplus" occurs in the future, it will likely enlarge the salary range by tending to keep down the salaries of new teachers. Future research on the impact of unions might well take a·more critical look at using base salary as the appropriate source to study the effect of bargaining.

DANIEL S. HAMERMESH

The Effect of Government Ownership on Union Wages

Economists have long recognized that government regulation often aids unions in achieving higher compensation and greater control over employment. (See Friedman, 1951; Lewis, 1951; and for a specific example, Lurie, 1960.) Only recently, with the rapid growth of militant public-sector unionism, has it been argued (Wellington and Winter, 1971) that unions in government inherently have more power than in the private sector. The demand for services provided by government is often quite inelastic, so they claim, and wage setting there is inextricably involved in political decision making. (This latter point is quite consistent with Reder's argument in this volume.) The resulting tendency toward large union relative wage effects implies a need to impose drastic restrictions on the use of unions' bargaining power. Before such a policy is instituted, it is essential to know whether relative wage effects are greater in government and, if so, how important each of the two possible causes is. If the first, then restrictive policies should be applied to all sectors characterized by inelastic product demand; only if the second cause is important is there an economic basis for restricting unions' bargaining power in the public sector alone.

   In this study we analyze whether workers in the same unionized occupation receive higher compensation in government than in private industry. Previous work has discussed the effect of unions on wages of white-collar workers (Hamermesh, 1971) and of government employees generally (Schmenner, 1973), on firemen's wages (Ashenfelter, 1971), and on teachers' wages (Kasper,

Note: The work in this study was financed by a grant from the Ford Foundation to Princeton University for the study of urban labor markets. Joshua Greene and Frank Lysy provided helpful research assistance.

1970, Frey in this volume, and Landon and Baird, 1972).[1] While such measurement is interesting in its own right, only the comparative method of estimating these effects allows us to separate out the effects of government ownership and thus provide information designed to guide policy for bargaining in the public sector.

We present empirical estimates of the effect of public operation on union wages in the same occupation. The study thus abstracts from differences in demand elasticities for workers in different occupations and concentrates instead on the effect of involvement in the political process. The first part deals with unionized bus drivers, the second with unionized construction workers, and the third with a large sample of individual workers from many occupations. The first two parts of the study are especially interesting because they isolate wages in narrow occupations; the third should be useful in providing results based on a broader data set that allows us to abstract from differences in the quality of labor between sectors. Since part of the Wellington-Winter argument suggests especially large extra wage effects for public-employee unions where demand is inelastic, our use of transit (where the demand elasticity is probably low) should provide a good estimate of the upper bound of this effect. The other two parts should give estimates that are less likely to overstate the Wellington-Winter effect.

I. Unionized Bus Drivers, 1963-1971

Local bus drivers have been unionized in nearly all major cities since the 1940's.[2] We are thus dealing with an occupation which, though not highly skilled, also does not face serious threats from nonunion labor in most areas. Despite this lack of

---

[1] There is a small, roughly 5% relative wage effect of unions of clerical employees; the International Association of Fire Fighters' main effect has been the reduction of the work week. Evidence on the effects of teachers' unionization is quite mixed, but few researchers show effects of more than 5%.

[2] Lurie (1961) analyzes historical trends in unionization in this industry and discusses the relative wage effect of the ATU.

TABLE 1. Number of Cities in the Sample (N = 48) with Publicly Operated Bus Systems

Year	Number	Year	Number
1963	7	1968	14
1964	9	1969	18
1965	10	1970	21
1966	12	1971	24
1967	13		

change in the labor market in the past quarter-century, the structure of the product market has undergone rapid change. Not only has there been substantial consolidation of bus lines in each city, there has also been a large and continuing increase in the fraction of local bus companies that are municipally owned. As Table 1 shows, in our sample of 48 cities only 7 had bus lines in government-run systems in 1963, while by 1971 the figure had risen to 24. Moreover, bus lines in several other cities in the sample were scheduled to be taken over by the city during 1972. This change in market structure must be considered when we estimate the difference in union wages between the government and private sectors.

Data are available annually for 48 cities from 1963–1971 on the beginning wages of unionized bus drivers, w_U. All the cities contain between 100,000 and 1,000,000 inhabitants, so we are explicitly excluding possible unusual effects of bargaining in the largest cities. The American Transit Association provided unpublished data on the date when each publicly operated transit system came into government ownership. These data were used to form the variable G_{it}, taking the value one if the system in city i is owned by the government in year t and zero otherwise.[3]

To estimate the effect of government ownership, we need to hold constant those extraneous factors specific to each city in the sample. Many studies of this sort (see Fuchs, 1967, and Pashigian, 1972) include variables for region and city size as a means of holding the cost of living constant. Even if this were the only

---

[3] The wage data are available in Bureau of Labor Statistics Bulletins 1431, 1486, 1589, 1667, and 1745. Ownership information is from *Publicly-Owned Transit Systems in the United States*, March 1971.

other factor causing differences in wages across cities, the method would still be imperfect, for it ignores *intra-regional* variation in living costs. Rather than taking this route, we have chosen to deflate the wage of unionized bus drivers by the average hourly earnings of manufacturing production workers in the particular city, w_M.[4] This method removes cost-of-living biases and the effects of other differences across cities, such as nonpecuniary effects, that might affect wage levels.

Having introduced the deflator w_M, we need to account for differences in the quality of labor in transit and manufacturing across cities and in the extent of unionization in manufacturing. Our basic model, following the work of Lewis (1963), is thus:

$$\log w_U/w_M = \alpha_0 + \alpha_1 G + f(X) + \alpha_N UM,$$

where UM is the fraction of manufacturing workers unionized and X is a vector of variables to be discussed below. As a check on the consistency of our model, the coefficient of the measure of manufacturing unionization should lie in the range of estimates produced in studies of unions' effects on manufacturing wages. (Cf. Lewis, 1963; Rosen, 1969; and Hamermesh, 1971.)

One factor affecting manufacturing wage rates and, to a lesser extent, transit wages is the level of educational attainment in the city. Numerous studies have shown the relation between earnings and education; since manufacturing is a fairly broad classification, the manufacturing wage should be strongly positively related to the level of education. Bus driving is a much more homogeneous occupation and, given the technology, the quality of workers in this occupation is less likely to vary across cities as educational attainment varies. We can therefore assume that the greater effect of education will be on manufacturing wages, so that the effect on w_U/w_M will be negative. The actual measure used for each year in our sample is the interpolated value of the median educational attainment of males in the *i*th standard metropolitan statistical area for the appropriate year between 1960 and 1970. We use this area-wide variable, *MED*, rather than one restricted

[4]These data are from Bureau of Labor Statistics, Bulletin 1308-8, and from *Employment and Earnings*, May 1972.

to the city itself, because the manufacturing wage is area-wide and the labor market extends beyond the limits of the central city.

The fraction of nonwhites, NW, in the population may also affect our relative wage measure. There is a large and increasing proportion of black bus drivers in many cities; one would thus guess that their importance in the union implies less discrimination in this industry than in the average of manufacturing (cf. Ashenfelter, 1972b). Moreover, in cities with public bus lines or those with private bus lines having close public supervision of operations, there is likely to be less wage discrimination than in the broad range of manufacturing. For both of these reasons, the nonwhite variable should have a greater negative effect on the manufacturing wage and should thus be positively related to the relative wage measure. The measure used is the fraction of nonwhite males in the male population in the particular SMSA; for each year in our sample the measure is interpolated linearly between the values for 1960 and 1970.

Two additional variables are used to account for possible differences in the arduousness of bus driving in different cities. As population size increases, the complexity of bus routes and their length also increase, and drivers must devote more effort to learning the route. Other things equal, this must either be offset by attracting more capable workers or by paying current ones a higher wage to compensate them for their efforts. In either case we expect population size, POP, to be positively related to the relative wage measure. For this variable, the appropriate measure is the population of the city itself, since the bus lines are often restricted to the individual central city. The actual measure used here is again the interpolated value of the city's population in 1960 and 1970, measured in thousands. Population density may also increase the difficulty of bus driving by requiring more frequent stopping or more crowded buses. To account for this positive effect on w_U we also include $DENS$, the city's population in thousands divided by its area in square miles.

Data on the variable UM, the fraction of manufacturing workers unionized, are available only in selected years. For the

231

intervening years the data used are those for the adjacent years for which the data are available.[5]

The basic model to be estimated is:

$$(1) \quad \ln w_U/w_M = \alpha_0 + \alpha_1 G + \alpha_2 POP + \alpha_3 DENS$$
$$+ \alpha_4 MED + \alpha_5 NW + \alpha_6 UM + \epsilon,$$

where ϵ is a random error term. Ordinary least-squares estimation was first applied to the data for each year, and then a generalized least-squares method proposed by Zellner (1962) was also applied. This technique is essential here because the error terms for an individual city are likely to be correlated across the years and because the same measure of UM appears in several years' equations. Results are presented only for these estimates. In addition to estimating the equation for each year in our sample, we also estimate a pooled version of it for all nine years.

Table 2 lists the estimates of equation (1) for each of the nine years and then for the pooled equation. By far the most remarkable result is the constancy of the relative wage effect of the public ownership variable, G. It varies only between 3 percent and 6 percent, and there appears to be little trend in it after the first two years. This is especially surprising given the large number of firms that went over from private to public ownership in the years studied. The relative wage effect is significant in all years, again indicating the great stability of this result.

We can check on the validity of our method of deflating transit wages by those of all manufacturing workers by examining the relative wage effect of manufacturing unionism. In the pooled sample it is roughly 16 percent, quite consistent with past work

[5]The education data are computed from *Census of Population, 1960*, PC(1)-C, Tables 73, and *Census of Population, 1970*, PC(1)-C, Tables 83; the population and density data are computed from *Census of Population, 1970*, PC(1)-A1; and the data on the fraction nonwhite are from *Census of Population, 1970*, PC(1)-B1, Table 66. Unionization data, measuring the fraction of blue-collar manufacturing workers in plants where a majority of workers are covered by collective bargaining, are from Bureau of Labor Statistics, Bulletins 1435, 1530, 1575 and 1660.

TABLE 2. Estimates of (1), Local Transit Bus Drivers: Dependent
Variable is Ln (w_U / w_M) [a]

Year	Constant	G	POP	DENS	MED	NW	UM
1963	.263	.027	.000026	.0074	-.019	-.027	-.246
	(1.0)	(2.1)	(.3)	(2.1)	(1.6)	(.3)	(4.7)
1964	.207	.032	.000012	.0085	-.015	.047	-.248
	(1.4)	(2.9)	(.1)	(2.5)	(1.2)	(.5)	(5.1)
1965	.138	.051	.000001	.0091	-.010	.0002	-.226
	(.7)	(2.4)	(.02)	(2.4)	(.6)	(.2)	(4.1)
1966	-.098	.058	.000001	.0094	.004	.185	-.175
	(.6)	(6.2)	(.02)	(3.0)	(.3)	(2.5)	(4.2)
1967	-.154	.045	.000002	.0106	.007	.197	-.151
	(.8)	(3.8)	(.03)	(3.3)	(.4)	(2.2)	(3.6)
1968	-.148	.039	.000074	.0088	.003	.123	-.117
	(.6)	(3.6)	(1.2)	(2.6)	(.1)	(1.3)	(2.6)
1969	-.116	.060	.000107	.0074	.0001	.206	-.117
	(.4)	(6.0)	(1.7)	(2.1)	(.00)	(2.1)	(2.5)
1970	-.078	.047	.000092	.0087	-.005	.164	-.041
	(.2)	(3.6)	(1.3)	(2.2)	(.1)	(1.4)	(.7)
1971	-.079	.039	.000141	.0063	-.003	.094	-.055
	(.1)	(2.3)	(1.9)	(1.5)	(.1)	(.7)	(.8)
Pooled	.145	.051	.000072	.0079	-.016	.00076	-.160
	(1.3)	(4.5)	(3.0)	(6.1)	(1.8)	(.5)	(6.7)

[a]Absolute values of t-statistics in parentheses here and in the next table.

on this subject.[6] The effect ranges from 20 percent in the first
two years of our sample down to 5 percent in the last two years.
While the drop in the effect of manufacturing unionism between
1969 and 1970 is probably an overestimate, the direction of
change is certainly what we would expect. In a rapid inflation
unionized workers in manufacturing lose compared to their nonunion counterparts (see Throop, 1968); the extent of loss would
hardly be 7 percent in one year, but some decline in this relative
wage effect is to be expected. The magnitude of the effect and
its change over time suggest that potential biases introduced by

[6]Hamermesh (1971) finds an effect of 20% for blue-collar workers;
Lewis (1963), in summarizing much of the previous work, concludes that
15% is a good estimate of the magnitude of this effect; Rosen (1969), using
data for 1960, finds an effect of 16%.

our use of the manufacturing wage to deflate the entry-level wage of unionized bus drivers have been adequately removed by the inclusion of the independent variable *UM*.

The education variable, *MED*, produces the expected negative sign in all but three years; moreover, in the pooled equations, the effect is negative and significantly different from zero. The fraction of nonwhite workers in the labor force, *NW*, generally produces the predicted positive effect on the wage of transit workers relative to that of manufacturing workers. Interestingly, the effect is most strongly positive just after the passage of the Civil Rights Act of 1964. Since the act's most immediate effect was probably on public and publicly visible employment, such as transit, the timing of the act can explain the pattern of coefficients on *NW*. These variables also appear to justify our method of deflating the transit wage and imply that we can interpret the coefficient of the public ownership dummy, *G*, as being uncontaminated by effects introduced by our deflation procedure. Density produces a significant positive effect on the wage relative in all years; population size has a positive effect, and it is nearly significant in the latter half of the sample. Since we have accounted for cost-of-living differences through our deflation procedure, we may conclude that density and population size can, as we postulated, be acting as proxies for the degree of difficulty and thus the skill required of bus drivers.

A dummy variable for the South was tried in place of the *NW* variable with results even less satisfying than those presented in Table 2. Undoubtedly, other variables could be included, but those we have used appear to perform quite well and in a manner consistent with one's expectations.[7]

Our estimate of the coefficient on the public ownership dummy, *G*, could be biased downward because we include as publicly owned those systems that were recently bought from the private sector. It may be that it takes time for the public ownership wage effect to reach its peak. We can test for this

---

[7]A set of eight dummies, each taking a value 1 for one year's observations and 0 for all others, was included in the pooled equation; its effects on the estimates presented in Table 2 were minimal.

possibility by including in equation (1) the additional variables:

$$G1_{it} = \begin{cases} 1 \text{ if } G_{it} - G_{it-1} = 1; \\ 0 \text{ otherwise} \end{cases};$$

$$G2_{it} = \begin{cases} 1 \text{ if } G_{it-1} - G_{it-2} = 1; \\ 0 \text{ otherwise.} \end{cases}$$

By examining the coefficients on the variable G after these changeover variables are included, we should be able to estimate the steady-state public ownership effect.

Table 3 presents estimates of equation (1) after the variables $G1$ and $G2$ have been included. The methods of estimation are identical to those used in Table 2. The quality variables, MED, NW, $DENS$ and POP, perform roughly as they did in the estimates of equation (1). Most interesting is the magnitude of the coefficients of G, $G1$, and $G2$. As we expected, there is a slight increase in the steady-state value of the coefficient on public ownership. Once we have accounted for recent switchovers to public ownership, we find an effect ranging from 3 percent up to nearly 9 percent on the wages of unionized transit workers. The coefficients of the two switchover variables, $G1$ and $G2$, are usually negative; moreover, the value of the coefficient $G1$ is generally more negative than that of $G2$, suggesting that it takes several years for firms taken over by the public sector to increase wages up to the steady-state level. The coefficients on $G2$ are not significant as frequently as those on $G1$, and the pattern of coefficients suggests that most of the effect of public ownership is reached after two years. We have thus not bothered to experiment with additional variables of this sort.

One might object that our estimates are biased down by the failure to include data for the 6 cities with more than 1,000,000 inhabitants. The estimates in Tables 2 and 3 were recalculated including such data. In no case did the coefficient on G (the steady-state public ownership effect) increase by more than .8 percentage points over the estimates in the tables; in the early years in the sample the coefficient actually decreased.

Having shown that the steady-state effect in transit is no more than 9 percent, one can ask whether there is a contagion effect

235

TABLE 3. Estimates of (1), Expanded, Local Transit Bus Drivers: Dependent Variable is Ln (w_U/w_M)

Year	Constant	G	G1	G2	POP	DENS	MED	NW	UM
1963	.301	.032	-.057		.000033	.0078	-.022	-.007	-.265
	(1.8)	(1.9)	(1.2)		(.4)	(2.2)	(1.7)	(.07)	(4.9)
1964	.250	.032	.001	-.051	.000021	.0091	-.018	.059	-.271
	(1.5)	(2.1)	(.06)	(1.2)	(.3)	(2.7)	(1.3)	(.6)	(5.3)
1965	.129	.070	-.046	-.006	-.000014	.0094	-.007	.0002	-.258
	(.6)	(2.6)	(.8)	(.1)	(.1)	(2.5)	(.4)	(.2)	(4.4)
1966	-.058	.072	-.017	.053	.000001	.0099	.002	.178	-.208
	(.3)	(4.7)	(.6)	(2.7)	(.00)	(3.1)	(.1)	(2.4)	(4.6)
1967	-.124	.080	-.090	-.029	-.000011	.0102	.007	.176	-.175
	(.6)	(4.7)	(3.5)	(1.1)	(.1)	(3.2)	(.4)	(2.2)	(3.9)
1968	-.188	.070	-.062	-.048	.000057	.0088	.008	.152	-.137
	(.8)	(3.8)	(1.7)	(1.9)	(.9)	(2.7)	(.4)	(1.6)	(2.9)
1969	-.135	.086	-.019	-.042	.000091	.0078	.003	.242	-.148
	(.5)	(4.7)	(.9)	(1.1)	(1.4)	(2.3)	(.1)	(2.4)	(3.0)
1970	-.168	.080	-.063	-.009	.000070	.0087	.005	.174	-.079
	(.4)	(3.9)	(1.6)	(.4)	(1.0)	(2.2)	(.1)	(1.5)	(1.3)
1971	-.102	.067	-.068	-.021	.000129	.0061	.0004	.106	-.095
	(.2)	(3.0)	(2.2)	(.4)	(1.7)	(1.4)	(.01)	(.8)	(1.4)
Pooled	.157	.065	-.058	-.032	.000062	.0076	-.017	.00076	-.159
	(1.5)	(5.1)	(2.3)	(1.1)	(2.55)	(5.9)	(1.9)	(.5)	(6.7)

from the increasing extent of public ownership.[8] It could be that, as this increases, there is an increased spillover of the higher wages from the government sector to workers in privately operated lines. This effect could be due to competition among union leaders in different cities to achieve higher wage increases and to decreased management resistance, although the geographical separation of the union locals suggests that the effect may be small. It is also often thought that large wage increases are granted prior to a government takeover as a way of hastening it.[9]

We can test for this phenomenon by studying whether the wage in privately-run bus lines rose relative to that in manufacturing as the extent of government ownership increased. Using the coefficients on the variables G, $G1$, and $G2$ from the yearly estimates of equation (1) in Table 3 and the means of these variables, we estimate in the last column of Table 4 the wage in privately-run bus lines, w_{PU}, relative to the manufacturing wage, w_M, in each year in our sample. The results suggest that there is an increase of at most 3 percent between 1963 and 1971 in this relative wage. That the entire effect is due to spillovers is unclear, as it could be that the supply or demand curves for labor in bus driving relative to other occupations shifted upward for reasons we have not specified in our estimates. Suffice it to say that this result shows that there was no unusually large change in

---

[8] This is analogous in some ways to the threat effect of unionization on nonunion wages discussed by Rosen (1969). Here we postulate that unionized employees of privately operated lines push for the higher wages obtained by their counterparts in publicly operated lines.

[9] By inference this was in the minds of local ATU leaders during the long strike in 1972 against Transport of New Jersey. (See *New York Times*, April 24, 1972, p. 39). The owner of the Connecticut Company implied as much in his comments during a recent strike. (See *Hartford Courant*, November 15, 1971.) If this effect exists, it implies that G cannot be treated as exogenous in our model and that there exists a simultaneous-equations bias on its coefficient. However, simple calculations show this bias to be positive, so that we have probably *overestimated* the magnitude of the raw public ownership effect. On the other hand, were there no chance of public takeover, there would be no incentive to raise private transit wages and the estimated effect would be larger.

TABLE 4. Mean Public ànd Private Bus Drivers' Wages Relative to Manufacturing Earnings

Year	Ln (w_U/w_M)	Ln (w_{GU}/w_M)	Ln (w_{PU}/w_M)
1963	-.0852	-.0650	-.0886
1964	-.0817	-.0599	-.0867
1965	-.0808	-.0389	-.0918
1966	-.0775	-.0218	-.0961
1967	-.0733	-.0233	-.0919
1968	-.0769	-.0332	-.0949
1969	-.0593	-.0096	-.0892
1970	-.0310	-.0010	-.0544
1971	-.0293	-.0012	-.0574

wages in private firms coincident with the rise in the extent of public ownership.

Combining the results in Tables 3 and 4, we conclude that in the sample period the total effect of public ownership is between 9 and 12 percent. This result is, of course, qualified by the possibility that extraneous factors correlated with G could have shifted dramatically over time. It is unlikely, however, that such factors, even if they were present, could have produced a very large downward bias in our estimate of the public-ownership effect. Although it is not very large, the sign of this effect suggests that the Amalgamated Transit Union has been quite sensible in arguing for a public takeover of private bus lines.[10]

II. Construction, 1970–1972

Construction tradesmen are the second group for which we estimate the relative effect of public ownership upon union wages. Union organization is quite complete in the public sector in construction trades with the exception of a few southern cities. In many of the cities studied the tradesmen are organized into locals of the American Federation of State, County and Municipal Employees (AFSCME), but in a few they belong to the appropri-

---

[10]In a recent convention the ATU resolved that "the delegates . . . urge and support the prompt acquisition of all private transit companies by public bodies." *Proceedings of the 41st Convention of the Amalgamated Transit Union, AFL-CIO*, Las Vegas, September 27, 1971.

ate craft unions.[11] A long-standing policy of both the construction unions and AFSCME has been to seek to have wage rates in the public sector tied to those of private construction workers. In many states, wages of construction workers employed in the public sector have been based on other public-sector wages, and substantial lobbying efforts were used to force municipal governments to switch to private-sector comparisons.[12] The reason for this is obvious: by applying the hourly wage rate of the private sector, where hours worked are unstable and often quite low, total earnings can be raised to a very high level. In the empirical work here, we examine the success of this lobbying and ask: what total hours would have to be worked in the private sector to make earnings equal those in the public sector? To the extent that this hours figure is above that actually prevailing in the private sector and that other relevant factors are equal, there is a positive relative earnings effect of public ownership.

We proceed here in a manner similar to that of the previous section. The wage rate of government construction tradesmen is computed as 12 times the monthly salary divided by 2000 hours. In all the cities studied the scheduled work week for public construction craftsmen was 40 hours. This wage, w_G, is deflated by w_{PU}, the wage of private unionized construction craftsmen *in the same trade* in the city. The dependent variable in this study is the log of the wage of government craftsmen relative to that of unionized private craftsmen in the same trade; we are thus estimating relative supply curves to a very narrow set of occupations. Because of the narrow definitions of the trades being

[11] The cities in the sample are Atlanta, Baltimore, Birmingham, Boston, Buffalo, Chicago, Cincinnati, Columbus, Dallas, Denver, Houston, Indianapolis, Kansas City, Los Angeles, Milwaukee, Memphis, New Orleans, Omaha, Philadelphia, Pittsburgh, St. Louis, St. Paul and San Antonio. Of these, only Dallas, New Orleans, and San Antonio have nonunion public employees in the construction trades.

[12] AFSCME has insisted that laborers employed by New York City receive the same wage rate as those employed by contractors working on city projects (*The Public Employee*, August 1967, p. 3). In both Washington state and Sacramento County, California, pressure was exerted to induce government to interpret the prevailing wage as the private-sector wage (*ibid.*, April 1965, p. 8, and November 1966, p. 8).

studied, these curves must be very nearly infinitely elastic. The use of a relative wage measure obviates the need to worry about cost-of-living differences across cities.[13]

The four trades studied are carpenters, electricians, painters, and plumbers, the only ones having detailed data for public employees. There may be differences in the public-ownership wage effect in these trades. Since in many of the cities the trades are all organized into the same local in the public sector, this more centralized form of collective bargaining may result in a narrower wage structure across trades than does the decentralized bargaining in the private sector. Our estimates should provide evidence on whether this phenomenon occurs.

Because construction tradesmen in the public sector in several of the cities are not unionized, we need to control for the presence of public-sector unionization. We do this by including a dummy variable, U_G, that takes the value 1 if public construction tradesmen are unionized. Not only does this variable allow us to include observations that otherwise would have to be deleted, it also enables us to check on the consistency of our data by producing an estimate that is a measure of the relative wage effect of unionism in government construction. Previous estimates of this measure in private construction suggest it is rather high—on the order of 20 to 30 percent.[14] If the data we are using are reasonable, our estimate should be somewhere fairly close to this range.

Additional variables are used to hold constant potential differences across cities in the relative wages of public and private construction workers. As a compensating differential for working in the public sector, where variation in hours is low and the job is fairly secure, wages should be lower as the probability of un-

[13] The municipal salary data and information on unionization of municipal employees are from the Municipal Government Wage Surveys conducted between 1970 and 1972 by the regional offices of the Bureau of Labor Statistics. Private union wages are interpolated from BLS data published quarterly by Bureau of National Affairs, *Daily Labor Report*.

[14] Sobotka (1953) uses cross-section data from 1939 and historical data to produce estimates of this size. Ashenfelter (1972b) uses microeconomic data from 1967 and finds similar large effects.

TABLE 5. Means and Standard Deviations of Means of Hourly Wages

	Pooled	Carpenters	Electricians	Painters	Plumbers
w_G	5.00	4.91	5.23	4.70	5.22
	(.1)	(.2)	(.3)	(.2)	(.3)
w_{PU}	6.77	6.61	7.20	6.06	7.32
	(.1)	(.1)	(.1)	(.1)	(.2)

employment facing private-sector employees is higher. (Cf. Rees' (1973b) discussion of the literature on this effect.) There are no published data on unemployment rates in construction by city so we use instead the average unemployment rate for the entire city as a measure of this probability. It is included in our regression estimates as a means of adjusting for this rather obvious source of intercity variation in relative wages. Implicitly we are assuming that unemployment of government construction craftsmen varies less with labor-market wide unemployment than does that of private craftsmen. The basic equation estimated is thus:

$$(2) \qquad \ln w_G/w_{PU} = \beta_0 + \beta_1 U_G + \beta_2 UN + \nu,$$

where ν is a disturbance term.

We estimate (2) for the 23 cities for which the data are available between the years 1970–1972.[15] Because in several cities there are no data for certain trades, the total number of observations is below the maximum possible, 92. In addition to this equation, estimated separately for each trade, we also estimate a pooled equation containing dummies $D1$, $D2$ and $D3$, taking the values 1, respectively, for carpenters, electricians, and painters. Plumbers are thus the reference group for this particular set of dummies.

Table 5 lists the means and variances of the means of the two

[15] The unemployment data are from *Manpower Report of the President, 1972*, pp. 237–239. Admittedly, there are problems of comparability in these data across areas that weaken any conclusions based on them. Data on total numbers of craftsmen and black craftsmen, from *Census of Population, 1970*, PC(1)-C, Tables 86 and 93, were used to form an estimate of the fraction of black workers in all construction in each city. This measure and a dummy variable taking the value 1 in the South and 0 elsewhere were both added to (2), but neither ever had a coefficient with a t-value greater than 1.00, and none affected greatly the magnitudes of β_1 or β_2.

TABLE 6. Estimates of (2), Construction Trades: Dependent Variable is Ln (w_G/w_{PU}) [a]

	Constant	U_G	UN	D1	D2	D3	R^2	NOBS
Pooled	−.364	.209	−.039	.041	.015	.090	.180	85
	(3.0)	(3.2)	(1.9)	(.6)	(.2)	(1.3)		
Carpenters	−.303	.228	−.046				.182	22
	(1.2)	(1.6)	(1.1)					
Electricians	−.288	.233	−.056				.197	21
	(1.1)	(1.6)	(1.2)					
Painters	−.340	.147	−.013				.095	23
	(1.8)	(1.3)	(.4)					
Plumbers	−.375	.228	−.040				.164	19
	(1.4)	(1.5)	(.8)					

[a] Absolute values of t-statistics in parentheses.

wage measures for the four trades separately and pooled. Not surprisingly, the hourly wage in the public sector is lower than in the private sector, although these estimates are an overstatement of the difference because the public-sector wage includes some observations from nonunionized public employment. The variances of the means are quite low; the differentials between the hourly wages in the two sectors are significant.

Table 6 presents the estimates of equations (2). The unemployment term is always negative and is significantly different from zero in the pooled regressions. This sign was predicted by the theory of compensating differentials. The relative wage effect of unionism in public-sector construction ranges from 16 percent among painters to 25 percent for electricians. This set of estimates is close to that produced in previous studies and suggests that a similar ability to raise wages exists in the public and the private sector. There is no possible bias here because of intercity differences in the cost of living, as we are using a relative wage variable.

The reference group of the three dummies in the pooled equations is plumbers, the highest-wage trade among the four. The positive coefficients on the dummies thus suggest that there is some narrowing of craft differentials in the public sector; this is made particularly clear by the large coefficient on $D3$, the dummy for painters, the lowest paid of the four crafts. This phenomenon may well be a result of their organization into AFSCME locals in most of the cities in the sample. Finally, while our results suggest that there are some differences in the wage relatives among the trades, these are not significant, and we can use the estimates of the pooled equations in further discussions in this section.

We now use the estimates of β_0, β_1, and β_2 in equation (2) to estimate the hours needed in the private sector to equalize earnings of unionized workers in the two sectors. We wish to isolate the effect of government ownership on union earnings. This effect may be produced by an hours differential that is more favorable to the public sector than the wage differential is to the private sector. Construction unions in the public sector may take advantage of government by securing steady full-time work with only slight reductions in hourly rates.

We can write earnings in each sector as a product of wage rates and hours worked:

$$E = wH.$$

Denote the log of relative earnings, E_{GU}/E_{PU}, as:

$$(3) \qquad \ln E_{GU}/E_{PU} = \ln \frac{w_{GU}}{w_{PU}} + \ln \frac{H_{GU}}{H_{PU}}.$$

If this expression equals zero, then earnings in the two sectors are equal. The log of the relative wage of unionized workers in public compared to private construction, $\ln w_{GU}/w_{PU}$, is:

$$\gamma = \hat{\beta}_0 + \hat{\beta}_1 + \hat{\beta}_2 \, \overline{UN},$$

where $\overline{UN}$ is the mean unemployment rate. We can substitute into (3), set the expression equal to zero and derive:

$$H_{PU}^* = H_{GU} \cdot e^\gamma.$$

Assuming that H_{GU} is 2000, as it is in the cities in our sample, it is a simple matter to calculate H_{PU}^*, the number of hours needed in the private sector to equalize earnings between the two sectors.

Before estimating H_{PU}^*, let us examine some estimates of the actual number of hours worked by unionized private construction employees. Estimates of hours worked are not produced on a

243

TABLE 7. Mean Annual Hours for Craftsmen with more than 700 Hours Worked[a]

Trade	Detroit	Omaha	Milwaukee	So. California
Bricklayers and Masons	1470	1471	1486	—
Carpenters	1542	1530	—	1430
Ironworkers	1524	1590	—	1572
Laborers	1540	1467	1416	—
Plasterers	—	1756	1611	—

[a]From Bureau of Labor Statistics, *Seasonality and Manpower in Construction*, Bulletin 1642, p. 71.

TABLE 8. Estimates of γ and H^*_{PU} From (2)

	Weighted	Carpenters	Electricians	Painters	Plumbers
γ	-.298	-.290	-.316	-.254	-.334
H^*_{PU}	1485	1496	1458	1551	1432

regular basis because of the casual nature of work in this industry.[16] The Bureau of Labor Statistics has, however, produced occasional estimates for a few cities and trades on this by following up payments to retirement funds by employers. Table 7 reproduces these data for four areas and for a number of larger trades for which they are available. The data are presented only for individuals who worked more than 700 hours per year; this subsample enables us to concentrate on those workers whose main occupation is in the construction industry. As one can easily see, even among this subsample, hours worked are quite low. Only in one case, plasterers, whose work is generally indoors, does the figure substantially exceed 1600 hours per year. In most of the trades the data imply an average work week of 32 hours or less; if individuals work a full 40 hours each week they are employed, they are unemployed for 10 weeks of the year.

Table 8 presents estimates of γ and H^*_{PU} based upon Table 6. The estimates are presented both separately for each trade and for a weighted average of the individual regressions. The weights used are the fractions of the total workers in the four trades

[16]Mills (1972) presents the most up-to-date discussion of this and other aspects of work in this industry.

accounted for by each individual trade.[17] In all the trades studied and in the weighted average of these four trades, the hours required fall between the lowest and highest values listed for outdoor trades in the private sector in Table 7. Using the extreme values of hours in Tables 7 and 8, we find that the earnings effect here lies between $-.09$ and $.10$; there is no evidence of a positive effect of government ownership on union earnings.

There are a number of possible downward biases in our estimates: (1) construction tradesmen in public employment are engaged in maintenance work, while those in private construction are more often involved in new building. Insofar as the latter is more arduous, the private sector will have to pay a premium to attract workers. Failure to account for this possible difference in quality will thus bias downward our estimate of the relative wage differential. (2) We have also failed to consider differences in fringe benefits. A recent survey by the National League of Cities shows that, for public workers in general, the ratio of fringes to total compensation is higher by .8 percentage point in the public sector. If this holds for construction, it also implies that we have underestimated the relative compensation of public versus private unionized construction workers. (3) If wages of black construction craftsmen are lower than those of equally skilled whites, and proportionately more blacks are employed in the public sector, the average wage there will be lower for reasons having nothing to do with unions' ability to raise wages.

There are factors that could have caused us to overestimate the relative earnings effect of public employment: (1) in calculating hypothetical earnings in the private sector, we have used the straight-time hourly wage rate. Certainly, though, some of the hours worked in the private sector are paid on an overtime basis. We cannot get evidence on this, and our failure to do so biases upward our estimate of relative earnings. (2) Another possible bias results from assuming that leisure has no value to the individual. Insofar as this assumption is incorrect, we are wrong

---

[17]Estimates from *Census of Population, 1970,* PC(2)-7C, were used to make these calculations.

TABLE 9. Percent Distribution of Employed Male Construction
Craftsmen, by Industry and Age, 1970[a]

	Government				Private Construction			
	16–24	25–44	45–64	65+	16–24	25–44	45–64	65+
Carpenters	2.9	23.9	69.6	3.6	11.6	43.2	40.7	4.5
Electricians	7.1	41.3	49.5	2.1	14.7	51.9	30.5	2.9
Painters	6.3	24.9	64.8	4.0	11.0	40.8	41.9	6.3
Plumbers	3.1	31.6	63.1	2.1	12.0	47.0	37.2	3.8

[a]Computed from *Census of Population*, 1970, PC(2)-7C.

in concluding that earnings plus the value of nonworking time
are no greater than in the public sector.

Since the potential downward biases to our estimates have more
interest for policy, and since two of them can be measured at
least partly, we deal with them here. The remaining biases are
ignored because of our inability to measure them. Although
measures of the relative arduousness of the work performed by
public and private construction workers cannot be obtained, we
can find the age distributions by trade. These enable us to
estimate differences in wages between the sectors due to differences in experience and education and also to discuss how
workers might self-select into the two sectors.

Table 9 presents the age distribution by trade of craftsmen in
government and private construction. The government employees
are much older on average, and this difference is especially
pronounced among carpenters. Possibly because of differences in
pension benefits (discussed above) or because the work of construction employees in government is less strenuous and more
secure, older workers, who can be expected to prefer these
characteristics more than younger workers, elect to work in the
public sector. The differences in age distributions thus provide
some inferential evidence that work in government construction
is less arduous.

The data in Table 9 also present the opportunity to adjust for
public-private wage differences due to sectoral differences in
average age and educational attainment. (The latter difference
exists because, due to the secular rise in average educational
attainment, younger workers are more educated than older

workers.) Data on the educational attainment of craftsmen and on their experience (age – education – 6) were computed, and the expected education and experience of the average craftsman in each of the four trades in public and private construction were calculated. Using an equation relating income to education, experience, and experience squared, we find that wage rates in public construction are 3 to 5 percent lower then they would be if workers in both sectors had the same skill (as measured by education and experience).[18] This adjustment for differences in skill suggests that the bias on the estimate of log w_{GU}/w_{PU} is positive, or that our estimates of H^*_{PU} in Table 8 are slightly high. Although government craftsmen are probably less well educated than private construction craftsmen, this difference is more than compensated for by their greater average experience.

We can also account for differences in the relative wage, w_{GU}/w_{PU}, due to differences in the extent of black employment in the two sectors. Although we cannot measure it directly, we can write the relative wage of unionized white workers in the two sectors, w_{GUW}/w_{PUW}, as:

$$(4) \qquad \frac{w_{GUW}}{w_{PUW}} \cong \frac{w_{GU}}{w_{PU}} + \Delta,$$

where
$$\Delta = e_G \left[\frac{\delta_G}{1 + \delta_G} \right] - e_P \left[\frac{\delta_P}{1 + \delta_P} \right] ;$$

δ_i is the fraction by which wages of white workers exceed those of blacks of equal skill in government (private) construction, and e_i is black employment as a fraction of total employment in the sector. In 1970 the averages of e_G and e_P were .098 and .052, respectively, where these are computed using all four trades.[19] It is unlikely that the measure of wage discrimination

---

[18] The equation, based on the work of Mincer (1970), was estimated for craftsmen in 1960, using aggregated data from Census of Population, 1960, PC(2)-7A. The estimates are:

$\ln Y = 7.65 + .0478\,ED + .0392\,EX - .00060\,EX^2 - .189\,SO, R^2 = .99,$
$\qquad (.07) \quad (.004) \qquad (.003) \qquad (.00006) \qquad (.02)$

(where the standard errors are in parentheses.)

[19] The raw data are presented in Census of Population, 1970, PC(2)-7C.

(δ) is greater in government than in private construction or that it is greater than .5. Substituting these assumptions into (4), we can conclude that Δ is less than .015. Failure to account for differences in racial composition imparts a downward bias to our estimates of the true w_{GU}/w_{PU}, but it is minute. The corrected estimates of H^*_{PU} would thus be no more than 1.5 percent greater than those listed in Table 8.

Our admittedly indirect estimates suggest there is no difference in earnings between public and private construction employees. This statement takes account of the adjustments made to account for several possible biases, although other biases in both directions could not be dealt with empirically. At the very least, we may conclude that earnings of publicly employed construction craftsmen are not overwhelmingly greater than those of their privately employed brothers, other things equal.

III. Microeconomic Data, Survey of Consumer Finances, 1968

Having investigated differences between unionized workers in the public and private sectors in two narrow occupations, we have gotten fairly good evidence on whether excessive union power exists in the public sector. Unfortunately, we have not been able to control for the possibility that these differences may exist even in the absence of unionism, i.e., that the government may simply pay more to workers of equal ability. There is some evidence (Oaxaca, 1971) that, holding constant individual and regional characteristics, earnings in government and most major private industries do not differ. However, no study has simultaneously examined the existence of wage differentials in unionized and nonunionized employment in both the government and private sectors.

In the previous two sections of this paper, the paucity of data forced us to slight possible differences in the quality of labor between the public and private sectors. Using microeconomic data, we can hold these differences constant and examine the Wellington-Winter hypothesis. We do this at the cost of being unable to isolate wages within narrow occupations. The data we use are from the University of Michigan's Survey of Consumer

Finances, 1968, a household study providing detailed responses from nearly 3,000 family units. This is the only one out of the many existing data sets of this variety that provides information on union status for all workers, regardless of whether they are employed in the government or private sectors. Since this information is crucial to our study, this data set is the only one usable.

The subsample consists of white, male heads of families. While undoubtedly there are differential effects for women and for blacks employed in the public and private sectors, the majority of employees are white males. We thus concentrate on them both because any significant differences between the two sectors should become apparent and because introducing other demographic groups could well bias the results for all groups. To decrease heterogeneity in the sample, only individuals who worked at least 40 weeks during 1967 and who worked between 35 and 60 hours during the week preceding the survey are included. These criteria result in a total of 1143 workers in our study. As one can see in Table 10, a relatively large fraction of these are unionized as compared to the population in general. Because the government sector is only a small fraction of the total and the majority of government workers are nonunionized,

TABLE 10. Sample and Subsample Sizes, Survey of Consumer Finances, 1968, White, Male Full-Time Workers

Total	1143
Private	
Union	395
Nonunion	623
Government	
Medical and Educational	
Union	13
Nonunion	38
Other	
Union	14
Nonunion	60

we are left with few individuals who are both unionized and in government. This will naturally lead to large standard errors on the estimated effects of unions in government.

Data are not provided on the hourly wage rate of these workers; instead, we are given the hours worked in the previous week, weeks worked in the previous year, and total earnings for the previous year. All of our estimates are based both on annual earnings, Y, and on an hourly wage rate, w, defined as annual earnings divided by the product of hours in the previous week and weeks in the previous year. (When Y is used, we include weeks worked as an explanatory variable.) Since we do not know whether hours in the previous week are typical of the entire year or whether data on weeks worked include time off for vacations or illness, we use both w and Y as measuring earnings.

Our goal is to explain differences in annual (or hourly) earnings among the individuals in our sample. The data in this survey enable us to measure union relative wage effects within the private and government sectors and also differences in these relative wage effects between the two sectors. Furthermore, the data allow us to make these estimates while holding constant the relative wage difference between nonunionized workers in the two sectors. Because the data are available and also because there may be differential effects, the government sector is divided into: (1) medical and educational services; and (2) other government services.

Using the model of Mincer (1970), we hold differences in labor quality constant by using education, ED, a measure of the years of schooling for each individual; experience, EX (age minus education minus 6), an estimate of the period of time the individual has been working and thus investing in himself, and the square of this variable.[20] While undoubtedly there are other differences in quality across workers, these measures have in past

---

[20]The Survey of Consumer Finances tape gives educational attainment as a range of years, e.g., 0–5, 6–8, etc. We assign the highest value in the range for each individual as his value of the ED variable. This method is equivalent to the introduction of measurement errors into ED; in such a case, there is no necessary bias on the coefficients of other variables in the equation.

studies captured a large fraction of individual differences. If there are quality differences between labor in the government and private sectors, inclusion of these variables should remove some of the errors in estimating the magnitude of union wage effects between the two sectors. Two variables designed to represent differences in the cost of living are also included in our model. (These are essential because the theory is based on real wages, while we observe only money wages.) These are: (1) SO, a dummy variable taking the value of 1 in the South and 0 elsewhere; (2) $SMSA$, a dummy variable taking the value of 1 if the individual resides in a metropolitan area with a population of 50,000 or more and 0 otherwise.

The essential variables are those representing individuals' union or government status. These are: (1) $G1$, taking the value of 1 if an individual is employed in government hospitals or educational facilities and 0 otherwise; (2) $G2$, taking the value of 1 if an individual is employed in some other governmental function and 0 otherwise; (3) U, a variable taking the value of 1 if the individual is a union member and 0 otherwise; (4) $G1 \cdot U$, a variable taking the value of 1 if the individual is a unionized employee in a government hospital or educational facility; and (5) $G2 \cdot U$, taking the value of 1 if the individual is a unionized employee in some other part of the government.

Although we cannot hold constant the occupation each individual works in, there are sufficient data to allow us to hold broad occupational classifications constant. Therefore, in some forms of the equations we include a set of five occupational dummy variables, each taking the value of 1 if the individual is in a particular major occupational category and 0 otherwise. (Laborers form the base group for this set of variables.) This allows us to account for possible failure of our variables to capture all individual differences in quality and thus to remove potential biases to our estimates of the union and government wage differentials.

Table 11 presents the estimates of the individual wage equations both with and without the set of occupational dummies and for both dependent variables. Compared to most studies using microeconomic data, a fairly large proportion of the variance is

TABLE 11. Estimates of Individual Wage Equations, Survey of Consumer Finances, 1968[a]

Dependent Variable	Regression			
	(1) Log w	(2) Log w	(3) Log Y	(4) Log Y
Constant	−.035	−.107	7.402	7.236
	(.4)	(1.4)	(31.9)	(30.1)
ED	.054	.075	.053	.074
	(9.6)	(14.9)	(9.6)	(14.8)
EX	.023	.027	.023	.027
	(7.0)	(7.8)	(7.1)	(8.1)
EX^2	−.00035	−.00039	−.00037	−.00044
	(5.1)	(5.7)	(5.6)	(6.3)
SO	−.148	−.138	−.139	−.132
	(5.6)	(5.0)	(5.4)	(4.8)
SMSA	.220	.249	.183	.214
	(9.6)	(10.5)	(8.1)	(9.1)
G1	−.082	−.095	−.099	−.132
	(1.3)	(1.5)	(1.6)	(2.1)
G2	.120	.113	.035	.023
	(2.4)	(2.2)	(.7)	(.4)
G1 · U	−.073	−.015	−.043	.016
	(.6)	(.1)	(.3)	(.1)
G2 · U	−.119	−.100	−.112	−.080
	(1.1)	(.9)	(1.0)	(.7)
U	.164	.093	.116	.043
	(6.5)	(3.8)	(4.7)	(1.7)
Professionals	.372	—	.358	—
	(7.4)		(7.2)	
Managers	.442	—	.512	—
	(8.9)		(10.5)	
Clerical and Sales Workers	.167	—	.192	—
	(3.3)		(3.9)	
Craftsmen	.239	—	.252	—
	(5.8)		(6.3)	
Operatives	.114	—	.139	—
	(2.6)		(3.3)	
Laborers and Service Workers	—	—	—	—
WEEKS			.006	.008
			(1.3)	(1.8)
R^2	.398	.338	.424	.353

[a]Absolute values of t-statistics in parentheses.

252

TABLE 12. Approximate Percent Relative Wage Effects of Unions in Each Sector [a]

Regression	(1)	(2)	(3)	(4)
(1) Private	16.4	9.3	11.6	4.3
	(2.5)	(2.4)	(2.5)	(2.4)
Government				
(2) Medical and Educational	9.1	7.8	7.4	2.7
	(11.1)	(11.8)	(11.0)	(11.7)
(3) Other	4.5	-.8	.5	-3.8
	(10.5)	(10.9)	(10.3)	(10.7)

[a]Computed from Table 11; standard errors in parentheses.

explained by our equations. Furthermore, although the implied rates of return to education (.053 to .075) are low, they are within the range of previous estimates. The coefficients on the experience variables suggest an earnings profile that peaks after approximately 30 years of experience, also about what has been estimated in the past. The cost-of-living dummy variables, *SO* and *SMSA*, have the expected signs and are significant. They imply extra effects on wages that are roughly what one would expect.

We can calculate the relative wage effects of unions in the two government sectors using the estimates in Table 11. These calculations, presented in rows (2) and (3) of Table 12, indicate that the effect of unions in government medical and educational services on wages is between 3 and 9 percent, depending upon which of the four specifications we use. The relative wage effect for unions in other government services is approximately -4 to 4 percent, again depending upon the equation estimates utilized. The estimates for medical and educational services in government do not differ greatly from those for teachers by Frey in this volume. Insofar as we have captured differences in the quality of workers by also holding education, experience, and occupational classification constant, these estimates are free of biases that might result from a correlation of union status and worker quality. The relative wage effects for government in Table 12 are generally lower than for the private sector, even holding these other variables constant.

There are a number of reasons why our negative estimates of the difference between union wage effects in the government and private sectors must be discounted. Biases of unknown direction may be caused by our inability to hold constant the detailed occupation of each worker as we did in Sections I and II. Moreover, the standard errors on the wage effects in government in Table 12 are very large. However, this section does provide strong additional evidence that the excess of government over private union wage effects is not large and may be zero or negative.

IV. Conclusion

Only in one of three different sets of data have the earnings of unionized workers in an occupation in government exceeded those of private unionized employees in the same occupation. While that extra effect was no more than 12 percent, in the other two parts we found no difference between the earnings of the two unionized groups. Although there are a number of potential biases in these estimates, there is no evidence that any one of these overwhelms the possible errors in the opposite direction. We may therefore conclude that these estimates are quite reasonable.

The results here say nothing about union effects on work rules and the quality of the service provided by the government. It could be that unions in the public sector do have excessive power, but that they choose to exercise it by controlling technology rather than by raising earnings. Insofar as this behavioral difference exists, it implies that unions in the public sector raise costs more than do their private counterparts in industries characterized by similar demand conditions. It is difficult to quantify this hypothesis and thus to test its validity. There is, however, inferential evidence against it in the form of the casual observation that in those industries (construction, rail transport) receiving most attention for having archaic work rules, union relative wage effects are fairly large. If this admittedly weak evidence carried over into the public sector, we could conclude that our failure to find a large difference between union earnings effects in the two sectors also implies the absence of significant differences in effects on technology.

Let us assume that the estimated relative earnings effect of public ownership is as large (12 percent) as it is in our highest estimates for unionized bus drivers. Whether this effect is large enough to justify arguments such as those of Wellington and Winter (1971) for well-enforced laws limiting the right to strike in the public sector is debatable. On one hand, a 12-percent extra effect implies, once we account for labor's share in the production of the service, that expenditures on it are at most only 6 percent higher than if it were operated privately. If we consider also the non-zero price elasticity of demand for the service and the resulting drop in quantity consumed when wages rise because of the public takeover, the effect on expenditures is even less.[21] On the other hand, this small positive effect may still exist, and people may feel that municipal budgets are so strained already that any increase in taxation resulting from the effects of strong public-sector unions must be avoided. Although I disagree with this position, it is surely a tenable argument. It is strengthened by the recognition that current laws, although they are enforced only weakly, may have had some effect in mitigating the power of public employee unions to produce larger relative wage effects than their private counterparts. If our estimates are interpreted favorably to this position, its adherents might be justified in urging harsh restrictions on public employee unionism and attempts to transfer ownership to the private sector.

[21] See Ohls and Wales (1972) for an outline of how these calculations should be made. The study by Ashenfelter and Ehrenberg in this volume presents estimates of the wage elasticity of labor demand in the public sector.

COMMENTS

PAUL F. GERHART

Using a novel approach, Hamermesh has presented some convincing evidence that the union wage effect is *not* substantially greater in the public sector than in the private. If we are prepared to accept the balance of power existing in the private sector as appropriate for the public sector, there appears to be no need for additional policy restraint on public-sector unions at this time. The inference that follows, however, is that relaxation of present policy restraints on public-sector unions (particularly as regards the right to strike) would upset this power parity.

For reasons more ideological than empirical, I am predisposed toward Hamermesh's conclusion: union-management relations in the public sector should be regulated to about the same extent as in the private sector. The unique features of public-sector bargaining can generate their own solutions, much as the unique occupational groups and industries of the private sector have. In some instances my comments weaken this ideological position he and I share, but more often I think they support it.

Only in transit was Hamermesh able to discover a disparity between public- and private-sector union wage effects, with public-sector unions exhibiting greater relative bargaining power. There may be an institutional explanation for this result. Public transit has a history of being private transit. As Hamermesh notes in Table 1, only 7 of the 48 transit systems observed in his study were publicly owned in 1963; by 1971, half were publicly owned. This history of private ownership distinguishes transit from other functions of government. The Federal Urban Mass Transportation Act of 1964 actually provides for the continuation of private-sector bargaining practices and procedures after private transportation companies have been acquired by public agencies. To comply and thereby qualify for federal grants to support the purchase of mass transit facilities by public agencies, the state of

256

Louisiana, for example, passed Act No. 127, "Public Transit Employees: Protection of Rights, 1964." Among other provisions, the act: (1) emphasizes the need to minimize changes in employer-employee relations as a result of the change of ownership; (2) guarantees the employees' right to form unions; and (3) requires the employer to bargain. The continuation of a historical relationship gives transit workers an advantage over the typically fledgling unions in other functions of government that have received bargaining rights only recently.

The frequency of strikes among public-transit employees has been greater than among other public employees. (Data are available in the 1962 and 1967 *Census of Governments* and the report of the Advisory Commission on Intergovernmental Relations.) In 1962, the strike rate of transit employees standardized for the number of employees in the function was approximately ten times higher than for public employees in general; in 1967, the rate for transit was approximately three times higher. Since public-sector managers are likely to project the future on the basis of their experiences, they should find strike threats by transit workers more credible; this enhances transit workers' bargaining power.

This conclusion, relating strike frequency and relative bargaining power, is supported by data from my own study of the scope of bargaining in local government labor agreements. A contract index based on the scope of bargaining including noneconomic as well as some economic issues was calculated. The index was intended to represent the relative power of the union vis-à-vis management and was highly correlated with the strike incidence within a state. Even after other correlates of the contract index are introduced into the equation (e.g., public policies toward collective bargaining and strikes, and patterns among other public sector contracts within the state), the strike incidence variable is reasonably important in predicting the contract index.

I believe the greater wage effect of transit unions is at least partially explained by the higher incidence of strikes in transit. If this conclusion is correct, it adds credibility to the argument that union power is a function of strike frequency. If the aim of public-policy makers is to constrain union power, one approach

257

is to constrain the right to strike. Wellington and Winter (1971) apparently reach the correct conclusion as regards the direction of impact that increased strike activity has. Hamermesh provides some evidence that the size of the impact is not as great as Wellington and Winter may have anticipated.

Hamermesh concludes that there is no difference between the union wage effect for building trades employees in the public and private sectors. As before, I rely on what is essentially an institutional argument to question this conclusion. The building trades are not completely organized. More often than not the recruitment of city "craftsmen" occurs among the nonunion segment of the industry. When this occurs, I would argue there is a de facto difference in the skill levels required for the jobs, although the titles may be the same. Recruitment from other than building trades hiring halls is especially likely where an "industrial type" union (e.g., AFSCME) represents city craftsmen in a general city-wide bargaining unit. When craftsmen are included in city-wide units, the concept of prevailing rates is given little more than lip service. Therefore, the public-sector union wage effect is biased downward when public-sector craftsmen (though unionized) are compared with private-sector crafts that are unionized by the building trades.

It would be useful if Hamermesh would estimate the differences in the union wage effect for each craft by union affiliation. Based on the field work of the Brookings Studies of Unionism in Government, I would anticipate a considerable difference between the "industrially organized" craftsmen and the craftsmen organized by the building trades. The union wage effect is likely to be substantially greater in the public sector than in the private for cities in which craftsmen are organized by building trades unions.

In the broad sense in which the author is investigating union wage effects, the impact of the structural differences among cities may not be relevant. That is, the overall impact of unions in the public-sector crafts may not be any greater than the general impact of unions in the private-sector crafts. Differentiation among the cities on the basis of bargaining structure would be useful for policy-makers, however. If the impact of structure I have hypothesized is correct, the encouragement of consolidated, industrial-type structures may be a useful device for those who wish to constrain union wage effects.

If unionized public-sector employees do in fact receive more pay than their counterparts in the private sector, is it because *unions* have a greater wage effect in the public sector than in the private? To the extent that other factors related to public ownership lead to higher wages for public employees, the union wage effect is overstated. It was impossible for Hamermesh to obtain an estimate of the union (as opposed to public ownership) wage effect for transit since there are no nonunion public transit workers. The estimate for building tradesmen is suspect, since the only nonunion public-sector tradesmen appeared in a "few southern cities." Only in Section III, using the Survey of Consumer Finances, did he produce a satisfying (to me) estimate of union wage effects as between the two sectors. There, as Hamermesh notes, fine occupational breakdowns are not possible, so the unionization variable may simply be a proxy for higher-paying occupations. (This last point is not very significant in my opinion, though it must be noted.)

There are both theoretical and empirical reasons to question the hypothesis that unions are inherently more powerful in the public than in the private sector, even if the methodology employed by Hamermesh shows that unionized employees are paid more than their unionized private-sector counterparts. On the theoretical level, patronage machines buy the skills of the transit worker or building tradesman as well as his vote. Given equal skill levels in the public and private sectors (an assumption Hamermesh makes for transit workers and craftsmen which might be questioned by some), higher pay should be expected. Perloff (1971) shows that local, public-sector employees tend to receive higher rates of pay in most occupations than do similar employees in the private sector in the same labor market. This was true in nine of eleven cities studied. The occupations included accounting clerks, payroll clerks, stenographers, computer programmers, and keypunch operators, as well as carpenters, electricians, painters, and plumbers. Since many of the occupations are not generally unionized, it is clear that factors other than

PAUL F. GERHART

unions in the public sector are raising wages relative to the wage
rates paid in the private sector at the local level. Unless a sufficient nonunion base is available against which to measure the
union wage effect, it is impossible to sort out whether the wage
effect is due to public ownership or unionization.

Even if unions do have a greater relative wage effect in the
public sector than they do in the private sector, there is reason to
question whether this greater relative wage effect is due to the
reasons—demand inelasticity and political vulnerability due to
potential strikes—cited by Wellington and Winter. Arvid Ander-
son, Chairman of the New York City Office of Collective Bargaining, in a recent speech to the Midwest Regional Assembly in East
Lansing, contended that compulsory arbitration is a mechanism
for enhancing the wage rates of many groups of public employees.
In some functions of government such as police, fire, and health
care, the political vulnerability of public officials who decide to
take a strike may be great. In addition, the demand function for
such services may give striking unions substantial bargaining
power. On the other hand, many functions of government are
not so essential that unions in these functions can use them to
generate the same degree of political leverage. Compulsory arbitration is likely to lead to higher wage rates than the employees
in such functions would receive if they were forced to rely upon
their bargaining power generated through the strike weapon.

Hamermesh uses the wage rate or earnings of public employees
and private employees in order to measure the differential effect
of unions in the two sectors. I have some reservations regarding
the sole reliance on wages as a measure of the possible differential
effect of unions in the two sectors. In the course of bargaining,
there may be other tradeoff items on which union influence can
be exercised, but where the visibility of the item may not be so
great to the taxpayer. In other words, public officials may be
more willing to negotiate less visible benefits with public employees than they are to grant wage increases. The taxpayer-wage
earner may find it somewhat more difficult to compare his own
situation with that of the public employees if this approach is
used by the public officials.

One such area is fringe benefits. The Edward H. Friend survey

260

of benefits in the public sector indicates that a slightly larger fringe package is negotiated in the public sector than in the private.[1] This is not a serious problem for Hamermesh, since the difference between the public and private sectors was on the order of 3 or 4 percent. If the total wage-fringe package were taken as a whole, and if there is no substantial wage differential, as Hamermesh's study suggests, this would mean that the difference in the total package for wages and fringes is less than 1 percent.

An area in which no data are available is the "effort bargain." The question is whether the amount of effort required in the public sector is the same as the amount of effort required by similar private-sector employees. Productivity measurement is only beginning to be considered in the public sector. While Hamermesh mentions possible differences in work rules and the quality of services performed by employees, I believe this area provides considerable potential for a union effect.

Finally, the area of job security is difficult to evaluate. The public sector generally provides civil service protection for public employees. While I have no evidence on local government employees, the Bureau of Manpower Information Systems of the U.S. Civil Service Commission provides comparative turnover rates for federal employees and manufacturing employees in the private sector. For the most recent two and a half year period, these data indicate that the category "separations except for quits" is 2.5 times higher in manufacturing than it is for federal civilian employees. Even more important than civil service protection may be the economic condition of the employer and the lack of cyclical behavior in public employment. While it is difficult to place an economic value upon job stability, it is an important consideration.

On the basis of these three kinds of tradeoff items, public employees appear to be somewhat better off than private employees. One would expect that markets adjust accordingly and that public-employee wages would be somewhat lower than private-

---

[1] Bureau of National Affairs, *Government Employee Relations Report*, October 16, 1972.

employee wages for the same kinds of occupations. To establish that unionized public employees have about the same rates of pay or earnings as private employees indicates that the relative wage effect of public-sector unions is actually greater than the relative wage effect of private-sector unions.

In the last paragraph of his paper, Hamermesh notes that there are now a number of constraints on public-employee unions, particularly in the area of restraints on the right to strike. These restraints may in part explain why the strike incidence in the public sector is still less than half that of the private sector, and hence why the union wage effect is no greater than it is.

There are a number of other constraints on public-sector unions that also reduce their bargaining power. First, union security provisions are limited in the public sector. (Only a few states permit the agency shop or maintenance of membership types of provisions.) The open shop prevails. Second, the scope of bargaining in the public sector is restrained relative to that in the private sector. In the Pennsylvania Labor Relations Board case involving the State College Area School District, the teachers' association was denied the right to negotiate on locker space, hall and bus duty, and job descriptions, among other items.[2] Furthermore, civil service commissions continue to fight a holding action against the invasion of their prerogatives by unions and management in negotiations. While this appears to be a losing battle, the immediate effect is to restrain the expansion of union power. Finally, a substantial number of states still have no comprehensive statute providing the right to unionize, and only a minority of states provide mandatory collective bargaining.

Since Hamermesh finds little support for a larger union wage effect in the public sector than in the private sector, there is reason to question whether the present restraints should be relaxed. As Wellington and Winter (1971) noted there may be other areas where public unions have an advantage over their private-sector counterparts. These other areas may help to explain the unusual success public-sector unions have been able to achieve in the face of their shortcomings and restraints. One of these is political ac-

[2] *Ibid.*, November 8, 1971, and August 7, 1972.

tivity; alternative channels of influence over the terms of employment are available to public-sector unions. These may be cataloged as lobbying at the state level, lobbying at the local level where negotiations are not conducted by the legislative body but rather the executive, electing "friends" to office, and finally, by the threat to expose the public officials' "dirty linen." (That public-sector unions have considerable potential through the political activity route has been documented in a recent study reported in UCLA Law School, 1972, pp. 946–957.)

It is possible that these alternative channels may compensate for the limitations presently placed on public employees; the data presented by Hamermesh indicate that they do. Therefore, it may be in the best interests of the taxpayers to continue to restrain the public-sector unions in the ways presently used. To allow unions to continue to use the political channels and the more conventional collective bargaining techniques in the public sector may in fact provide these unions with more power than it is in the public interest to give them. While this is not my own position, it is one which can be justified by Hamermesh's results.

I have come to a conclusion over the past several years that the position one takes on public-sector bargaining has substantial normative overtones. This is not to say it has no empirical basis; on the contrary, the experience with illegal strikes over the past ten years has undoubtedly led to a softening of anti-strike policies in some jurisdictions. As Professor George Taylor has said, however, the position one takes on the question of whether unions have too much power depends largely on whether one views what unions have been able to achieve as legitimate. To a major extent I am sympathetic with Hamermesh's views in that some further experimentation with the reduction in restraints on public-sector unions would appear to be warranted. Hamermesh's data indicate the price would be quite low, and even the insidious effect that property ownership and tax bills have had on me does not lead me to believe that equity for public employees might not be worth a slightly higher price.

COMBINED REFERENCES

Alchian, A.A., and Kessel, R., 1962. "Competition, Monopoly, and the Pursuit of Pecuniary Gain," in NBER, *Aspects of Labor Economics.* Princeton: Princeton University Press, 157–75.

Amacher, F., and Freeman, R.B., 1973. "The Youth Labor Market," Unpublished Manuscript, M.I.T. Center for Policy Alternatives.

American Association of University Professors, 1950–1972. *The Annual Report on the Economic Status of the Profession.*

Ashenfelter, O., 1971. "The Effect of Unionization on Wages in the Public Sector: The Case of Fire-Fighters," *Industrial and Labor Relations Review* 24 (January), 191–202.

——, 1972a. "Demand and Supply Functions for State and Local Employment: Implications for Public Employment Programs," Unpublished Manuscript, Princeton University.

——, 1972b. "Racial Discrimination and Trade Unionism," *Journal of Political Economy* 80 (May/June), 435–464.

Ashenfelter, O., and Johnson, G., 1969. "Bargaining Theory, Trade Unions, and Industrial Strike Activity," *American Economic Review* 59 (March), 35–49.

Barro, R.J., 1972. "An Economic Theory of Politics and Government Spending," Unpublished Manuscript, Brown University.

Barten, A.P., 1968. "Estimating Demand Functions," *Econometrica* 36 (April), 213–251.

Barzel, Y., 1973. "Private Schools and Public School Finance," *Journal of Political Economy* 81 (January), 174–86.

Bayer, A.E., 1970. *College and University Faculty: A Statistical Description.* Washington: American Council on Education.

——, 1973. *Teaching Faculty in Academics: 1972–73.* Washington: American Council on Education.

Becker, G., and Lewis, H.G., 1973. "On the Interaction between the Quantity and Quality of Children," *Journal of Political Economy* 81 (March/April), S279–S288.

Benson, C.S., 1968. *The Economics of Public Education.* Boston: Houghton Mifflin.

Bergstrom, T., and Goodman, R., 1973. "Private Demand for Public Goods," *American Economic Review* 63 (June), 280–297.

Borcherding, T., and Deacon, R., 1972. "The Demand for Services of Non-Federal Governments," *American Economic Review* 62 (December), 891–901.

Bronfenbrenner, M., 1947. "Price Control Under Imperfect Competition," *American Economic Review* 37 (March), 107–120.

Burton, J.F., Jr., 1969. "Reply," *Industrial and Labor Relations Review* 23 (October), 84–88.

Burton, J.F., Jr., and Krider, C., 1970. "The Role and Consequences of Strikes by Public Employees," *Yale Law Journal* 79 (January), 418–40.

Cartter, A., 1966. "Supply and Demand for College Teachers," *Journal of Human Resources* 1 (Summer), 22–38.

_____ , 1971. "Science Manpower for 1970–1985," *Science* 172: 132–140.

Chamberlain, N., and Kuhn, J., 1965. *Collective Bargaining.* New York: McGraw-Hill.

Cleland, S., 1955. *The Influence of Plant Size on Industrial Relations.* Princeton: Princeton University Industrial Relations Section.

Downs, A., 1957. *An Economic Theory of Democracy.* New York: Harper and Row.

Dubin, R., 1965. "Industrial Conflict: The Power of Prediction," *Industrial and Labor Relations Review* 18 (April), 352–63.

Eckaus, R.S., 1973. *Estimating the Returns to Education: A Disaggregated Approach.* New York: McGraw-Hill.

Ehrenberg, R., 1972. *The Demand for State and Local Government Employees: An Economic Analysis.* Lexington, Mass.: D.C. Heath.

_____ , 1973a. "The Demand for State and Local Government Employees," *American Economic Review* 63 (June), 366–380.

_____ , 1973b. "Municipal Government Structure, Unionization and the Wages of Fire-Fighters," *Industrial and Labor Relations Review* 27 (October), 36–48.

Feldstein, M., 1971. *The Rising Cost of Hospital Care.* Washington: Information Resources Press.

Freeman, R., 1971. *Market for College-Trained Manpower.* Cambridge: Harvard University Press.

———, 1972. "Labor-Market Adjustments in Psychology," *American Psychologist* 27 (May), 384–392.

———, 1973. "Supply and Salary Adjustments to the Changing Science Manpower Market: Physics, 1948–1973," Discussion Paper No. 318, Harvard University.

Frey, D., 1972. "Wage and Employment Effects of Collective Bargaining in Public Schools in New Jersey." Unpublished Ph.D. Dissertation, Princeton University.

Friedman, M., 1951. "Some Comments on the Significance of Labor Unions for Economic Policy," in D.M. Wright, ed., *The Impact of the Union.* New York: Harcourt Brace, 204–234.

Fuchs, V., 1967. *Differentials in Hourly Earnings by Regions and City Size, 1959.* New York: National Bureau of Economic Research.

Goldfeld, S., and Quandt, R., 1965. "Some Tests for Homoskedasticity," *Journal of the American Statistical Association* 60 (June), 539–547.

Gönensay, E., 1966. "The Theory of Black Market Prices," *Economica* 33 (May), 219–225.

Gould, J.R., and Henry, S.G.B., 1967. "The Effects of Price Control on a Related Market," *Economica* 34 (February), 42–49.

Gramlich, E., 1969. "The Effect of Federal Grants on State-Local Expenditures: A Review of the Econometric Literature," *National Tax Association Proceedings* 62:569–593.

Gramlich, E., and Galper, H., 1973. "State and Local Behavior and Federal Grant Policy," *Brookings Papers on Economic Activity* 4:15–67.

Hall, W.C., and Carroll, N.E., 1973. "The Effect of Teachers' Organization on Salaries and Class Size," *Industrial and Labor Relations Review* 26 (January), 834–841.

Hamermesh, D., 1971. "White Collar Unions, Blue Collar Unions and Wages in Manufacturing," *Industrial and Labor Relations Review* 24 (January), 159–170.

Harberger, A., 1962. "The Incidence of the Corporation Income Tax," *Journal of Political Economy* 70 (June), 215-240.

Harris, S., 1962. *Higher Education: Resources and Finance.* New York: McGraw-Hill.

———, 1972. *A Statistical Portrait of Higher Education.* New York: McGraw-Hill.

Hicks, J.R., 1932. *The Theory of Wages* (Original edition), 2nd edition. New York: Macmillan, 1964.

Hinich, M., and Ordeshook, P., 1970. "Plurality Maximization vs. Vote Maximization: A Spatial Analysis with Variable Participation," *American Political Science Review* 64 (September), 772-791.

Hirschman, A., 1970. *Exit, Voice and Loyalty.* Cambridge: Harvard University Press.

Horton, R.D., 1973. *Municipal Labor Relations in New York City.* New York: Praeger.

Houthakker, H., 1952. "Compensated Changes in Quantities and Qualities Consumed," *Review of Economic Studies* 19:155-164.

Johnson, D., and Mohan, C., 1971. "Revenue Sharing and the Supply of Public Goods," *National Tax Journal* 24 (June), 157-168.

Johnson, H.G., 1971. *Two-Sector Model of General Equilibrium.* Chicago: Aldine.

Johnson, H.G., and Mieszkowski, P., 1970. "The Effects of Unionization on the Distribution of Income: A General Equilibrium Approach," *Quarterly Journal of Economics* 84 (November), 539-561.

Kasper, H., 1970. "The Impact of Collective Bargaining on Public School Teachers' Salaries," *Industrial and Labor Relations Review* 24 (October), 57-72.

———, 1971a. "On Political Competition, Economic Policy and Income Maintenance Programs," *Public Choice* 10 (Spring), 1-21.

———, 1971b. "On the Effect of Collective Bargaining on Resource Allocation in Public Schools," *Economic and Business Bulletin* 23, (Spring/Summer), 1-9.

267

REFERENCES

——, 1972. "Reply," *Industrial and Labor Relations Review* 25 (April), 417–423.

Kerr, C., and Siegel, A., 1954. "The Interindustry Propensity to Strike—An International Comparison," in A. Kornhauser, et al., eds., *Industrial Conflict.* New York: McGraw-Hill, 189–212.

Korman, A., 1971. *Industrial and Organizational Psychology.* Englewood Cliffs, New Jersey: Prentice-Hall.

Kramer, G., 1971. "Short-Term Fluctuations in U.S. Voting Behavior," *American Political Science Review* 65 (March), 131–143.

Krider, C., 1971. "The Patterns and Determinants of Public-Sector Strikes," Unpublished Manuscript, University of Chicago Graduate School of Business.

Krislov, J., 1961. "Work Stoppages of Government Employees, 1942–59," *Quarterly Review of Economics and Business* 1 (February), 87–92.

Landon, J.H., and Baird, R.H., 1971. "Monopsony in the Market for Public School Teachers," *American Economic Review* 61 (December), 966–71.

——, 1972. "The Impact of Collective Bargaining on Public School Teachers' Salaries: Comment," *Industrial and Labor Relations Review* 25 (April), 410–417.

Lewis, H.G., 1951. "The Labor-Monopoly Problem: A Positive Proposal," *Journal of Political Economy* 59 (August), 277–287.

——, 1963. *Unionism and Relative Wages in the United States.* Chicago: University of Chicago Press.

——, 1972. Unpublished Lecture Notes, University of Chicago.

Lipsky, D.B., and Drotning, J.E., 1973. "The Influence of Collective Bargaining on Teachers' Salaries in New York State," *Industrial and Labor Relations Review* 27 (October), 18–35.

Lurie, M., 1960. "Government Regulation and Union Power: The Case of the Boston Transit Industry," *Journal of Law and Economics* 3 (October), 118–135.

——, 1961. "The Effect of Unionization of Wages in the Transit Industry," *Journal of Political Economy* 69 (December), 558–572.

McCall, J., 1971. "Probabilistic Microeconomics," *Bell Journal of Economics and Management Science* 2 (Autumn), 403–433.

Metzger, W., 1973. "Academic Tenure in America: A Historical Essay," in Commission on Academic Tenure in Higher Education. *Faculty Tenure.* San Francisco: Jossey-Bass.

Mills, D.Q., 1973. *Industrial Relations and Manpower in Construction.* Cambridge: The M.I.T. Press.

Mincer, J., 1970. "The Distribution of Labor Incomes: A Survey with Special Reference to the Human Capital Approach," *Journal of Economic Literature* 8 (March), 1–26.

Moynihan, D.P., 1972. "Equalizing Education: in Whose Benefit?" *Public Interest* 29 (Fall), 69–89.

_____, 1973. " 'Peace'—Some Thoughts on the 1960's and 1970's," *Public Interest* 32 (Summer), 3–12.

National Education Association, 1972. *Faculty Salary Schedules in College and Universities,* Report 1972-10.

_____, 1958–1972. *Salaries in Higher Education,* various editions.

National League of Cities, 1972. *1970 National Survey of Employee Benefits for Full-Time Personnel of U.S. Municipalities.* Washington: National League of Cities.

National Opinion Research Center, 1965. *The U.S. College Educated Population: 1960.* Chicago: NORC.

National Science Foundation, 1970. *American Science Manpower: 1970.*

_____, 1972. *First-year, Full-Time Graduate Science Enrollments Continue to Decline,* NSF Report 72-308.

Nerlove, M., 1972. "On Tuition and the Costs of Higher Education," *Journal of Political Economy* 80 (May/June), S178–S218.

Nilon, J., 1973. "Where Have All the Ph.D.'s Been Going," Unpublished Manuscript, Cornell University.

Oaxaca, R., 1971. "Male-Female Wage Differentials in Urban Labor Markets," Working Paper No. 23, Princeton University Industrial Relations Section.

Ohls, J., and Wales, T., 1972. "Supply and Demand for State and Local Services," *Review of Economics and Statistics* 54 (November), 424–430.

O'Neill, J., 1971. *Resource Use in Higher Education.* New York: McGraw Hill.

Owen, J.D., 1972. "Toward a Public Employment Wage Theory:

Some Econometric Evidence on Teacher Quality," *Industrial and Labor Relations Review* 25 (January), 213–22.

Pashigian, B.P., 1972. "Public Versus Private Ownership," Unpublished Manuscript, University of Chicago.

Pauly, M., and Redisch, M., 1973. "The Not-for-Profit Hospital as a Physician's Cooperative," *American Economic Review* 63 (March), 87–99.

Pencavel, J.H., 1970. "An Investigation into Industrial Strike Activity in Britain," *Economica* 35 (August), 239–56.

Perloff, S., 1971. "Comparing Municipal, Industry and Federal Pay," *Monthly Labor Review* 94 (October), 46–50.

Perrella, V.C., 1970. "Moonlighters: Their Motivations and Characteristics," *Monthly Labor Review* 93 (August), 57–63.

Perry, C.R., and Wildman, W., 1970. *The Impact of Negotiations in Public Education.* Worthington, Ohio: Wadsworth Publishing Company.

Polsby, N., 1963. *Community Power and Political Theory.* New Haven: Yale University Press.

Porter, R.C., 1965. "A Growth Model Forecast of Faculty Size and Salaries in U.S. Higher Education," *Review of Economics and Statistics* 47 (May), 191–197.

Rapaport, A., 1970. *N-Person Game Theory.* Ann Arbor, Michigan: University of Michigan Press.

Rees, A., 1952. "Industrial Conflict and Business Fluctuations," *Journal of Political Economy* 60 (October), 371–82.

———, 1973a. *The Economics of Work and Pay.* New York: Harper and Row.

———, 1973b. "Compensating Wage Differentials," Working Paper No. 41, Princeton University Industrial Relations Section.

Roomkin, M., 1972. "Some Findings on the Performance of the Ashenfelter-Johnson Strike Model." Unpublished Manuscript, University of Chicago Graduate School of Business.

Rosen, S., 1969. "Trade Union Power, Threat Effects and the Extent of Organization," *Review of Economic Studies* 36 (April), 185–196.

Ross, A., 1948. *Trade Union Wage Policy.* Berkeley and Los Angeles: University of California Press.

270

_____, 1961. "The Prospects for Industrial Conflict," *Industrial Relations* 1 (October), 57–74.

Schmenner, R.W., 1973. "The Determination of Municipal Employee Wages," *Review of Economics and Statistics* 55 (February), 83–90.

Scully, G., 1971. "Business Cycles and Industrial Strike Activity," *Journal of Business* 44 (October), 359–374.

Smith, D.A., 1973. "The Determinants of Strike Activity in Canada," *Industrial Relations (Industrielles)* 27:€⁻3–678.

Sobotka, S., 1953. "Union Influence on Wages: The Construction Industry," *Journal of Political Economy* 61 (April), 127–143.

Stigler, G., 1950. *Employment and Compensation in Education.* New York: National Bureau of Economic Research.

_____, 1973. "General Economic Conditions and National Elections," *American Economic Review* 63 (May), 160–167.

Stone, R., 1965. "A Model of the Educational System," *Minerva* 3 (Winter), 172–186.

Theil, H., 1952. "Qualities, Prices, and Budget Enquiries," *Review of Economic Studies* 19:129–147.

_____, 1967. *Economics and Information Theory.* Chicago: Rand McNally.

_____, 1971. *Principles of Econometrics.* New York: John Wiley and Sons.

Thornton, R.J., 1971. "The Effects of Collective Negotiation on Teachers' Salaries," *Quarterly Review of Economics and Business* 11 (Winter), 37–46.

Throop, A., 1968. "The Union-Nonunion Wage Differential and Cost-Push Inflation," *American Economic Review* 58 (March), 79–99.

Tullock, G., 1967. *Towards a Mathematics of Politics.* Ann Arbor: University of Michigan Press.

Tinbergen, J., and Bos H., 1965. *Econometric Models of Education.* Paris: OECD.

UCLA Law School, 1972. "Collective Bargaining and Politics in Public Employment," *UCLA Law Review* 19 (August), 887–1051.

REFERENCES

U.S. Bureau of the Census. *Statistical Abstract, 1972.*

U.S. Department of Labor, *Manpower Report of the President, 1972.*

U.S. Office of Education. *Digest of Educational Statistics: 1971.*
———. *Projections of Educational Statistics to 1971–80.*

University of Minnesota. "Survey of Economics Departments," Unpublished Manuscript, Department of Economics, annually 1957–1972.

Veblen, T., 1934. *The Theory of the Leisure Class.* New York: Modern Library.

Walton, R.E., and McKersie, R., 1965. *A Behavioral Theory of Labor Negotiation.* New York: McGraw-Hill.

Ward, B., 1958. "The Firm in Illyria," *American Economic Review,* 48 (September), 566–589.

Waud, R., 1968. "Manhour Behavior in U.S. Manufacturing: A Neoclassical Interpretation," *Journal of Political Economy* 76 (May/June), 407–428.

Weintraub, A., 1966. "Prosperity versus Strikes: An Empirical Approach," *Industrial and Labor Relations Review* 19 (January), 231–38.

Weisbrod, B., 1975. "Toward a Theory of the Voluntary Non-Profit Sector in a Three Sector Economy," in E.S. Phelps, ed., *Economics and Altruism.* New York: Russell Sage Foundation.

Wellington, H., and Winter, R., 1971. *The Unions and the Cities.* Washington: The Brookings Institution.

West, E.G., 1967. "The Political Economy of American Public School Legislation," *Journal of Law and Economics* 10 (October), 101–128.

Wittman, D.A., 1973. "Parties as Utility Maximizers," *American Political Science Review* 67 (June), 490–498.

Young, J., and Brewer, B., 1970. "Strikes by State and Local Government Employees," *Industrial Relations* 9 (May), 356–61.

Zellner, A., 1962. "An Efficient Method of Estimating Seemingly Unrelated Regression Equations and Tests for Aggregation Bias," *Journal of the American Statistical Association* 57 (June), 348–368.

Library of Congress Cataloging in Publication Data

Main entry under title:

Labor in the public and nonprofit sectors.

   Papers presented at a conference held May 7–8, 1973, at Prince-
ton University and sponsored by the Industrial Relations Section,
Princeton University and the Manpower Administration of the
U. S. Dept. of Labor.
   Includes bibliographical references and index.
   1. Employee-management   relations   in   government—United
States—Congresses.   2. Trade-unions—Government   employees—
United   States—Congresses.   3. Civil   service—United   States—
Congresses.   I. Hamermesh, Daniel S., ed.   II. Princeton Uni-
versity. Industrial Relations Section. III. United States. Dept. of
Labor. Manpower Administration. IV. Title.

HD8008.L3   331.7'61'353   74-22495
ISBN 0-691-04203-9